Preflection

by Ron Fry

[whose generative listening unleashed the i̶n̶t̶e̶n̶t̶i̶o̶n̶ ̶t̶o̶ ̶?

My first journey through this work by Cees was a wonderful ride. It was full of inner 'yes,' 'aha,' 'never looked at it that way,' and outer smiles, with some thoughtful frowns. Overall it is a tour-de-force into a deeper view of generativity, generative connections, and the novel idea of the "genarrator" to help those interested in nurturing, transforming, changing or developing human systems toward being spaces for everyone to flourish within. A few things I am appreciating most about this contribution to our global community of practice:

Wordplay

Like Cees and many of us in the Appreciative Inquiry and Social Constructionist domains, I adhere to the powerful notion that words create worlds. Cees has given us a masterclass in the power of intentional-yet-playful reframing, rewording, and inventing words to stimulate new ideas and images. This is not just limited to the new Genarrator role. Everywhere there are delightful twists and turns with language to awaken us from mechanistic reading and thinking.

Communitas

Every time I have encountered Cees, and now in his writing, I am reminded of community. He lives and "be's" for communing with equal voice, shared power, and true appreciation for diversity and inclusion. But now I think he is highlighting even more the moments of communitas that Victor Turner first described. Those emergent moments where a collective finds themselves in a space of true concrescence, or simultaneous "growing along with." The unknown is embraced, everyone shares a type of bond I would describe as a generative connection, and all join in co-inquiry. The Genarrator can be a positive change agent for these moments.

Power-with

Several times during my reading, I found myself thinking of Mary Parker Follett's sage distinction between power-over and power-with. One occurred when Cees described the Genarrator role as being about the other(s), not about oneself.

I would extend this a bit to suggest it is about our relational space and the beauty, love, influence, curiosity, creativity, difference, etc. that emerges or resides in that relationship. It is beyond any personal ego agenda, not just the Genarator's.

I look forward to the next time and space to wander through this book again. Like every time I view my garden, there are likely to be experiences of newness and sameness, but always an inviting and fertile space for discovery and growth.

Ron Fry

Professor of Organizational Behavior
Case Western Reserve University
Cleveland, Ohio, USA

.

GENARRATIVE

super cali fragilis tic
expli cali docious

Right to Copy
02022*

Being 35 years in organizational change and development, I have witnessed that a fulfilling job coincides with high performance. Easier said than done, always rewarding. Humanization is my mission, generativity my expertise, subtle disruption one of my qualities. Every organization houses like-minded professionals who want all the stakeholders to flourish. Does this resonate?

Cees Hoogendijk
Organizational Perspectivist

www.ceeshoogendijk.com

Right to Copy 02023
Publisher OrgPanoptics (NL)
Author Cees Hoogendijk
Cover artwork Regis Berchet @Clad63
ISBN 9789083318714

(Photo by Carmen Marsal)

www.genarrativity.org

GENARRATIVE

*future forming practices for
building better legacies*

**How do organizations and
communities stay alive?**

Cees Hoogendijk

Pragademic memoir of an emerging research journey

INTENTION

Intention is the driving force behind all meaningful action.

Ralph Waldo Emerson

This book is intended to propel three life-giving practices that emerged from a mixture of experience, curiosity, future-forming research, and love for life.

Practice 1   To use the word 'generative', and language in general, in such a way that it contributes to social and organizational flourishing.

Practice 2   To recognize, facilitate and accelerate generative relational processes.

Practice 3   To understand, appreciate, see and enhance the generativity of organizations and other kinds of communities.

Do these practices seem a bit abstract to you? It will all become clear, but don't expect an easy ride. Human progress is all about communication: one of our most complicated activities. Bear in mind that not many words contain so much life as generative. For a specific reason, which will be explained in this book, I named the corresponding practices *genarrative*. With an a and two r's. After reading this book you may call yourself a Genarrator. For the sake of life itself.

The book is also an attempt to connect the organizational world of managers and professionals with the academic domain of researchers and professors. The former are rewarded for checking, talking and getting things delivered, the latter for researching, teaching and getting published. In between are the groups, teams and communities that deserve to be beneficiaries of both parties. Perhaps the specific group of people called PhD candidates may show a special interest in this book. I sincerely hope it will show up in class as well as on the CEO's desk.

Proclaimer: genarrativity may very well enhance your personal well-being; however, it is primarily a practice to serve the well-being of the people around and beyond you.

NAVIGATION

Are you going to get lost with me?
I know the way

Loesje.org

My good friend and knowledgeable co-creator Joep C. de Jong wrote to me:

"I was at times lovingly-wondering whether I was reading (a) an autobiography (which in this case I truly enjoyed – it was very nice to be offered the opportunity to learn more about your story, (b) a chapter for the new edition of the Handboek Buitenpromoveren (Basten, E.M.R.C., & Tiggelen, K.B. van, 2013), a guide for the ones who combine a PhD next to their job, or (c) an inspiring search for (new) elements that will help us to 1. Find new, positive ways of using generativity to create new ways of understanding and new images of possibilities and 2. To become a Genarrator, an ambassador of organizational generativity. It probably is in the best of the AI traditions not an 'either/or' but real 'both/and'. However, it might be helpful to the reader to make these distinctions a bit clearer. In some parts of the book, I saw attempts to distinguish between the different elements, but often it was left up to me to decide whether I was reading a, b or c. It might help to manage the expectations if you offer up front what it is they are reading. I'm just imagining a book where it says if you want to read only a) just follow the blue text, if you are primarily interested in b) read the black text and in your interest is with c) read the green text. Just a co-creative thought!"

Esteemed reader, although you won't find colored text, I think that Joep's words may have sharpened your focus already. Yes, being a manager or OD professional, you might be interested in how to enrich your practice. The scholar in organization studies could prefer the research elements and findings. As a PhD candidate you may feel strengthened by the idea that you are not alone. You may also enjoy parts of this book because of being a language lover, an appreciative inquiry practitioner, or a social constructionist. More likely, you may have a bit of all of these perspectives, and who am I to direct you beforehand?. Nevertheless, you will soon find out that the structure of this book allows you to easily skip (and return to) paragraphs as you like. Through this, you will probably create the best way to navigate, even co-create your own unique reading journey.

...

...

...

from the ancestors of our ancestors
from the teachers of our teachers
from the sources of our sources

...

to the clients of our clients
to the students of our students
to the children of our children

...

to the successors of our successors

...

Scheveningen-Viladrau-Llavaneres
02023

...

...

...

CONTENTS

Part Zero - Giving Life to Humanization

PREFACE & PRE-PHASE   3

So What?   5

To PhD, or not to PhD?   6

Humanization of Organization   7

The People's Side of Change   9

Queuing up for Vertical Dialogue   9

What is the Definition of a Definition?   10

Ich bin ein Practitioner!   11

Appreciative Inquiries of the 3.0 Kind   11

www.genarrativity.org   13

PREMISES & PROMISES   15

Confused? Ask Confucius   17

Part One - In Search of Generativity

LIFE CHANGES   21

Spreading Appreciative Inquiry in my Town's Hall   22

Owls and Storks Co-creating in Leiden Living Lab   23

Rise and Fall of my AI Freedom Lab   25

Starting my Journalley   27

64 Pages of Integrity   28

Cees, What Is It You Want to Research? (x10)   31

GENERATIVITY   33

Preliminary Framing   34

In Dialogue with my Sources   35

More Titles than Body Text   36

Organizational Healthy Aging   39

Organizing Generativity: a Conceptual Framework
to Appreciate and Inquire
the Fitness of Organizational Interventions   42

Highlights of DPC Chapter 0   45

TO FRAME OR NOT TO FRAME   49

Philosophical Investigations   50

A Framework Named Generativity   52

Big Bang   59

Apotheosis   61

FIRST APPENDIX TO PART ONE   65

Extended guidelines for applying
the Conceptual Framework Generativity   65

SECOND APPENDIX TO PART ONE   79

My Primary OD Sources   79

My Ancestor Sources   82

Part Two - Processual Generativity

DIALOGIC TEAS WITH MY PROFESSOR   89

A Welcome PhD Ceremony   90

A Seemingly Simple PhD Plan   92

THE DRILL OF PRAGADEMIC WRITING   93

Running for AoM Paper Presentation   95

Muddling Through JABS Journalism   101

Digging Up the Darling   104

Knowledgeable Co-creators   106

Published At Last   107

HOW TO ASSESS A GENERATIVE PROCESS   109
    Apotheosis: Conceptual Framework of   111
    Generative Processes in Organizations   111
    Now is the Time for Your Own Journaling   113
    Thank You Again, for Your Kind Attention   115
    Sampling Processual Generativity   116
    More Examples of Generative Processes   118
    ODJ Requested More Guidelines   120
    Not so Big a Bang anymore: message from Viladrau   126

Part Three - Organizational Generativity

GETTING INTO PART THREE   131

CONCEPTUAL FRAMEWORK
ORGANIZATIONAL GENERATIVITY   133
    Retroperspective Structurization   135

FUTURE FORMING INQUIRY,
A WELCOME RESEARCH PRACTICE   141
    Imagine Yourself a Knowledgeable Cocreator   145
    "Cees, how do you see the five factors yourself?"   150
    Would You Perhaps Consider Interviewing an OA Yourself?   162
    Future Forming Inquiry Accomplished? Well ...   170

ORGANIZATIONAL GENERATIVITY
PLAUSIBLE? DISCOVER AND DREAM   171
    Processing the Interviews   172
    Sitting with the Prints   176
    A Quickstep with Google Scholar   177
    Counting and Filtering   180
    Coding to Compare: a New Frame   181
    Statistics   184
    Proper Logic   186

BREAKING: Unexpected Intermezzo ###   187

[Zzzzzzzzzz....]   188

Old School or Good Science? You tell me.   192

Fast Forward to Organizational Reality   198

Five Factors, Five Natures   198

About (in)completeness   200

The 3 Degrees Enhanced   201

About the Parts and the Whole (of this book)   202

The Research Journey Revisited   203

Part Four - Genarrativity as a Practice

PRACTICING THE FRAMES   207

Practicing the Word Generativity   209

Practicing Processual Generativity   210

Practicing Organizational Generativity   211

GENARRATIVE INSPIRATORS   213

Michael Puett (02016)   213

Umair Haque (02011)   214

Roman Krznaric (02021)   214

Peter Senge a.o. (01990)   214

Margaret J. Wheatley (02017)   215

Timothy Gallwey (01979)   215

Benjamin Smith a.o. (02017)   215

David Bohm (01990)   216

Matthew B. Crawford (02009)   216

Yuval Noah Harari (02018)   217

Gareth Morgan (01986)   217

(P)REFLECTIONS BY MY CO-MAKERS   218

Lara Carminati   218

Lars Doyer   218

Kenneth J. Gergen   219

Joep C. de Jong   220

Jeffrey Hicks   222

Miriam Subirana Vilanova   225

Gert Veenhoven   229

Cisca Hoogendijk   230

Celeste Wilderom   231

Geert Heling   232

Erica Harpe   233

Peter Brinkman   237

Ronald Fry   239

WHEN AI MEETS AI ...   241

A Not so Genarrative Chat with ChatGPT   241

Finally One of my Genuine AI Interview Questions   251

Quod erat Demonstrandum   251

LET'S GET GENARRATIVE   253

Five Steps Interview with your Co-worker   254

Three Degrees Questions as a Common Practice   255

ENDNOTE & ANDNOTE   257

PART ZERO

02004-02021

Giving Life to Humanization

*"Let us make our future now,
and let us make our dreams tomorrow's reality."*
Malala Yousafzai

*"There's nothing more fundamentally disruptive to the status quo than a
new reality."*
Umair Haque

"The way we talk to our children becomes their inner voice."
Peggy O'Mara

*"Start using flourishing as the primary indicator of successful human
existence. Homo curitans is the authentic caring human being that can bring
forth and exhibit flourishing."*
John Ehrenfeld

"Nothing is impossible, the word itself says "I'm possible!"
Audrey Hepburn

"We live in the world our questions create."
David Cooperrider

"I'm not afraid of storms, for I'm learning to sail my ship."
Louisa May Alcott

*"What about research, not as a mirroring,
but as a making of the world?"*
Ken Gergen

PREFACE & PRE-PHASE

The Greek root gen bears two meanings: to beget and to arise.

A book paragraph caused my eyes to get wet: an unprecedented experience. Not that I would consider myself an icy reader. Ken Follet's cathedral trilogy makes me submerge in medieval romance and suffering, and I feel Tom the Builder carving his stones. By speaking her songlines, Margareth Wheatley invites me to reflect on my path and on who I choose to be. Plenty of books turned my silent reading into inner silence. ('Hola, I was talking to you!', says my wife.) My friends and clients (my professional friends) consider me a sensitive being. It took me half a life to find out that being sensitive is not the same as showing emotions. Some people judged me for my lack of visible emotion and touched me deeply by calling me unsensitive. But they didn't get my tears. Only a few intimate friends notice subtleties in my expression, when I feel sad or uncertain, and when they are at their best. Crying is not my core competence. And yet, reading those particular pages made me want to weep.

The last movie that made me swallow, printed the eyes of Bambi in my brains. In Fiddler on the Roof, where Tevye sings: 'If I were a rich man, ya ba dibba dibba dibba dibba dibba dibba dum', his humor and optimism compensates for the terrible fate of his people in such a way that possible eye wetness may as well be caused by laughter. I really sense *Anatevka*, *The Sound of Music*, *Billy Elliot*, not to mention *Watership Down* in my very guts, besides showing poker face. Newspaper stories full of sadness and injustice make me gnash, but not snivel.

My face may be mostly dry, still nothing wrong with my sensitivity. And through my unexpectedly moist eyes I experienced *The Good Ancestor* by Roman Krznadic as touching. Because, at 16 percent of the e-book, a mind blowing and heart glowing exercise triggered my senses. You might experience the same in about a minute or two. But let me first give you some context. According to Krznadic, we humans seem to prefer the short term, whilst we're the only species wired for envisioning the future. Our marshmallow brain wants rapid satisfaction and creates questionable short sighted decisions. Our acorn brain can make us plant a seed of a tree that may protect our grand-grandchildren from the sun, or heat their stove, depending on climate development. Roman Krznadic urges us to develop deep-time awareness and cathedral-thinking. He wants us to be time rebels who offer next generations a future instead of borrowing it from them - without payback. This was far too brief for describing such a promising book. You better go and read it. And, like me, on page 66 you may suddenly find yourself immersed in the following impressive time-machine[1]:

You begin by standing in an open space. The first instruction is to take a step backwards, with your eyes closed, and imagine someone you know and care about from an older generation, such as a parent or grandparent. You then step further back again and imagine them as a young adult, picturing their life, their thoughts and feelings, their hopes and struggles. After a minute, you take a third step backwards and imagine their fifth birthday – everyone who is there, the looks on their faces, the emotions in the air. When I did this, I was picturing my five-year-old father in his tiny village in Poland, just a year before the outbreak of the Second World War turned his life upside down. There was laughter, warm embraces from his grandmother, the first strawberries of spring from the forest.

For the next stage, you return to your original starting position and imagine a young person in your life who you care about and feel connected to, like a niece or godchild or one of your own children. Again with your eyes closed, you take a step forward and conjure up their face, their voice, the things they love doing. Then take another step forward and you've traveled 30 years into the future – what's happening in their life, what are their joys and troubles, what is the state of the world around them?

Then take a final step and it's their ninetieth birthday party. You picture them surrounded by their own children and grandchildren, their closest friends, neighbors and work colleagues. They stand up, slightly doddery, with a stiff drink in their hand, about to make a birthday speech. Suddenly, over on the mantelpiece, they see a photograph of you, and decide instead to tell the gathered group about the legacy you left them: what they learned from you about how to live and the ways you inspired them. At this point, the final instruction is to sit down and write out the speech they would give, a memorial to you, their departed ancestor.

---

[1] From Roman Krznadic, 02020, The Good Ancestor, recalling his participation in a workshop called Human Layers, created by cultural activists Ella Saltmarshe and Hannah Smith, and inspired by the deep ecologist Joanna Macy.

How was that? Did you walk the time-line? In the open air, or mindful in your chair? Was it as good for you as it was for me, as it was for Roman? Did you stop reading, to reflect on your thoughts or perhaps to share your feelings with others? Did you ever *before* think about any *future* speech remembering the *late you* framed in a photo? Are you wondering how a "future *in-memoriam*" would describe you? Did you actually write that speech, as suggested in the time-machine practice? A first attempt perhaps? Where are your thoughts at the moment? Are you planning proper action? Did your mind change a bit? I wouldn't be surprised.

Perhaps you already forwarded the practice to a family member or a friend? Just imagine: Roman did the exercise and described it in his book; then I read it, experienced something similar and copied the instruction in my book; then you read it, perhaps practiced it and brought it further. How many people would have done the time-simulation by now already? And Roman wasn't the first. The exercise is alive and being reproduced for at least two years now, probably much longer. I sense generativity here. What? Generativity, the phenomenon about creating some kind of life that creates offspring: new life. Do I consider Roman Krznadic a generative person? No. (I will explain later.) Can we call that exercise script a generative story? Not yet; time will be the judge of that. Let me tell you this: In the past five years I have been studying almost every book that uses the word generativity, for the purpose of finding out how we can make the world, in particular the organizational world, a better place. There was - and still is - a lot to discover around that magical adjective *generative*. Regarding Krznadic's time-travel exercise, I can reveal that the interaction between its description and you - the exercising - is likely to be qualified as generative.

So What?

According to one of my former PhD-supervisors, one always should ask this question after putting the results of your inquiries on paper: "So what?" Why do I consider generativity so important that I should write a book about it, with a seeming typo in the title? Well, 35 years of working in and with organizations made me clear that (i) my level of organizational sensitivity is high, (ii) there's too much suffering among the workers, and (iii) sound working conditions create the best possible performance. I wish organizations and communities to be safe, healthy, inspiring to live and to work in. I want them to grow the capability to thrive, to flourish, to leave a promising future behind for their successors. This should be normal. My concern addresses leaders, managers, coordinators, supervisors, facilitators and enablers of these hopefully generative social movements; especially their abilities, their craftsmanship, their intentions, their *genarrativity* to contribute succes(sor)fully to what I care so much about: flourishing, life-giving organizations and communities, thriving through uncertainty, antifragile. Five years of inquiry into the concept of generativity, and how to apply this in a future-forming way, strengthened my convictions. It all starts with the Greek root *gen* and its double meaning to beget and to arise. It feels like my research is not more than halfway. According to HH Dalai Lama, half the knowledge is a good point to start forwarding it. Therefore this book. Perhaps it can be an accelerator. Does this resonate? The well-being of humanity is at stake. There's work to do. Join the club. Active members only.

To PhD, or not to PhD?

What happened before? Until Saturday 13th November 2004, almost twenty years after becoming a Master of Science in Mathematics, I thought that getting a PhD was supposed to make me a doctor in mathematics, for which I consider myself not the best candidate. I never even thought so much about PhD back then. My sister however, one of the rare papyrologists on the globe, and working most of her life in academia, did achieve her doctorate. I happened to be her paranymph at the defense ceremony, with my parents as proud witnesses. Every year I appreciate my mum and dad more, not in the least for the gentle way they guided us on the path of learning to our potential, something they themselves had missed because of world war circumstances, also being kids of large families in which work came before school. During the course of their lives they compensated fairly for their own disturbed schooling, and as I see it now, they projected their educational dreams on my sister and me. I am deeply grateful for their subtil and loving efforts. So, attending pre-academic high school seemed for me the normal thing to do, as going to university, which was not a common thing in the large families of my parents. But their aspirations reached even beyond that.

When my sister Cisca, in line with her job, became a philosophical doctor in ancient languages, I sort of felt a responsibility to also give it a try. From the side of my work as manager-slash-consultant I wasn't really invited to high level learning. At least not more than the occasional project management training or leadership development weekend. It was therefore a surprise that my pragmatic boss directly agreed to finance my enrollment in a part time PhD program, when

I proposed such; I suspect that it had to do with his power position and corresponding budget within the profitable express logistics industry. I don't think he agreed for the sake of keeping me on board, because only a year later he fired me as easily as he granted me the study. Long story. I learned a lot about corporate politics and power games. That I should keep my opinion to myself. That I better be loyal to my bosses than to the organization's objectives, if I wanted to reach my retirement. That I am not a company man. That freedom is one of my driving values. That organizational change is about people. Confronting but valuable lessons. Thank you, very last of my bosses, first for granting me an initial study budget into a PhD adventure, and second for your humble golden handshake that facilitated me to jump into the rabbit hole called entrepreneurship. It was just enough to bridge the finances for the mortgage and our six children's household of that time, until my first client appeared. I named my company *OrgPanoptics - Managing the Whole*. My mission was - and still is:

Humanization of Organization

I saw this beautiful imperative on a poster at the wall of the University of Humanistics in Utrecht, The Netherlands, where I visited an open day. It was 13th November 2004, I was DHL Express's Director Organization Transition Support, responsible for the people side of the change, and I considered Humanization of Organization a very attractive title for a seminar, workshop or masterclass. It turned out to be a PhD/DBA program. That very afternoon I decided to enroll, right after I understood that my research topic didn't need to be of a mathematical nature. I consider this decision the start of the awakening of my right brain half. Some people in their forties decide to buy a motorcycle and/or to end their relationship. I already had a motorbike in my twenties through summer and winter until my first real job granted me the luxury of a company car. My first marriage would encounter a premature ending, but only many years later. So, at the age of 45, I took up this PhD journey and I never expected that it would be such a rewarding and bumpy ride. The journey was surely generative, although I embraced that word not before 15th March 2018, fourteen years later, when the first seed was planted for the book you are reading now. Quite a journey, ey? And still traveling.

My two years at the University of Humanistics have been foundational, as well as my two years at DHL turned out to be life changing. My PhD lead-professor Hugo Letiche consecrated his students in the world of social constructionism: a philosophical view in which meaning is created - and obviously recreated - through conversation among people. Words create worlds. We don't see the world as it is; we see the world as we are. Where my earlier truth had been a more mathematical one, fixed and flavored with logic, my new understanding of truth was fluid: something we make up together; or: what is useful in the moment. Fake news was not an issue in those years, but I am sure it would have influenced our discourse. Among a variety of inspiring and mind blowing guest lectures (by Harry Kunneman, David Boje, to name just a few) was also a speech by Kenneth Gergen, who showed us a plastic bottle, asking: "What is this, a plastic bottle, or perhaps more?". He elaborated on endless manifestations of that bottle for about six hours. I can't have a drink anymore without my thoughts drifting away to Gergen. Never thought that ten years later, on 30th August 2015, he and I would be having lunch in Amsterdam, and that he would re-ignite my PhD spark plug that I had left behind on the back burner.

In the meantime, Letiche was researching the concept of group flow: in particular circumstances in which a team becomes high performing. In 2011 he published *Coherence in the Midst of Complexity*, and since then I read one or two pages of it every trimester. On the blurb, some professor says that 'every manager should read this book, and take it to heart'. Well, I have met, interviewed, mentored or accompanied at least a thousand managers in my professional life, and I can't think of one of them that would know about the existence of Letiche's book, let alone reading it. He and his co-authors provide at least one valuable insight: the difference between ascribed and emergent coherence. To put it simply: there is 'acting in the present with old knowledge' and there is 'acting in coherence with what is emerging'. Managers better embrace the latter. The book breathes generativity as I see it now, but I don't remember the word having been addressed in Letiche's classroom.

Two years at the Humanistic University's hot tub of social constructionism brought me to a nearly finished PhD proposal on Vertical Dialogue. I had given this name to an inclusive and dialogical way of co-creating business plans within DHL, which turned out to be very successful, and made me a popular guy, to the extent that I only had to serve two years of my three year contract. Being me and popular in a competitive environment can be risky. I memorized the full experience in an essay that stayed under embargo for five years. Let me give you a glimpse of my adventures. The following fragments seem relevant as background for what I want to bring forward in this book.

The People's Side of Change

Around 2003, DHL Express Worldwide merged with (or was taken over by) Deutsche Post World Net, and Danzas Logistics was in the deal as well. The former burgundy-white DHL colors would turn into the present red and yellow. The merger also included local transportation companies, in order to create a full service proposition in each country. Only in Europe, hundreds of millions of euros were involved - read: to be saved - in this huge reorganization that consisted of 250 major change programs. In my region, about 15.000 people were affected. As newly assigned Director OTS (organization transition support) it was my team's role to look after the people's side of the change. This meant so much that I should oversee the whole organization, report to the Regional Director Human Resources, and that the Regional Change Manager, responsible for the financial side of the merger, didn't want to speak with me. I may have been the only one that actually studied the 500 presentation slides - two for each major change program - to detect at least 70 doublures; to begin with. However, headquarters in Bonn was not easy to reach with such reflections. To my gut feeling, the organization would not cope with so many change impacts, but how to bring that to the table of senior management? First we decided to go for the gentle approach: based on research and the book *What Really Works*, we designed a template for a departmental business plan, easy to use and promising in terms of getting timely results; actually, the foundation for achieving any organizational change. After all, during the reorganization, the business had to be run as well. This "mother of plans" titled Mastering Integrated Growth unfortunately didn't reach proper consideration in the senior management team.

Queuing up for Vertical Dialogue

The management team had already a busy agenda, and our OTS issues were constantly postponed. Our promising template ended up in a drawer (not for too long happily, as you will see soon). We needed a plan B. We called it the Human Impact Analysis Tool (HIAT): an official checklist, to assess an upcoming change project on its possible human impact. We managed to make this checklist part of the project initiation procedure. Depending on the answers, the spreadsheet would show green, yellow or red flags to items such as performance decrease, motivation, sickness rate and risk of strike.

Call it coincidence or mastery, but we actually got the strike and had the increase in sickness rate that our HIAT had predicted. This caused at least some respect, and finally an invitation at the table of the big change manager. Even more, 'human impact' was added as an indicator on the change management dashboard. Some thought this would support the change, others said the opposite. So be it. Little steps are steps.

Another coincidence was that I met a former client in the corridor who had just accepted the position of business unit director. After he learned about my - still fragile - position in transition support, he shared his desire to launch a quick win with his unit. I took him to my office, opened my drawer and showed him the master template and he said "let's go for it".

To shortcut the story: through a process of *vertical dialogue* involving most of the workers in his unit, my assistant Ronald and I facilitated the co-creation of a practical How-to-plan. I don't think it was pure luck - since it was diversity and inclusion that did most of the trick - that this very business unit made speedy progress in workers motivation and results. Subsequently, the other business unit managers queued up for a similar treatment. I still don't know if all this made my position more fragile or more robust. After two years of change, and under diffuse circumstances of a political nature - don't ask - the OTS team was dismantled, and I became self-employed. My bright assistant became an operations manager and made a beautiful and fully deserved career until at the moment of writing this being Managing Director DHL Express The Netherlands. I think he is a great humanizer and genarrator, making DHL a great place to work, if it's up to him. One anecdote about him brings us back to some of the essences of this book: the meaning of a word. Ronald, a triple graduate in military academy, business and organization, had the habit of asking "What is the definition of ... ?" (a process, an objective, a system, a vision, etcetera). One day I got a bit annoyed and asked him the ultimate question: "What is the definition of definition?"

What is the Definition of a Definition?

One day in the spring of 2005, when DHL offered me a great new job in the morning, and withdrew the offer in the evening, I decided to stop being an employee and, thanks to a bit of funding, started to be self-employed. Then, by 2006, life had other plans with me than writing a thesis. Partly because the UvH's tuition fee was too expensive for a beginning entrepreneur with a big family to support. Partly because I had ideas to write a not so academic but very practical book - offering twenty management recipes with the flavor of Vertical Dialogue. This conflicted with the regular PhD journey, because: first the thesis, then the book. Since I prefer practice above theory, I chose to produce the book, in Dutch titled *Kracht zonder Macht*, best translated as *Strength without Power*. It was printed early 2008, and I consider it as a fruitful outcome of my first PhD attempt. History would repeat itself fourteen years later, but that I didn't know yet.

Ich bin ein Practitioner!

I love to dive into relevant sources. I always study the technical manual before working on my motorcycle. I like to understand more than I need. I am interested in the whole context. Of course, in the end it is all about a smooth running engine and making some fine curvy miles. I think that proper information makes a better mechanic. I am getting to know myself as a perfectionist, a wannabe craftsman, who likes to seek underpinning for his activities, but prefers to turn the research findings into relevant practice - perhaps a tutorial - rather than into scientific papers. I am a practitioner! The internalization of this self-awareness reached its apotheosis on the 2nd August 2021, the day that I officially decided that I still would pursue my research on generativity, but not strive anymore for the certificate that would automatically turn me into a member of the club of scholars. I don't (need to) belong to that family, although I want to maintain a friendly relationship with science. And if it comes to titles, I'd rather call myself a master of science than a philosophical doctor.

Appreciative Inquiries of the 3.0 Kind

To conclude this pre-phase I think you should know a bit about my professional humanizing journey. From my father I probably inherited my preference for 'power to the people'. He was a genuine craftsman in the print industry, when newspapers still were delivered on your doorstep. Strong in his values, he was highly appreciated as a progressive and people driven manager. I must have carried that human orientation with me across various jobs, and in some confrontations with 'bosses'. Two years at the University of Humanistics provided me with a huge extra body of knowledge, infinite sources, and basic research skills, all valuable for my further practice in organization development. It gave me the inspiration and courage to write my first book, with more to follow.

Two exciting years at DHL, paid for three, fueled my strong intentions to focus on - and fight for - humanization of organizations. Between 2008 and 2017 my social enterprise generated more or less the necessary income. In line with emerging new propositions, I produced five more books. Besides *Society 3.0*, of which I was the editor and ghostwriter on behalf of another bright Ronald, none of them were bestsellers. I roughly sold enough copies to compensate for the production costs, and was happy to use my books as give-aways. Call them my extended business cards. Compare it with today's Spotify model: make your work accessible and hope that someone invites you to give a concert. All five books are of a practical nature; I didn't think of adding a list of references at the end. The ones with my name on the cover are now downloadable for free, and right to copy. I'm quite fond of my 2015 book called *Appreciative Inquiries of the 3.0 Kind, How to Connect, Share and Co-Create for Tomorrow's Human Wholeness*.

To explain myself as a co-creating self-employed knowmad, you should know that I built my first website after a weekend of studying the HTML manual. Then, around 2009, it was the under-appreciated but over-complicated platform *Mindz.com*, invented by the visionary Ronald (3.0) van den Hoff, in which I created and maintained 37 different homepages. From 2012 onwards, I used Wordpress as a template to generate my 3rd generation website, still showing far too many different products and services. (Humanization of Organization needs more than a single-method approach.) When you are reading this, you will find me on ceeshoogendijk.com - a one pager with one call to action: "book a meeting with Cees for a generative conversation". Would this book still be around for some decades more, and I might not be present anymore, perhaps some successor is keeping *genarrativity*.org in the air.

If I would dare to already speak of a professional legacy from my efforts so far, then this would include: a systematic approach to assess and develop organizational learning; a new way of understanding and improving (work) processes; the *Connective Leadership Mirror*; and the *Dutch Appreciative Inquiry Academy*. Besides, I can only hope that my future forming research into (organizational) generativity will have the potential to live beyond me.

What year is it for you? Please share your comments on this book. And would I be gone, let my children know. They may use it in a sudden speech some day... Writing down these last sentences touched my feelings again. It also gave me the idea of opening a guestbook, where you at any time can leave your reflection. Take a moment to visit the corresponding website.

www.genarrativity.org

HORA EST! Proclaiming these two words (meaning: "it's time") is at Dutch Universities the way for the beadle to immediately end the doctorate 'defense', after which the highly learned opponents leave the room, to decide about granting you the PhD certificate. Defense? Opponents? How deconstructive! Stay with me, highly appreciated reader. You are my appraisal committee.

Nevertheless it's time. Time to co-create the content of this book. Co-create? Yes. In his meta-book *On Writing, Memoir of a Craft*, Stephen King describes the process between author and reader as sheer telepathy. Just imagine for a moment. At a certain time and place, the writer translates his or her ideas in words, and at a totally different time and place, some reader translates these words into similar ideas again. Thoughts and visions traveling over time from one brain into the other, isn't that surreal? So, while reading this book, allow my ideas and intentions to mingle with yours, and turn you into a fellow genarrator, equipped for building better legacies.

GENARRATIVE

PREMISES & PROMISES

"What about research, not as a mirroring,
but as a making of the world?"

Ken Gergen

Five premises are to be made. Unlike theses or theories, that can be tested as true or false, premises are like assumptions. Whether they are valid can only be tested over time. They also contain a certain logic in itself that makes them plausible, trustworthy. That's why we are willing to take them as given. Beware. Don't take the following premises for granted. Please try them for yourself.

Premise 1: reading this book is for you an act of co-creation. By reading my mind, you make up your mind. The moment you start applying the content of this book, like telling others about it, or doing the suggested genarrative (with 'a') practices, you initiate another co-creation with new people. This will ignite new ideas that will make a change in the way things are going. In that sense, both the reading and the applying of this book can be regarded as generative (with 'e') processes. Let me promise that slowly but gently you will get more comfortable with the difference (differance?) between that 'a' and that 'e'. For sure this will be accomplished when you reach the Andnote of this book!

Premise 2: this book is important. This perhaps sounds a bit blunt, but the more I inquired into generativity, the more promising it became. I dare to say that studying Generativity is as important as studying Love; and how many books, movies, poems, songs (and therapies) have been created upon that four-letter concept? Furthermore, this book has been built upon genuine academic research. Quoting Richard Sennet, author of The Craftsman, I would regard my five years of inquiry as *"doing things well just for the sake of it"*. The word generative demands clarity, where most of its use so far is technically incorrect or its meaning taken for granted. Collecting the evidence for this bold statement took proper study: literature review, engaging experts, interviewing leaders, and so on. Clarifying is one; translating into practice is two. Having published a few academic articles on organizational generativity might be considered impressive;

articulating the concept to become actionable for practitioners, represents the real importance of this book.

Premise 3: learning to do is different from learning to know. This book is intended to give you something to do. Not only the why and the what but also the how, so to say. And in doing such, you probably will learn, which can be understood as: doing something better than before, or doing something you didn't do yet. Telepathy is not enough. This book heads for telekinesis; to make you move; to make your organization or your community move. When performed in a conscious way, the doing is the learning.

Premise 4: diligent use of language is crucial. I've seen so many strategic plans that didn't prevent organizations from stagnating. Too many job profiles are being matched with even more C.V.'s and do we really know that the chosen co-worker will flourish? How do we go from reading to doing? When asked what he would do if he would rule the country, Confucius answered: "I would use the language well." I don't think that he desired language to be so perfectly clear that everybody would exactly understand, because such may not exist. I do think that unclear language can bring uncertainty and stuckness among people. If you ask me, language should be just clear enough to bring people into action, from which understanding will follow. Inspiring words are nice; mobilizing words are better. Some of my client-friends say: "If we take care of the coffee, Cees will take care of the confusion." Confusion happens where multiple perspectives meet. You could call this the opposite of tunnel-view. To confuse this conversation for the full, I think that language doesn't necessarily need to be clear; it better be performative: inviting to act. Confusion may very well be beneficiary to action. That is: if we use the language well.

Premise 5: this book can work for you. If you have reached here, and it is your intention to keep on reading, this book can work for you - with you - through you - for others.

Confused? Ask Confucius

"Cees, you should know that academic readers are not interested in you or your research journey, so just stick to your question, method, data, analysis and conclusions. Furthermore, it's not a detective story, so please start with a resume of your findings, don't let your reader wait for it until the end."

After this feedback on my first serious writings, from one of my early Leiden University mentors, I separated my diary from my data and tried to focus on the content, keeping the notes of my research journey aside and for myself. Years later, when I finally managed to pass the peer reviews and publish a genuine academic article, with the help of esteemed scholars, muddling through almost a hundred manuscript versions, the majority of my revisions had only to do with document structure and text formatting. Nobody seemed to be interested in organizational generativity itself.

I understand that scientific papers should be structured for the purpose of traceability. But what about the intentions of the researcher? What to think of reporting the research as a seemingly logical series of steps, whilst the reality is much more chaotic and full of emergence? Not to forget the doubts, the difficult decisions, what to in- and what to exclude? Or the necessary transfer from theoretical findings to practical guidelines? To cut this short, I came to a point where all this scholarly work seemed little rewarding, besides the fact that none of my clients ever would find or read such an article. From that moment on, I knew that all my stuff had to be blended into a book. You are about to finish reading *Part Zero* of it. Four parts will follow.

In **Part One, In Search of Generativity**, we will travel toward and across my extensive review of almost every piece of literature that uses the word generativity. It was actually quite exciting to see that this word is taken for granted so much, but not very well explained. I dare to say now that the adjective 'generative' is often used incorrectly, and clearly in the need of re-framing or even un-framing. This part of the book is foundational. It may be the first time that the word generativity finally has been given a genuine user manual. It may be your first time to be taken on a journey in which one word is being studied. Be prepared for a generative journey that will make you reflect on your own use of language.

Part Two, Processual Generativity, invites you to take a closer look at processes going on in organizations and communities. Some of the relational interactions are more generative than others. Generative processes can be recognized in seven possible manifestations. This part of the book may very well be a transformational experience for you, since you might not have looked at processes this way at all, let alone bother about their generativity. Through examples, reflections and challenging guidelines, you will be enabled to observe, with completely new eyes, relational processes that make organizations and communities thrive and flourish. Whether you are a family member, a community leader, a manager in an organization, or a coach or consultant of any kind, you will benefit from a new capability to not only recognize generative movements, but also promote and facilitate them.

Part 3, Organizational Generativity, stretches your newly gained observational capabilities to the level of organization or community as a whole. Its organizational generativity is determined by five elusive factors. You need to embrace emergence in your own reasoning to become comfortable with them. (Compare it to getting comfortable with the fact that water molecules are not wet, but together they are. The relation between the molecules and the water is emergent.) Again you will be guided by examples, reflections and practices to make this new view valuable for you. You actually are invited and facilitated to do the research yourself. At this point you can claim your membership of the circle of knowledgeable co-creators of organizational and social generativity.

In **Part 4, Genarrative as a Practice**, finally you will get some clues about that "a" and that "e". Moreover, this part is intended to provide pathways for practical personal development, after which, at some self determined point in time, you will find yourself qualified as genarrative: capable in future forming practices for building better legacies. Of course, the corresponding learning is preferably a generative process, and how could we better organize this than accompanied by profound genarrators and their immense wisdom?

PART ONE
02017 - 02019

In Search of Generativity

Practice 1

To use the word 'generative', and language in general, in such a way that it contributes to social and organizational flourishing.

Universe

The farther one viewed, the larger it seemed.

This poem by the Dutch[2] poet Jules Deelder can be considered as addressing the generativity of viewing. In the course of my emergent inquiries I once encountered the term generative image, in the sense that the admirer of the poem becomes inspired, and carried away in unexpected new thinking towards appealing ideas that invite to act upon, perhaps even completely forgetting about the universe.

Would the words of this poem have the same generative effect to any reader? In what way would they influence the thoughts of an astronomist? Is the poem likely to cause a degenerative experience to the agoraphobic? Can this or any poem, or any image, be considered generative in or by itself? Or might it be the observer who needs to contain or express sufficient generativity, for the poem to generate a creative or even transformational experience?

Furthermore: could the poem, or perhaps better: the process between the poem and its reader, be generative to such an extent that it provokes the latter to start writing poems themselves? Poetry giving birth to poetry, a surviving art; quite generative, so to speak. Is it procreation, leaving behind for future benefits, what generativity should ultimately be capable of? So what? So whát? How can this question guide us to study life and giving life, in organizations and other kinds of communities?

---

[2] Humbly and appreciatively translated by your author, from the original Dutch version "*Heelal. Hoe verder men keek, hoe groter het leek.*" (J.A. Deelder, 1944-2019).

LIFE CHANGES

Yesterday I was clever, so I wanted to change the world.
Today I am wise, so I am changing myself.

Rumi

Early 2017, somewhere between clever and wise, I enrolled in the Orientation Phase of the Leiden University Dual PhD Center (DPC). The word dual refers to combining such a journey with a working life. The word generativity hadn't crossed my mind at all, let alone that I was in search of it. Perhaps I was searching, but not necessarily for the word itself and its miraculous meanings. When I think of it, it must have been my lunch meeting with Ken Gergen, August 2015 in Amsterdam, where he sensed and awakened my sleeping understream of PhD aspirations. The TAOS Institute he founded long ago offered the necessary support and connections with official academic institutions to get a doctorate. So I returned to the university where I once graduated in mathematics and physics: Leiden.

Seeing it from now, this fitted very well in the life changes I was undergoing since 2015. My mother passed away, and without my parents around anymore I felt officially the next generation. I just had published my first English book, full of Appreciative Inquiry practices in service of humanization of organizations and preferably of society as a whole; my world suddenly became much bigger than The Netherlands, as also became my urge for being more effective in my mission. In 18 months I had reduced my body weight from 120 to 90 kilograms, through a mixture of common entrepreneurial sense, consistent Pilates, a minimum of carbohydrates and being less sensitive to the smirking looks of my family. My biggest struggle (or learning) concerned my growing awareness that three decades of being a family man were coming to an end, followed by actually going through the free fall of marital separation, and gently growing into relational rise both with myself and my flourishing new life companion. Leaving my Dutch home base and following love towards Barcelona was a surprisingly logical move. Creating new forms of connecting and relating with my grown up children completed the 'grand reset'. Compared to all this, picking up the PhD challenge again was peanuts. And it had been waiting for me just around the corner.

Spreading Appreciative Inquiry in my Town's Hall

It's a five minute walk from The Hague Town Hall to Leiden Dual PhD Center, in short DPC. Leiden University located their faculty of Governance and Global Affairs as close as possible to the Dutch government and parliament, and the DPC was happy to use some of their office space. It was my contact Rudmer, senior organizational consultant within the The Hague administration, who told me about the DPC because quite a few of his fellow civil servants were doing their PhD there. I emailed my credentials and was invited for an intake.

The city council organization of the town where I was born counts 10.000 workers, in a huge variety of disciplines, most of them assigned to serve citizens; part of them managers and professionals supposed to serve the organization. In 2011, one of the senior directors invited his direct reports to send him a motivation letter for winning one of the five seats in a training Appreciative Inquiry[3] (AI). This course was provided by a young social enterprise which nowadays is called AI-academy.nl, of which I grew from co-founder to owner. Since that first group, and over the years, a few hundred civil servants have been trained in AI - mostly by myself - either in our certified practitioner program, or in a more pragmatic one day conversation training. As part of the learning journey, the students are supposed to design and facilitate a 'whole system summit'. For such a free, high quality consulting offering, it was easy to find problem owners, topics and participants in the organization. Through participating in these summits, many more co-workers of The Hague got a taste of AI. I really felt and feel grateful for being able to spread AI across that organization to such an extent. To be honest, AI is still far from mainstream, and has reached not more than a minority of the co-workers yet. A city council organization is inherently complex, and the realm of public management, politics, re-organizations and competing views on learning and development fuel that complexity to the max. The fact that AI still is present in town hall has more to do with the efforts of a few passionate and nonconform civil servants than with strategic vision or official policies.

---

[3] A.I. is a strength based, possibility oriented practice, fueled by guiding questions, to shape and facilitate positive change and, according to Peter Drucker: "to create an alignment of strengths in ways that make a system's weaknesses irrelevant". A.I. is also one of the few methods for action oriented, future forming research. Find all you need to know about Appreciative Inquiry in my free downloadable book at https://ceeshoogendijk.com/#appreciative-inquiry

Being 35 years in organization and their development, the last 20 years practicing humanization as my professional mission, I am not necessarily optimistic about the significance of my fragmentary interventions. But if something can contribute to a healthy organizational life, it is Appreciative Inquiry. With that conviction I began to raise the question of studying possible effects of AI in The Hague City Council organization in an academic way. And I wondered whether my client could provide a living laboratory for such a study. Speaking of such...

Owls and Storks Co-creating in Leiden Living Lab

On the 1st of February 2017 I entered DPC for the first time of my life to meet my new PhD mentor Mark. Besides getting to know each other, I told him that the next day I would be facilitating an AI event in the Living Lab of Leiden Faculty in The Hague. Mark took me one floor down and showed me the room: spacious, modern, flexible, comfortable: a perfect location for co-creation. If his agenda allowed, Mark would even join as a participant. Why? Because the next day's event was supposed to connect the researchers who work inside the city council with the researchers from various universities situated in The Hague. Let me tell you how I became the facilitator of that event, a nice illustration of Appreciative Inquiry in practice.

Two months earlier, one of my The Hague AI students asked me to visit the sixth or seventh meeting of a team assigned to organize a conference with the purpose of growing the cooperation between internal and external researchers. I was told that they were a bit stuck in their preparations, and could need some extra inspiration. The moment I stepped into the narrow meeting room in the city hall , I got the feeling that they saw me as a possible keynote speaker on the topic of professional cooperation. The chairman welcomed me and asked for my ideas on how to contribute to their conference. I observed about eight or nine faces and suddenly I heard myself asking: "Who of you is from the city council, and who represents the external researchers?" After a painful silence, I learned that all the people in the room were city hall workers. They must have felt my thinking about how on earth it could be that a conference to connect internals and externals is organized by only one of the partners. No need to emphasize their discomfort, I asked another question: "When the conference has been successful, what does it look like? What are the ideal outcomes and effects of it among the participants?" The silence took so long that I started to get a bit uncomfortable, but I clung to the principle that if a question needs time to get answered, it is a good question. I am not sure they agreed with this. After a while, one person uttered that at the end of the event, everybody should be well informed about the meaning and requirements of good co-creation. That was not the answer I hoped for, but I kept smiling appreciatively. Happily, another team member seemed to understand what I was inquiring into. He answered: "So far in our preparations, we didn't see it the way you put it, but now you ask, I do think that a good outcome of our conference - and I mean on the longer term - would be that our neighborhoods benefit, and our citizens feel served better because of the high quality of joint social research." This was the answer I was waiting for. Now others joined in, giving similar desirable effects of better co-creation among the various researchers. I proposed a scenario they never had thought of, and they agreed on it at that very same meeting.

On the 2nd of February, in the Living Lab of the The Hague location of Leiden University, about 30 internal and 30 external researchers found themselves in one of the comfortable seats that had been arranged in circles of eight. To keep the welcoming speeches of the esteemed leaders of both parties as short as possible, we had agreed that I would ask them some questions. And that was after that I had informed them that the event itself would do without keynote speakers, since all participants would be considered as such. It took us not more than five minutes to appreciate the people in the room for showing up. It took me another five minutes to introduce the metaphor of the owls and the storks. (The logo of The Hague contains a stork. It seemed nice to visualize the two groups as birds. Fill in the metaphor yourself.) It worked well. It had taken me four hours of searching for the proper images, especially some sort of wallpaper in which storks and owls mingle. Owls and ravens, yes. Storks and frogs, yes. Finally I got the images corresponding to my metaphor, what seemed a bit of a silly time investment. Nevertheless rewarding, because both groups felt appreciated and connected. Birds of a feather. In no time, pairs of participants, always one owl and one stork, engaged in a pre-scripted and tailor-made AI interview, inviting them to discover valuable experiences of cocreation - in general, and among researchers - and to visualize dreams about flourishing citizens and neighborhoods. In the next round, each group of eight shared the essences of the AI interviews, in such a way that the interviewer would share what he or she had heard from the conversation partner, and vice versa; the conversation partner being in the same circle. This was, of course, connectivity in action. Why talk about cooperation, when you can experience it? In the plenary, the groups presented their powerful discoveries of successful joint research, which showed that beautiful things were already happening. In the next round, every group took the podium to present exciting and sometimes hilarious dream performances. The atmosphere breathed co-creation. When it came to propose so-called Areas of Opportunity, and after participants regrouped to join design labs around the topics that got the most votes, the cooperation was at full speed. At the end of the day the walls of the Living Lab were spreaded with ideas, plans, and initiatives for 'purposeful joint action research' to strengthen my beautiful city. I saw participants exchanging business cards; others asked for the full list of attendees. And the only thing I had to say in my closing words was: "We envisioned a conference about cooperation. What we created together today was cooperation as a living experience. What did you appreciate the most?"

In two consecutive days I had entered the DPC premises and felt quite comfortable there.

Rise and Fall of my AI Freedom Lab

The Orientation Phase at the DPC goes before the two year Pre-PhD Phase at the end of which the candidate needs to produce a full PhD research proposal including a professor willing to supervise. The DPC serves as a portal to the university itself and is therefore positioned independent from the faculties. Aligned with the calendar of the academic year, DPC activities officially start in September. For me therefore, the orientation phase was as long as seven months, allowing me to make up my mind, discuss my ideas with my preliminary mentor, and work on my formal application. For which I had a brilliant idea.

Just imagine. Starting mid September 2017, I would practice AI as an 'intern' in the Public Services Department: the front office of The Hague City Council. I would join team meetings and ask guiding questions. I would be walking through the corridors and randomly invite workers for a short AI-interview: "Would you tell me about an experience in your work that illustrates the most why you are in this job?" People could book a meeting in my agenda for an extensive AI conversation. I had the idea of taking a picture of their face just before that conversation, and then afterwards another picture - with the excuse that the photo wasn't taken well. I would use face recognition software to find out whether specific elements in their expression had changed during the AI interview. I would spend hundreds of hours practicing AI, providing me with various kinds of research data to find out about possible effects: on the working atmosphere, quality of cooperation, and the personal well-being of the people in the department. I would be practicing my practice. This would represent the core of my research proposal for DPC. And even more, I would be paid a reasonable hourly fee for this. After all, studying at DPC is not for free, I am self employed, I was struggling through a divorce with the corresponding extra financial pressure. So this was going to be a win-win-win situation. In July, after having performed a typical AI interview with the director of that The Hague department, we shaked hands and it felt like a contract. I shared the details of my intended AI activities, I calculated the number and kind of hours when and where to spend, and they confirmed. My first meeting, to update and involve the management team, was due to happen.

In the meantime, building my DPC proposal, I had a series of constructive conversations with my future PhD mentor Mark. He resonated with my working title *Organizing Freedom* and saw the possibilities of "testing" the effect of AI in action. It would need a proper positioning of the concept of freedom and furthermore a clear introduction of what AI is about. But it made sense, since AI invites the other to see more possibilities (=freedom) than experienced before, when *situations* were still narrowed down to *problems*. My research question would be "What is the effect of a large-scale organization-wide Appreciative Inquiry intervention on the individual and collective behavior of the employees involved?" I even suggested the alternative term "innervention", but noticed that scientists rather seek robustness and security in language, than innovation. Creating new words is something that can't be supported by proper references. Mark was critical about the fact that AI would represent both my object as well as my method of research. That I, the researcher, also formed part of the process being researched, made it even more challenging. I think I really needed to include the work of Ken Gergen. At the time this all happened, Taos Institute and Leiden University were in contact about double PhD's and it was Ken who advised me to directly contact Mark. Things got sufficiently fluid to join into what DPC's director called "an exotic research".

I refer to Gergen's prize-winning essay at least once a week, was it just for the phrase *"What about research, not as a mirroring but as a making of the world?"* This quote would be my North Star to keep a clear focus on subject and object, the researcher and the researched, during my appreciative journey in that The Hague department. Unfortunately, this was not going to happen. One day before

I would start, the whole project was canceled, because of 'change in priorities'. I was disappointed, desperate, furious. Not my finest moment. It took me a while to recover my AI-capability and to practice even more its two main crafts 'to appreciate' and 'to inquire'.

Starting my Journalley

After I officially enrolled in the DPC Pre-PhD trajectory on the 1st of September 2017, it was an unexpected first task to completely revise the proposal that had made them accept me. It seemed dramatic at that time. I should have known better because, for decades already, my motto has been: "nothing goes without a plan, nothing goes according to plan". The last plan is the best plan, so I moved on with version two; expected delivery before Christmas 2017.

Slowly I came to the conclusion that to even produce a research proposal, already proper research should be done. It also became clear that I still was in the early stages of learning how to do research. Where is Baron von Munchhausen when you need him? I mean that famous book character, capable of lifting himself out of the swamp by pulling his bootstraps, also responsible for bringing the term 'booting the computer' into existence. "Where is the beginning of the beginning?", Ludwig Wittgenstein asked. We will meet him and his philosophical investigations again later. A new beginning of my research proposal had begun.

For me, the best thing to do seemed to keep a journal, a kind of diary just for this PhD journey. I had a few of those nice notebooks in stock - all gifts - and I chose the one from a client called Inspiralia, with the picture of an air balloon on the cover, saying "If the world has no sense, who's stopping us from inventing one?" My first writings filled the notes sheets by the end of September and before Christmas I had stuffed 64 pages with book titles, search words, names, inquiries, insights, ideas and reflections, lots and lots of reflections. My swamp was clear and present: an overload of information coming to and from my mind, constantly pulling me down in the sticky mud. My bootstraps were my pen, my journal and my notes. My pulling up consisted of jotting down - fixing, securing - my insights every moment I had - or I thought I had - progressed a millimeter. I continued filling three journal books and 420 pages; without these I wouldn't have been able to write the book you are reading. There's a tiny little piece of hope that reading my book also could help you to either pull yourself out of some swamp, or to get comfortable thriving in your juicy fertile mud.

Are you aware that the book you are holding is an attempt to deliver some scientifically obtained findings to everyone who cares about the wellbeing of future members of our organizations or communities? Did you read about my research findings already? Did you miss them? During my journey I was more than often surprised that, according to my PhD mentor, the honorable scholars don't seem to care so much about the character, the life experience nor the circumstances of the researcher, since that shouldn't have anything to do with what really matters: research niche, data, analysis, conclusions, and move on to the next paper, as crisp as possible and fully conform the latest APA restrictions.

It's as if Google Scholar would be interested in style, whilst searching for sources. Just think of research before the digital era: PhD candidates wandering across libraries and archives, articulating their search terms to librarians. No, today the searching is done by computers. It is of the utmost importance that in the rankings of citations all quotes are (ac)counted (for). Tripadvisor, but then for scientific papers. The number of likes as a search criterion. If - and only if - the ranking stars are honestly granted by real visitors, Tripadvisor at least gives a clue about the number of guests on a certain location, and the effort that location makes to seduce their visitors to add a like. Just remember that the most beautiful and relevant places may not be included in Tripadvisor. Nicholas Nassim Taleb stated that "a free person is to be defined as someone who is not dependent upon peer review". Given the fact that "independence" is considered a major pillar of academic integrity, this seems a bit contrary to being in the race for the highest H-index. I did a bit of research to find out that the H stands for Hirsch, which until now I only associated with the tuning kit on my old Saab and I guess I am drifting away, wondering about why and how academic life has become such a rat race.

64 Pages of Integrity

In my first semester at the DPC I attended a series of academic courses, I would mostly have forgotten about without my journal. I found them not very sophisticated but fairly useful. They provided fuel and a sounding board for my next version research proposal. Apparently I was not the only one struggling with this. The conversations with my fellow PhD candidates were inspiring and connective. The various courses informed me how to write, how to argue, how to do concept mapping, how to academically write, how to Create A Research Space (CARS), how to distinguish qualitative and quantitative research, and not in the least: how good research is defined. One particular course, regarding research integrity, was quite exciting. The official five academic principles are honesty, diligence, transparency, independence and responsibility. They sound to me quite obvious for any good work, including proper research. And still, the world of science suffers from the most juicy fraudulent scandals, falsified data and conclusions just for the sake of fame, or power, or other appearances of narcissism.

But then again: science also brought us Gödel's *Incompleteness Theorem*, stating that there's no such thing as a closed and therefore fully controllable system. (For me, O.M.G. means "Oh my Gödel.") My notes for example, especially when reading them again, are completely incomplete. However, they tell a whole story. This story; the integrity of it: impossible to deny. Integer means whole. So why has science become such a fragmentary occupation? Context is everything. My company name is OrgPanoptics, Managing the Whole. You reasonably can't ask from me just to pick a 'research niche' and forget about the rest. Can you? In the spring of 2018, I would be focussing on everything there is to know about one word. Apparently, every PhD is granted to their own specific meandering. And apparently the wise PhD mentors know that they should just let that happen.

So I was saying farewell to my first concept called Organizing Freedom, with myself both as organizer and researcher of that freedom, and using the very same practice - Appreciative Inquiry - as the intervention and as the research method. I couldn't escape anymore from the conclusion that this 'kind of niche' would bring me in scholarly trouble. To get out of my self-created mess I needed to bring multiple voices into my room: so I consulted all four mentors at DPC about my ideas. Mark said: "Search for the assumptions. Take organizational freedom as a conceptual starting point. Find out how to reach such a state, and to what extent AI can contribute to that." Pieter advised: "Delimit the discourse. Make sure that your research can be verified. Observe a completed case study from your past instead of creating a new one." Gijs lectured: "You contribute to theory building. Theory is a way of seeing, and it explains why we see what we see. AI is a method, a toolkit. What theory supports or explains AI? What makes the AI practitioner, which are his or her essential tools?" All this made me think deeper about what AI actually does, when it is applied, or practiced. And it occurred to me that practicing AI generates movement by means of specific high quality communication. One of my journal reflections sounds like "AI is sort of productive. Is it also re-productive?" What followed was pages with all kinds of synonyms for to reproduce: to copy, to duplicate, procreate, replicate, transfer, delegate, etc. I held on to the term forwarding. At some point I jotted down that I should inquire into the possible generative nature of AI. Does it touch the other person; does it even make the other person move? Then Maria Montessori entered my journal: "Teach them to do it themselves". A few pages further, I ask myself: "AI may be well-received by someone, would that someone also pass-on AI to others?" It is 15th December and the fourth PhD mentor Charlotte asks me: "Given a group of your The Hague AI alumni, how much AI do they pass on in their organization? To what extent and under which circumstances might AI have a certain effect in that organization?" I think she grabbed the essence of what I could investigate.

On the 21st of December 2017, the director of the DPC put his signature under our PhD contract. My (second) proposal was titled *Organizing Freedom, an Appreciative Inquiry into Organizational Enlightening*. The preliminary description of the research topic sounded like this: Appreciative Inquiry (AI) is a change method and human treatment aimed at tapping into and empowering strengths already present in people and organizations, through generative questioning and generative listening via a proven template, the so-called four-D model. The experienced AI-practitioner practices this craft: (a) as designer and process facilitator of inclusive and performative work conferences (AI summits); (b) as a constructive interlocutor, who in a high quality treatment invites the other to use his/her potential to the fullest; (c) to develop and deepen one's underlying AI attitude. The person who has been 'touched' by such an AI encounter, experiences this as having more possibilities for future action and as a certain enlightenment of his/her existence or functioning. You could call this an increase in freedom of movement. The 'mission' put forward by AI's founder David Cooperrider is to spread AI in the world. In his slipstream, several hundred experienced AI-practitioners are active worldwide. As true craftsmen, they learn with and from each other. Partly thanks to their work, it has been conclusively demonstrated that, because of AI, employees contribute to more initiative, more cooperation, more job satisfaction and ultimately to a better collective performance. You could say that AI *works*. If, within an organization of several thousand employees, you want to realize a broad reach, then it would be nice if AI not only works but also *works through*. The research question therefore could be: "To what extent and under what conditions will an AI intervention lead the person who experienced such, to start or want to practice AI themselves?" In other words, "Does AI harbor the potential for an inherent replicative effect?".

A new year awaited, and I had the feeling that I was up to something.

Cees, What Is It You Want to Research? (x10)

When I teach or facilitate Appreciative Inquiry, I often tell my audience that for about 40 years my personal development took place in my left brain half. I consider my time at the University of Humanistics as a shift, when my right brain half started to claim more attention. My little joke was that I would be in balance by the age of 80. But *The right way to flourish*, as John Ehrenfeld named his book, seems to make more speed. Of course, there's still plenty of left brain number crunching in my system, which made me aware of the fact that I needed exactly another 64 pages in my diary to be able to monumentalize the major breakthrough in my research planning. Eureka! I found it! Reaching that milestone would take the first three and a half months of the year 2018, filled with increasing confusion.

Zigzagging across more academic courses, about valorisation, research methods and the philosophy of science, the forest only grew bigger. My research was supposed to be valuable for society. So many methods and approaches seemed at hand: quantitative, qualitative, process analysis, engaged scholarship, discourse analysis, longitudinal case study; in the end I was convinced that when you just start exploring, you will find at least one article that describes your approach. So perhaps don't bother too much about the method, let alone the philosophy behind it. I've read articles about research methods on how to research research methods. From time to time I sent my mentor Mark a long email with my considerations. In return, if he responded, his reflections were not more than: "I don't understand you, please stick to the core question."

With all those courses I collected 30 ECTS (european credits representing 28 hrs of study) and all this knowledge didn't seem to help me much further. Two meetings with Mark took place, in which I presented my ideas, hoping to get some support, are at least a clue, but of course - I see now - the more you talk, the less you learn. In the few pauses I left, Mark repetitively asked me: "Cees, what is it exactly you want to research?" The struggle lasted until the first week of March, when I came to my senses. Good research is about asking the right questions, I read in another book about methods. Appreciative Inquiry is fueled by so called guiding questions. Slowly the idea grew that I might not study AI so much as well as practicing it, and perhaps better study the generativity of it instead of being constantly so generative in my preparations. The morning of 15th March, I took the 50 minute walk from my house to the DPC, where I would have my next 'session' with Mark. I had decided that this time I would be the one to ask questions, appreciatively of course, on which Mark could share his ideas and experiences. After all, I had been an AI practitioner for more than ten years. Why hadn't I thought of this before? Completely overwhelmed by the impressive academic environment? Wanting to be the best boy in the class? Practice what you preach, stupid. The long walk was purely to empty my mind, to focus on the person of Mark and Mark alone.

How powerful Appreciative Inquiry can be, when applied in the right way, and with the best intentions. Finally, there was our connective conversation. It happened because of my questions: inquiring into Mark's valuable life experiences, things to be proud of, and dreams to fulfill. Until that moment I only knew about his academic credentials. Now he showed completely different and beautiful sides of himself. His stories about Spain and his love for art really enlightened our meeting. The only thing I could do was listen. It was actually a pleasure to listen. Ten minutes before the scheduled end of our session, Mark suddenly came back to what we were here for. He said: "Cees, I know what it is you want to research. You want to research Generativity!" I thought "wow", and I showed him my latest notes, mentioning the same keyword. We smiled in silence. And he said: "First find out everything there is to know about the term generativity".

GENERATIVITY

Everything should be as simple as it can be,
but not simpler.

Einstein

And generativity it was! Only two days after the breakthrough I discovered a voluminous compendium, edited by 'AI-guru' David Cooperrider and others, titled *Organizational Generativity: the Appreciative Inquiry Summit and a Scholarship of Transformation.* This seemed a perfect starting point for a literature review. Enthusiastic I was, it would take me a while to find out that this needed to be a *critical* literature review. But so far, the book gave entrance to various sources related to my topic. Finally my research got a bit of a direction. Wasn't it for an unfortunate postal mistake, I would even have been the proud owner of a hard copy, signed by David himself. He was so kind to send it to me after I practiced a round of engaged scholarship, consisting of emailing professional friends in my network to ask them what resonates when I mention the term generativity in the context of organization.

New sources and references appeared in my notebook. The search word generativity guided me to the psychologists Erikson and McAdams, who use it for explaining life stages of individuals, but no hits came when I entered 'generativity in organization', except for that promising compendium. According to my journal I was still very stuck to my 'beloved AI practice' and the assumed generativity of it when I read myself pondering: "Is AI inherent generative?"

Another two months were needed to gently convert my thinking, from checking the generativity of AI to inquiring into the organizational generativity of The Hague city council, possibly caused by AI-interventions. I compare this with the organization as a garden, and the difference between checking its health by taking a soil sample, or by observing the growth and flourishing of its plants. In other words: don't watch the input, watch the process. The plant or flower on a certain day is just a temporary output; but watching the process of growing tells more about the garden's future. These notes were jotted in May 2018, exactly one year after finishing my 2017 book *Organize your processes, and you will never have to (re)organize again.* Clearly a book about the art of process thinking in order to improve general performance in the chain of organizational processes. In my mentor meeting with Mark, we now spoke of organizational generativity, and he assigned me to start writing the first chapter of my future dissertation, about generativity and organization. From that moment, the research proposal, the research and writing the dissertation went parallel. Panta rei, everything flows. I now fully adopted Mendeley as a reference manager, because it is one of the few that works on multiple devices. (I am a Chromebook believer.) Still, according to my growing collection of sources in Mendeley, I seemed to believe more in AI than in generativity.

Preliminary Framing

On July 6, a model - my first - appeared in my journal and it looked like this.

Survey Model for AI Summits To what extent are they…?					
Connective? (quality of the personal encounters)					
Constructive? (positive, valuable)					
Productive? (something decided or produced)					
Performative? (ownership, progression)					
Generative? (sustained, repeated, brought forward)					
Some kind of a scale (0 - 5 ?) and cumulate …					

Reading and copying this rough idea, I considered that taking notes of my research journey is already a kind of meta-research, which is more than just collecting data. Thinking afterwards, I'd better also had made meta-notes, in the sense that I am curious now what made me jot down that table.

During the summer of 2018, I was collecting more and more possible sources that refer to generativity. Even Darwin popped up: generativity as a biological way or procreation. Survival of the fittest. What about the fitness of organizations? What about the chances of survival for a good idea? I was constantly reading books and articles and not in a very structured way. I was learning that I should mark and fix and preferably code and correctly archive fragments of text that might seem relevant for my research into the concept of generativity. In reality, I may have read and re-read my sources multiple times to collect all this so-called data. The fact is, that I wasn't aware so much of doing research, I was just reading. And I am the kind of guy that first wants to retrieve an overview of what's there, the panoptical view - and not focus too soon on fragments.

In Dialogue with my Sources

By October I was working with twenty designated sources - books and articles - and struggling to make sense out of their existence in my Mendeley reference library. Should I put them on a timeline; or organize the lot by the type or number of relevant 'generativity' fragments they contain? Watching the fragments closer, I noticed that a fair amount of it are citations of the works of others. This gave me the idea of building a sort of genealogy; this is where I started to use the word *ancestor*. Some of the contemporary authors borrowed the word generativity from the work of psychologists or sociologists, took them out of their context and placed them in the organizational context they are writing about. Be aware that the number of (so-called) organization studies that refer to generativity is quite small. Actually, the total number of books and publications that use the word generative on purpose, may not reach far beyond one hundred.

The moment I reached my data saturation - that is when you don't encounter any more new sources that add to your data set, which was around January 2019 - I had collected 27 OD (organizational development) sources by 19 authors somehow using the word generative or generativity, as well as 45 'ancestor' sources by 30 authors, referred to by the 19 OD authors. At least, my genealogy gave an impression of who went before who; who made use of who; and since when generativity entered the OD domain. As far as can be found in digital sources, the word generativity was born in 1950, when Erik Erikson published his theory of life stages. The sixth stage, Generativity, can be obtained when we reach our sixties, and makes us 'giving forward' our knowledge, experience and wealth to next generations. Very generous, so to say. If we don't reach this stage, we get stuck in what Erikson called Stagnation. And all this can be 'measured' through a questionnaire called the *Loyola Generativity Scale*. And of course, when you want to use the word generativity in an non-biological abstract called organization, one takes the utmost care when tele-transporting the term from one academic domain to the other, wouldn't we?

Two important insights emerged during my process of extensively reading the text fragments that I marked in my growing set of sources. My first and most surprising discovery was that the word generativity is used in a somewhat sloppy way, referring to a variety of meanings. Where I first thought that I was just entering a pre-study to collect a proper working definition of generativity, I had to conclude that clarifying the term was going to be a major, or perhaps even a foundational challenge. The second insight was my growing awareness that I was not just checking sources to build an answer to my research question; every time I studied a new source, there was a chance that my question would change. This felt more and more like a co-creation, at least a dialogue between me and the authors. Not that they changed their minds - impossible, especially for the ones that don't live anymore - but where my keywords guided me to their path, their words and references directed me to different paths and new unknown sources. I think I saw some notes about this phenomenon in my journal, saying that what happened between me, my sources and my diary notes might be called generative. It would take me almost another year at DPC to be able to underpin this assumption with a lot more confidence and accuracy.

More Titles than Body Text

I must admit that being a PhD candidate is like taking lessons with the perspective of getting your driver's license. So perhaps for the ones that have passed their PhD (Philosophical Doctor) exam, the process of source selection is much more straightforward than my divergent (bloody) saturation adventure. Now you might think that all this research may take place behind curtains but actually, the DPC wants to show the world what their candidates are up to. (Something with validation, remember?) So I was warmly invited to fill my personal Leiden University webpage with an introduction to - and an explanation of - my research. In compact web language that is. I must have revised that page multiple times, trying to keep aligned with my emerging PhD plans. To give the visitor an idea of this emergence, I shared the history of my respective titles:

- *September 2017: Organizational Freedom.*
- *December 2017: Organizational Freedom, an Appreciative Inquiry into Organizational Enlightening.*
- *July 2018: An Appreciative Inquiry into Organizational Generativity.*
- *September 2018: Genarrativity: Reshaping the Generativity of Appreciative Inquiry in Organizational Life.*

- *October 2018: Genarrativity: Reviewing the Generativity of Appreciative Inquiry in Organizational Life.*
- *November 2018: Genarrativity: Reviewing the Generativity of Appreciative Inquiry in Organizational Life.*

The last one wasn't yet the final one. But the November version of my 'PhD-pitch' provided a fair impression of where I was at that moment; besides getting married to my beloved and the corresponding heavenly bath in the warm diversity of our family and friends. It was the most perfect excuse to freeze my research for a while and let the content of my DPC web page be my messenger. See an extract of it below. Points 1. and 2. are to refresh one's understanding of AI a bit. The place where I am *Creating A Research Space* is in point 3. Take good notice of point 4. And point 5 proves that the title of this book flowed from my pen into my journal way earlier than I assumed.

1. In short, Appreciative Inquiry (AI) is a possibility oriented, dialogical development approach to enable and enforce people and organization's well being. (source: David Cooperrider a.o., multiple publications) The method AI is mainly delivered in the form of coaching and large group summits, which I would call interventions. Less common is the delivery of AI in the form of teaching employees in organizations to become an AI practitioner themself, a process which I would call an inner-vention.

2. Appreciative Inquiry bears the promise to discover the life giving elements in organizations to further build upon. "To spread AI into the world" is the motto of AI-practitioners. Being an experienced AI practitioner myself, both in AI intervention and AI *innervention*, I am interested in the possibility of AI being generative in the sense of: does AI-behavior to another give rise to growing AI-behavior of that other? My research questions are: "What can be found about (this kind of) generativity of AI summits?" and "What can be found about (this kind of) generativity of the AI-innervention, going on in the City Council of The Hague?". My main research goal is to reveal the 'maximum' generative potential of Appreciative Inquiry.

3. To 'measure' the generativity of AI-processes requires a clear description of what it is to be generative. Surprisingly, as my first inquiries showed, there seem to be various different definitions, interpretations and applications of the quality

called generativity (source: 125 publications). Some of those support my own 'propagative' interpretation, which at least gives confidence for the relevancy of my inquiries. Within the domain of Appreciative Inquiry, generativity is frequently used (source: Gervase Bushe a.o., multiple publications), and mainly associated with producing new, unexpected and appealing ideas - not really my propagative, replicative interpretation. Furthermore, the variety in interpretations and applications - from Sociology to Information Technology, from Psychology to Organization Studies - is of such an extent, that I can't just 'choose' my definition and use it for my AI case studies. What my findings suggest to me is that my research, and perhaps organization studies in general - can benefit from a framework called Generativity (with capital G) that not combines but collects the most relevant meanings, and that can help to find out to what kind and which 'level' of generativity one is looking at.

4. The comments you are now reading are dated 9th October 2018. I am in the midst of preparing and writing my PhD chapter *In Search of Generativity* that should create the framework Generativity: the foundation for analyzing my two sets of case material (intervention/innervention). My research process into the meaning of generativity shows in itself various characteristics of generativity: constructive dialogue with my sources; giving birth to new knowledge, nurturing it and letting go of it; receiving unexpected insights that suddenly appear; becoming more of a researcher by doing research; affecting others with my inquiries to start inquiring themselves. In this I find myself meandering between Baron Munchhausen (who pulled himself up through his bootstraps) and Gödel (creator of the Incompleteness Theorem). I could scholarly refer to an article about explorative research (Stebbins, 2011), but I have to warn the reader that the definition of *explorativity* is also quite generative...

5. And what about *Genarrativity* (with an a)? Remember Derrida and let's see what this word tries to tell us.

Regarding some organizations, I will not further elaborate on here, I sometimes use the borrowed phrase "all chiefs, no indians". Regarding the production of my dissertation until November 2018, one could wickedly comment "all titles, no text". Not completely true. End of October 2018, I presented a first draft text to my mentor. It contained a description of my humanizing aspirations, my entanglement with AI, the discovery of

Organizational Generativity according to Cooperrider, an overview of my sources so far, and my early findings about the fragility of the word generativity.

I had produced a piece of writing. After all, my first academic year at the DPC had come to an end, and the idea was to be granted a pre-PhD certificate by then. For this, I needed to supply proof of having followed a certain amount of PhD-courses; I needed the approval of my proposal, preferably underpinned with a first chapter.

I checked all the boxes but for one: I should have already found a potential PhD supervisor, and I was still far from that milestone. Silly me, at that Christmas meeting, feeling a bit degraded when others were invited to the podium and received their certificate. The truth is that most of the PhD candidates don't reach their DPC goals within the officially given two years. A fair part of dual PhD students sees it as a hobby and doesn't mind about taking one or more decades to succeed. But in those days I wanted to be the perfect performer. Apparently I didn't so much consider the comments I received on my draft text: "Cees, give more attention to generativity and less to AI." (Ouch.) "A dissertation is not a journey nor a journal." (Pfoo.) "Your connection with AI should be no more than a slight remark in a preface." (Oink.)

I did it agAIn. Mark was right, and also gave me some practical hints: disconnect the research introduction from the main chapters; concentrate in the first chapter on the concept of Generativity. So, I cut my document in Chapter 0: *In Search of Generativity* and Chapter 1: *A Framework Named Generativity*, and this structure would hold for the next eleven months.

Organizational Healthy Aging

Yes minister! So right, mister Churchill. Writing a long letter (a.k.a. this book) is so much simpler than keeping the message crisp and brief. That's why I accept every challenge to shrink my propositions to the minimum. (A five minute video at the 2020 Academy of Management Conference, covering my whole research project, must have been my biggest achievement in that respect. But that's for later.) When the DPC sent out a Call for Posters, to illustrate the work of their PhD candidates at the walls of the building, I was the first to subscribe, also fueled by ideas that came out of a PhD course called Media Strategy. What makes the journalist pick out and publish your story? What is your message to the world you will be sharing at your press conference? It should be something that triggers the audience to ask "tell me more". The journalist's advice in brief: Seduce. Be efficient. Simplify.

Playing with ideas about healthy organizations, combined with not only being successful but also securing succession, I came to think of an organization's expiry date. And especially when it comes to (mostly) public institutions that don't seem to have an end date, I came with a draft (still too long) teaser: *The average public organization lives already for more than 100 years. Organizations are older than you think. Old and wise. Do they behave as wise as their age suggests? How about #OrganizationalHealthyAging?* Grumpy old organizations. Does that make me an organizational geriatrician? What to do when organizations become older but not wiser? Voila, beautiful content for a poster of 90 by 120 cm, portrait mode, and about 400 words.

I love to have a frame, a restriction. When I started being self-employed I decided to distribute a monthly newsletter among friends. A one pager, with nothing less than seven mini articles, all between 25 and 125 words. Such a nice puzzle to make! The DPC poster was a similar puzzle, and I completed it in one week. There's a proud photo showing it hanging on the wall, with the DPC director and me on both sides of it. The header of the poster said:

> "Many public domain organizations exist for such a long time that they can be considered 'old'. Seen as a metaphor they often behave 'older than wise'. They 'quarrel and complain' like 'grumpy old people', stuck in stagnation, not able to explore life's possibilities anymore. In real life, elderly people increasingly practice the art of healthy aging and seem to do better than 'old organizations'. What about organizational healthy aging? Generativity, both as measure and enabler of vitalizing organization development, is a promising new concept that requires more understanding and clarification."

Seeing it years later I love it as much as before. It grabs quite accurately what I was up to. And in a way I am still on the same track with the same aspirations.

Generative Organization

Many public domain organizations exist such a long time that they can be considered 'old'. Seen as a metaphor they often behave 'older than wise'. They 'quarrel and complain' like 'grumpy old people', stuck in stagnation, not able to explore life's possibilities anymore. In real life, elderly people practise increasingly the art of healthy ageing and seem to do better than 'old organizations'. What about organizational healthy ageing? Generativity, both as measure and enabler of vitalizing organization development, is a promising new concept that requires more understanding and clarification.

Organization in Stagnation

Healthy Ageing of Organizations: Reviewing Generativity

Research Motivation (-> 2018)

Organizational generativity not clearly defined

Today's organizations, especially the ones that exist in public domain, must adapt to rapidly changing circumstances. To survive in the present societal complexity, their organization development (OD) initiatives should aim beyond the usual criteria: efficient, effective, innovative and even sustainable[1].

In 2013 the term generativity[2] entered the OD vocabulary, suggesting an organization's capability to reproduce its life giving elements to benefit future generations. Studies that address organizational generativity show a wide variety of definitions and interpretations, and none of them include the propagating[3] quality; two reasons for further clarification.

[1] Sustainable is not enough (Marcuse, 1998)
[2] Organizational Generativity: The Appreciative Inquiry Summit and a Scholarship of Transformation (Cooperrider et al. 2013).
[3] Etymological Dictionary of Greek (Beekes, 2010)

Research Modelling (2018 -> 2019)

Framework to assess & promote generativity

While generativity is relatively young within Organization Studies, various other disciplines have included and studied the concept for a much longer period. The idea is to collect relevant academic definitions and include contemporary interpretations to construct a conceptual framework 'Generativity' aiming for more refined and nuanced understanding and assessment of how - and to what extent - OD interventions (potentially) contribute to organizational life.

$gen^3 \sim$ (Greek root) to give birth, to arise

Research Data (2019 -> 2020)

Two Appreciative Inquiry case studies

Appreciative Inquiry (AI) is a thirty year old, strength based and possibility oriented organization development method, which claims to be highly generative. Since the newly constructed draft framework Generativity is in the need[1] for validation before application, it seems the logical way to use AI samples for both purposes.

AI Summits ~ interventions	AI in-company ~ *inner*vention
- whole system intervention, based on diversity and inclusion	- longitudinal in-company training within The Hague City Council
- through Discover, Dream, Design and Destiny towards the implementation of best possible ideas	- inquiry amongst 40 trained internal AI-practitioners
- survey amongst experienced facilitators of the summits	- who did they 'touch' and what was the effect of their AI-skills?
- evaluation of specific summit characteristics and request for feedback on the survey questions	- survey[2] into the experience amongst the 'receivers' of the AI-gestures

[1] Building a Conceptual Framework: Philosophy, Definitions, and Procedure (Jabareen, 2009)
[2] Social Network Analysis (Steketee et al, 2015)

Research Ambition (2020 ->)

Enhance the effectiveness of OD-interventions

Imagine that OD-consultants and (change) managers are more aware of - and able to valuate - the possible impact of their interventions on the generativity of organizational life.

"What about research, not as a mirroring but as a making of the world?"[1]

As such, the instrument Generativity could serve as an extension of the extensive toolkit that has been generated within the domain of Organizational Studies.

[1] From Mirroring to World-Making: Research as Future Forming (Gergen, 2014)

Very preliminary still: because organization development is a construct of social interactivity, the concept of generativity, in terms of mutual benefit, could be enhanced to genarrativity...

genarrativity.org

Cees Hoogendijk
Leiden University Dual PhD Centre
mail@ceeshoogendijk.nl

It became end of December 2018 and the final revision of the originally revised revision of my dissertation title annex PhD proposal sounded:

Organizing Generativity: a Conceptual Framework

to Appreciate and Inquire

the Fitness of Organizational Interventions

It took me another six pages of diverging and converging journal notes to make sense out of what I jotted on that 26th of December: "Title Dilemma's". It was 22 months since my intake conversation with Mark, it was 12 months after my first PHD proposal, and I think I had a bit of a clue what I was doing and what I had to do. I thought. Therefore I was. (Descartes.)

Having reached page 200 of my journal, I had to inaugurate a new one: a distinguished booklet of 160 pages, with an imprint of Nyenrode University on the brown cover supposed to imitate wood.

When I now browse through both subsequent journals, I see an important difference in the general appearance of my notes: the older ones being quite

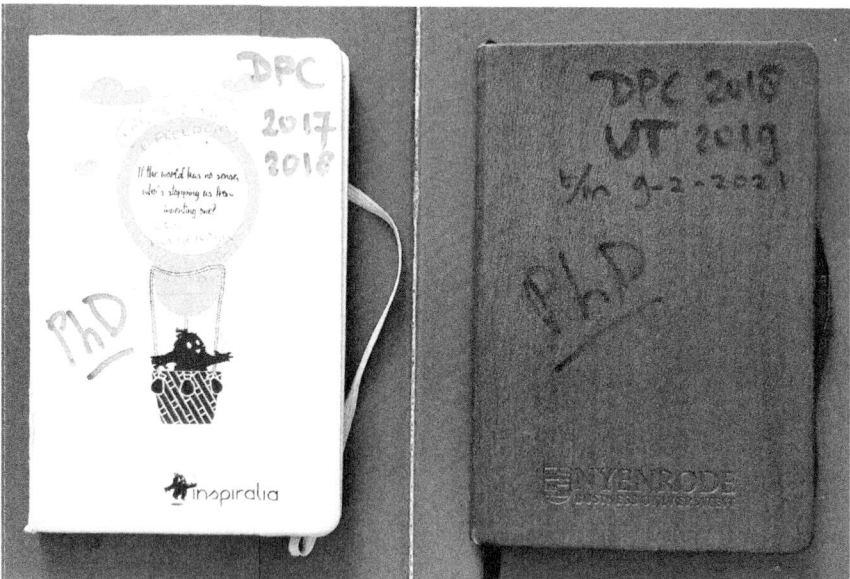

chaotic; the younger writings fairly structured.

Hopefully for you this book will take the same turn. Or do you like a bit of chaos? We're not done yet. All in all, my research began to deliver some results. Organizing generativity may be a bridge too far, but *clarifying* generativity - for proper and less confusing use in common and organizational language - was

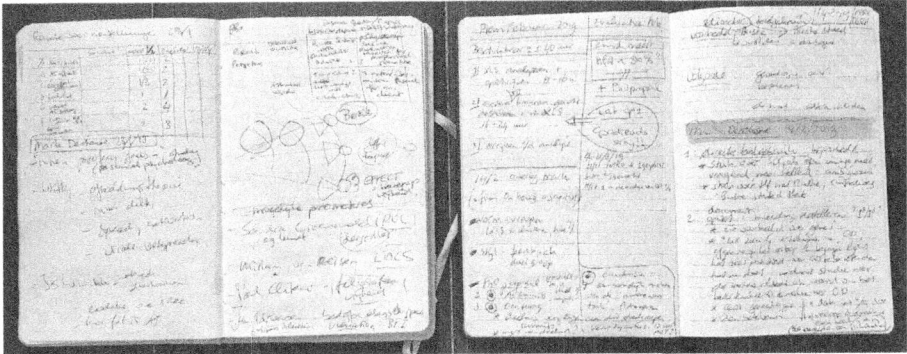

surely going to happen. It better be, because on 31st January 2019 my official half yearly DPC progress meeting was due, with the director and my mentor. A go-no-go moment. What would I bring to the table?

During that month of January - typically a period with fewer client work - I produced quite a lot. On the quantitative side of my research I was looking at 25 OD sources, out of which I had selected 150 text fragments that were using the word generativity or its adjective generative. I managed to organize these pieces of text in an excel spreadsheet, in this case to be seen as my database. A significant part of these fragments contained citations from another 40 ancestor sources.

On the methodological side of my research I could put my OD sources back on the bookshelf, because for my analysis of generativity I only needed to focus on the 150 fragments. (And if I needed more context, my database would help me to find the right book and page number.) I had a fair idea of the different layers in which I could analyze the text fragments from validation of the data, to the syntax into the semantics of my data. I also decided that I would use the ancestor sources not to extend my fragments, but as a sounding board to reflect on the findings from primary data. That would represent a fourth layer of investigation. And when a new search - not in Google Scholar but in Goodreads - delivered another 37 miscellaneous titles containing the word generativity, I saw the possibility of adding a fifth layer, just to find out whether I had missed something because of staying in the OD domain. Speaking about saturation. This would determine my chapter one, aiming for turning the word generative/ity into a (conceptual) frame. And against this frame I could assess the proceedings and impacts of two AI interventions in the organization of The Hague: to be captured later in dissertation chapters 3 and 4.

On the qualitative side of my research - I mean extracting findings and preliminary insights from the present data - I had noticed a few aspects I hadn't expected. I thought I was just using my OD sources to frame or define my keyword as a preparation for the real research: assessing my AI interventions. But getting the panoptical view of the use of generative/ity I became a bit disappointed. Other researchers would tell me that I was on to something. First there was the fragility of the term generative/ity: such a variety of different meanings and interpretations that at first sight no specific clue was to be derived from that; the term was "multi-framed". Moreover, I found conflicting definitions, and disputable statements about the generativity of something. Don't forget that I am citing academic sources here. Furthermore I found nothing about the procreative potential of generativity - the feeding forward. All associations with the term referred to effects in the here and now. And although the word was deliberately in use in organizational literature, it was constantly associated with people and objects in the OD context, but never with the organization as a whole. So in my journal I found notes like: "Shall we 'for a change' have a proper look at Generativity itself, instead of taking it for granted as a nice adjective on the side?" and "If we don't take care of the word, it might 'degenerate' to a synonym of an amplifier like 'terrific'; before we know, we call Agile a generative method" and "A nice but risky term, not to call it fragile: possible to negate with one counterexample". My assumed preparation for research seemed to become a research in itself.

On the logistic side of my research I progressed by implementing a monthly moment of evaluating the previous period, and planning the next. Plan-Do-Check-Act. Demming can be a welcome friend in times of divergence.

On the generative side of my research, by which I mean associations not directly derived from the data, but rather from my inquisitive process in general, I started to question the highly praised term 'sustainable' and to embrace the word 'emergence'. Sustainable - supported by scholarly statements like 'sustainable is not enough' - seems to be more circular, no waste, keeping at a certain level, where generative seems to refer to something further ahead. My encounter with emergence starts with the question: "What aggregation level do we study?" Do we study the ant or the anthill, and is there a clear relation between the two? A water molecule is not wet. Water is. Where does the transition take place, if we can speak of such? In the organization context we tend to speak of the world of management disconnected from the world of the workfloor. In all these examples the relationship between the two levels seems to be a fuzzy one, mutually influencing each other, the one not producing the other and vice versa. My journal note is brief but contains a meta-universe: "G on individual level / G on organizational level". (Two years later, this assumed distinction between generativity *in* organization and generativity *of* organization would cause me a lot of scholarly trouble.)

One day before the mid-term meeting I uploaded my draft to my tutors, covering my activities, data and preliminary findings so far. The essence of the feedback they gave me was twofold: "Well written, you are on the right path, continue like this," and: "with each possible supervisor you want to find, you will have only one chance; focus in your writings on the added value for them". The targets for the coming half year were clear: finish chapter 1 (everything there is to know about generativity); draw the attention of a candidate supervisor; revise your PhD proposal, include a planning; and earn your PhD Certificate.

Highlights of DPC Chapter 0

Quoting oneself is a popular academic practice. The citations below are quoted from draft material, which my DPC supervisors rated as well written; every word of it a result of various revisions; every word of it to be revised again in the future that was ahead of me. Are you ready for some ' academic' reading? I did my best to keep it as accessible as possible.

> Organizational generativity: a paradigm with potential? In these times of growing complexity, in which organizations are supposed to become adaptive to change, and therefore should be fitter than ever, it can be considered a good thing that the qualifier generative entered the organizational discourse. This term opens the doorway to consider organization development beyond the conventional business criteria productive, efficient and effective; the word generative provides easy access to the idea of a sustainable organization development. Although popular in organizational debate, we should look even further than sustainable (Marcuse, 1998; Wahl, 2018). Generative could or should refer to organizational flourishing, a concept still under construction but

strongly inspired by the idea of organizational health and well-being, in the sense of: vital, doing more than meeting the goals, providing extra value to society, metaphorically speaking: giving flowers that spread the seeds for procreation. (p. 4)

In 2013, Cooperrider et al. presented the compendium *Organizational Generativity, the Appreciative Inquiry Summit and a Scholarship of Transformation* in which generativity as a 'life giving' organizational feature is reviewed from a variety of perspectives. In this extensive work, generativity is said to be in the organizational air when - through generative inquiry, generative images, generative processes - new unexpected ideas have appeared that encourage the partakers to constructive or even transformative action; creating generative outcomes. One could say that by this book, generativity has officially been introduced in the organization development discourse. However, regarding the clarity of generativity, two observations can be made. First, the book still breathes an exclusive relation between organizational generativity and Appreciative Inquiry, which makes it hard to focus on organizational generativity as an independent concept. Second, the book seems to contain a contradiction between on the one hand the promising life-giving i.e. procreative, replicative, capability of generative action, and on the other side the actual definitions and examples of generativity which don't seem to reach farther than - simply stated - 'creating new, potentially transformative, appealing ideas'. How promising these types of ideas might be, they still insufficiently refer to sustainable well-being or to flourishing in the metaphorical sense of giving flowers that carry the seeds for potential outliving. (p. 5)

The general quest for organizations to become flourishing makes it very tempting to try and find a recipe for 'inherent generative organizations'. But such a research goal would again imply assumptions about the word generative: as being a quality of an organization, or even as being high on the ladder of organizational qualities. No, the question at stake here is to study generativity, and generativity alone, for the possible sake of better organizing. (p. 8)

The full thesis ambition includes a framework that is relevant for organization studies, in particular for organization development practitioners; a frame of reference that invites and enables these change managers - and their awarding authorities - to consider the fitness of their interventions, ideally before implementation. In this way, the tool called Generativity can be seen as a meta-intervention, appreciating all existing OD-interventions, enabling the inquiry of their effectiveness. The challenge is to turn Generativity not into a criterion, but into a language, a checklist perhaps, to make the OD practitioner more aware of his/her intentions, to invite the OD practitioner to reflect on the right tools for the right purpose before applying them, and by this to understand the added value of the interventions better and better. One could also speak of a conceptual "un-framework or re-framework", since the general idea is to invite change managers to review their own frames. (p. 8-9)

By the end of April, Mark graded Chapter 0 as 'perfect' which means that my research contained a foundation, and that I was allowed to spend my energy on the content. My next progress meeting was scheduled on 27th June and I was happy to spend about half a year fully on my Chapter 1: *A Framework Named Generativity*. To my opinion, the findings, conclusions and recommendations in that chapter, when reaching its final status by September 2019, were grounded and promising, until they got validated in a surprising big bang.

GENARRATIVE

TO FRAME OR NOT TO FRAME

One cannot guess how a word functions. One has to look at its application and to learn from that. But the difficulty is to remove the prejudice which stands in the way of doing so. It is not a stupid prejudice.

Ludwig Wittgenstein

In April 2019, the World Appreciative Inquiry Conference (WAIC) in Nice offered two great opportunities to enrich my research. I could hang my PhD poster on the designated wall for poster presentations, which enabled some constructive new encounters. And I had the honor and pleasure to have Gervase Bushe on my side as co-host in my workshop about generativity. I had Zoomed and emailed a few times with dr. Bushe, well known for his publications on Dialogic OD and - later - Generative Leadership, besides being the author of some sources in my database. By the time we did this workshop together, I didn't know yet that his use of the word generativity also would be facing some critical remarks from my side. And I am sure he would have smiled. He surely smiled in the course of our WAIC session which I had designed as a kind of field lab, to find out how people respond to the word generativity. We had - thanks to the presence of Gervase - about 40 participants. The chairs were put in three semicircles, and all had a piece of paper and a pen on it. From the 75 minute workshop only 10 were needed to show a few slides. The first presented the word Generativity. I asked the audience to draw intuitively the image that came to mind when seeing that word. The next slide showed three short poems. I asked the audience which of those they considered "the most generative". The same for images of paintings and of people. (Yes, this was a manipulative question. In a later version of this field research I added "in so far you would consider one or more of the three generative".) My next assignment was to rate their present level of generativity on a scale from 0 to 10. Then I asked them to complete the sentence "As far as I considered myself to be generative, until now I used to call that ... ".

They all jotted down their answers and were told that at the end of the session they could decide whether or not to hand their notes to me, for the sake of science. After a mini-introduction of Gervase and myself, he and I took a seat on two opposite chairs in the center, with an empty seat next to us, and we started a so-called fishbowl conversation. Gervase started the conversation, and it took just a few moments for one participant to join in on the third chair. A few minutes further Gervase and I had been replaced by participants, and I remember myself at some point standing behind the largest semicircle, just enjoying the lively conversation that took place by constantly changing speakers. The only thing left to do was to stop the process when the time was over, and to ask one last question: "What do you consider now your generativity, on a scale of 1-10?" I collected almost 40 pieces of paper: additional data for my research, and not yet really having a clue what to do with it, other than to fill a spreadsheet. At least I felt strengthened in my gut feeling that something like a painting or a poem can't be called generative in itself: each of the three alternatives in my slides got more or less the same number of votes for being most generative. In that period I had various opportunities to speak in public - mostly online - about my research, and two of those sessions also included my 'field lab'. I became more and more comfortable with presenting my intermediate findings before a live audience and answering their questions. Not in the least because I had really taken a deep dive in my dataset.

Philosophical Investigations

My research data saturated into 27 OD publications and 157 text fragments. My spreadsheet not only mentioned the page and title of the corresponding sources; I now was in the process of coding the fragments. For example, I distinguished four (syntactical) ways the word generative was being used in the text: either directly described, or only used as an adjective; or even more indirectly: as a precondition for generativity to appear, or in a way that you have to guess what generativity is about because the author writes about possible results of it. Quite a puzzle already, supporting the 'fuzziness', and raising the question to what extent such variety and indirectness in presentation is scientifically allowed to clarify the term generativity. Another aspect of the validity of the dataset is how many of the 27 authors were actually fans of Appreciative Inquiry, which could relate them to generativity and might cause bias. Graduated in mathematics, and with my basic knowledge of statistics, I looked into this question and concluded that my dataset was unbiased. However, two years later, a certain anonymous peer reviewer of the *Journal of Applied Behavioral Science*, would strongly question this.

This all was apparently needed to prepare for investigating the actual content of my text fragments. What did they tell me about the meaning and application of the term generative/ity? In short: I discovered that in some cases generativity is referred to as a quality of a thing, an object; in other cases the term is connected to people; but in the majority of the fragments the adjective generative is describing a process, an interaction. And even more: within that majority of examples of the generativity of processes, an extra layer of coding appeared, showing seven manifestations of processual generativity.

In the previous paragraph I did what my PhD mentor asked me to do when he saw my early draft of Chapter 1: "Skip the story, tell them what you have found, and then tell them how you found it." And somehow I suspect that in my brief paragraph above, about my semantical findings from 157 text fragments, you may not have created real understanding. And the point is - at least in this stage of the research - that words create worlds, that we should be aware of what we say, and that some words - like generativity - need even more care and attention than other ones.

I may have been the only one on this planet that has studied so many if not all publications regarding generativity. My data was telling me stories, and I tried my best to be brief in my reporting of it. But text is no math. You can count the number of text fragments, but interpreting their content is of a different nature. At least it includes the views and vocabulary of the researcher, so my findings and arguments should always be accompanied by examples taken from the samples. "Stay as close to your data as possible", I remember from one of the PhD workshops. So my Chapter 1 was growing, and the semantic layer was to be called either an analytical reflection or a reflective analysis. And yes, I know, even when I am writing this, that I am also dealing with readers that are used to watching 'slides and bullet points' and making decisions on the basis of that. Perhaps they stopped reading already many pages ago. But I need you to stand by me, when I share the highlights from Chapter 1. And where my DPC mentor made me start the chapter with the final product: a conceptual framework on generativity, I ask you to be patient in being accompanied in a (chrono)logical pathway to the apotheosis of Part One of this book: a practical and grounded guideline for how to use the word generativity properly and professionally for the sake of building better legacies. So we are heading now for both an apotheosis and a big bang. Shall we? After you.

A Framework Named Generativity

When I say highlights, I intend to give you a fair impression of 80 pages of my draft Chapter 1 in 'text bites'. Regarding the structure: the first five pages are to engage the reader for the topic and explain the research steps; in just more than two pages the end product is presented: the *Conceptual Framework Generativity*; then it takes another sixteen pages to elaborate on that framework with examples and arguments. Page 25 until 63 describe the various layers of the underlying literature study, under the consecutive heading titles: (1) Starting from gen: exploring the basics, (2) Exploring generativity addressed within OD, (3) Supplementary field research, (4) Genealogy of the OD sources, (5) Remaining sources on generativity: a supplementary spectrum. Eleven pages of references completed this draft, dated 27th August 2019.

The following selection of 'high bites' provides a brief document overview.

Two apprentices and their teacher are watching a flag on a windy day.
One apprentice says: "Look, the flag is waving."
The other: "No, the wind is waving."
The teacher: "It is your mind that is waving."
(p. 2)

The literature study reveals that appearances of generativity often are being addressed by words such as productive, creative or transformative; words that are mainly in use as isolated synonyms or definitions, and not as a certain level, dimension or capacity of generativity; words that also need a sufficient description for to be included in a conceptual framework. Further inquiry, analysis and reflection showed that generativity spans a field of possible - and impossible - perspectives, in which different meanings in their own specific way apply to different subjects or objects. Yes, a generator can be truly productive. We are allowed to speak of a generative person, but only under the right conditions. Can we call the assumed generative book transformative? Or would it be the combination of book, reader and circumstances that generates the transformation? When generativity is in the air, various manifestations are possible. This study into the meaning and use of generativity embodied more than pure text analysis; it required to include application, context and history. On the basis of the retrieved insights, this explorative research journey can now safely be qualified as a generative process. (p. 3)

Of course [the OD authors] are granted the freedom of choice. From a mathematical stance we could appreciate their chosen starting points as axioms. However, given the various 'definitions' of generativity used by the respective authors within the same academic discipline, it can't be denied that together they produced too many different, sometimes even opposing 'axioms' around the same term. (p. 4)

An example to illustrate this fragility is found in the term generative image (which in some cases could as well be perceived as *degenerative*). Bushe states: "One of the most iconic generative images of the past fifty years is sustainable development. Before that phrase showed up, environmental activists and business leaders had little to say to each other." (Bushe, 2013) Did this phrase really make the difference, did it really contain appealing new ideas to act upon? Has mother earth benefitted already substantially from it? In the cases that we did become sustainability activists, was it because of the phrase, or because the world showed to be increasingly unhealthy? Might it be that by having seventeen sustainable development goals (SDG's), we citizens think that governments and other big institutions are taking care of the problem, releasing us of our individual responsibilities? Could it be the case that, from such a perspective, the existence of SDG's is merely de-generative? Did it perhaps create more opponents than supporters? Is sustainable development at the moment still a generative image? These questions are probably not easy to answer. Which gives reason to think that it is debatable to declare sustainable development a role-model within generative images. (p. 5)

For the sake of generativity, this writing would rather continue as a meandering journal, slowly revealing findings, conclusions and recommendations, gradually or suddenly materializing into a framework, and thereby practicing what it is attempting to preach. For the sake of academic publications however, it starts with the introduction of the constructed framework and proceeds with the corresponding research itinerary, sources and substantiations. Let it nevertheless be known to the reader that the upcoming conceptual framework could not have been devised before having collected and examined all sources. Besides, it was not the researcher; it was the interchange between him and the data that gave birth to what is going to be presented here. (p. 6)

If only one conclusion could be drawn from this study, it would be that generativity – and the corresponding adjective generative – are promising words; containers of hope and aspiration. They point forward, upward. (p. 26)

Generativity is derived from the Greek root gen. It bears two meanings: to beget and to arise (Beekes & Beek, 2010, p. 272); to give birth and to become apparent. When someone or something A gives birth to someone or something B, at least it is very clear where that B came from. But when someone or something C (suddenly) appears, it is not very clear where C came from. By the way, the Greek etymology of gen doesn't say whether it is a good thing to have B or C among us. What it does suggest is at least two possible meanings of generativity: (1) the ability (of someone or something) to give birth in the sense of to reproduce or to procreate, and (2) the property of (someone or something) to appear. (p. 28)

Together, the 157 text fragments represent a diverse collection of empirical derived descriptions, citations of earlier definitions, definitions borrowed from different disciplines, freely combined and even self-created definitions. Looking just for (assumed) definitions would have been a too poor exploration: in an iterative process of reading and re-reading, structuring and restructuring, the 157 text fragments implied further division in four categories: Defining/explaining generativity; Generativity used as an adjective to something else; Pre-conditions for generativity and Effect/impact of generativity. This distinction amplifies the difference between direct and indirect meanings to be derived from the fragments. (p. 31)

Further exploration of the dataset, as referred to in Table 2 [with the 27 OD sources], includes analyses of consecutively: (i) the validity of the data, (ii) the nature of the text fragments and the occurrences over time, (iii) how and how often the authors referred to earlier sources, (iv) the extent to which the content of the text items supports the assumption of fragility, and (v) the extent to which the content of the text items reveals the first contours of a more robust conceptual framework. [...] To what extent can our text fragments be seen as equally distributed, enabling us to consider each text fragment as valuable as each other fragment? In other words: do we need to take account of certain preferences among certain (groups of) authors? After careful examination we are inclined to say that the dataset can be treated as non-biased. (p. 32)

How do the text fragments distilled from our set or OD sources address generativity? Analysis has been executed in three layers, revealing that generativity can be seen as a quality of something, someone or some in-between.

The first layer is about the categories representing the four different ways in which the text fragments refer to generativity. This opens a first level of understanding, mainly providing evidence to the assumption that the use of the term generativity within (academic) OD practices can be regarded as arbitrary and questionable. Nevertheless, with Wittgenstein in mind, the various explanations, descriptions and references are not stupid.

The second layer of analysis is based on a labeling system that distinguishes possible meanings of generativity referred to in the OD context. Two labels, coded "?" and "X", refer to text items that support the existence of flaws in the application of the term. Two other labels refer to generativity as a quality of something (code "Q_I") or someone human (code "Q_H"). The Q-coded text items present a huge variety of synonyms for the word generative; perhaps a rich source; yet another hint towards fragility.

The third layer analysis includes seven labels for text items that refer to generativity as characteristic of what happens in the in-between; to generativity as characteristic of a (relational) process.

R generativity representing relationships and communication, between or with people

C generativity representing continuous processes of change and development

D generativity representing disruption and/or disequilibrium

F generativity representing (a concern for) future generations; intentionality

I generativity representing the rise of new ideas

A generativity representing (people taking) action

P generativity representing procreation

To summarize: two labels refer to generativity as a quality of a thing or a human; seven labels refer to generativity as being (in) a process. Together they unleash a preliminary set of views on the meaning and utilization of the word generativity in the context of organizations, and from there a first glimpse at a conceptual framework under construction. All this, bearing Wittgenstein in mind. (p. 39)

Is generativity such a magnetic word that it creates an urge to be used? Is this to be considered "the generative nature of the word generative" in action; are we watching an onomatopoeia? (p. 40)

Why do all these authors and scholars pay such an effort to include generativity in their writings, whilst being so inaccurate in their descriptions? Could it be that the whole of the OD text fragments includes something beyond the study of phenomena? Do they possibly bear an intention? Do they manifest a sincere hope that we are able to build a better future than we have been describing and sustaining until today? Do the authors introduce their generative images, dialogues and moments for the purpose of (finally) creating generative organizations, led by generative leaders? Do the OD authors long for a future in which theory per definition equals generative theory, and research per definition equals generative research? Perhaps an image becomes (more) generative when we call it a generative image; is the use of the word generativity an exclamation of hope, or a prophecy meant to fulfill itself? (p. 42)

Have we been watching stupid statements? Or have we been reading propositions that are fueled more by hope than by logic? When we study the 157 text fragments beyond style and presentation, and consider the authors' hopes as valuable as their logics, we can allow ourselves to focus on actual content; not to define or describe generativity as such, but surely to obtain a better picture if not the elementary parts of a conceptual framework. The combined OD authors should be given the benefit of the doubt, and we should take the effort to distill the content related parts out of their writings for a noble purpose: more flourishing organizations. (p. 45)

What about someone, addressed as being generative, but not doing generative? Furthermore, what to say when a person acts in such a way that her or his actions are perceived as generative? Can we refer to this person as inherently generative? It is not the question whether he or she always shows that behavior; it is merely the question whether her or his behavior always contributes to an experience being addressed (by the other) as generative. Some considerations, just to enrich the analysis: "My boss is terrible!" must be considered as untrue; unless we agree that someone is terrible, when he or she *does* terrible during a substantial part of his or her doings. "That person is dangerous." may be true in the sense of potentially dangerous – aren't we all? – and if it be only for legal or privacy reasons, we should be careful with our formulation in this respect. (p. 46)

In general, this dataset provides some clues toward a better understanding and application of the term generative; it also proves that in many situations it is better to use a more clear and less confusing alternative. If someone shows productivity, please call that person productive, and preferably not "generative in the sense of productive". (p. 56)

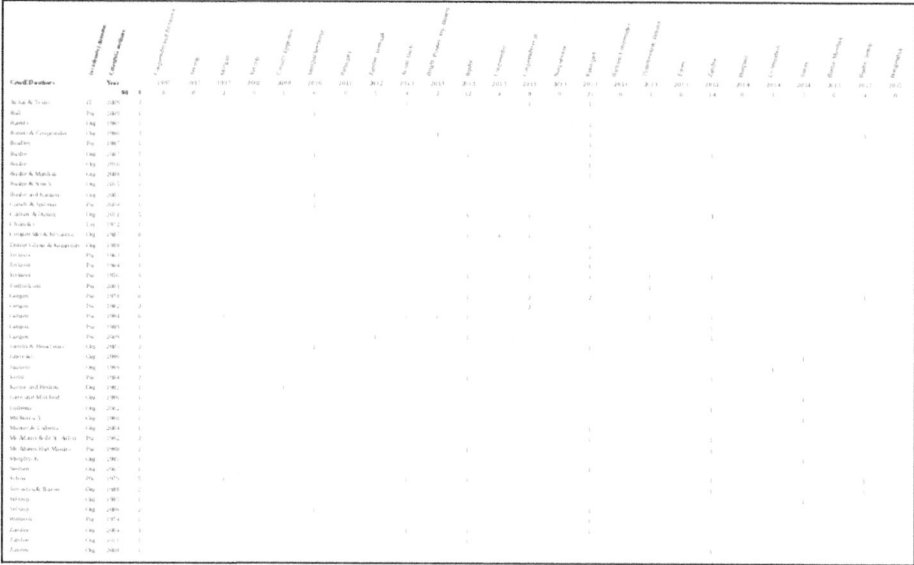

Figure 1. Impression of Genealogy Matrix

What do the ancestors add? Analysis, surprises and reflection. In general, the references to the ancestors are all relevant, be it that the citing authors for their work on generativity sometimes seem to use less substance than the ancestors have to offer. In some cases, the OD authors seem to present their citations for the sake of being polite or complete, after which they take their own stance when it comes to define, apply and study generativity. Where the ancestors substantially connect generativity with phenomena such as intentionality, human interchange, processes, initiatives, thought-to-action and procreation, the citing OD authors generally stay concentrated on the challenging of the status quo, the idea-giving, the appeal for change, and a bit of action (of which however the results on the short term and the effects on the long term remain unknown). (p. 57)

Besides dictionaries, 27 OD related sources and their 45 ancestor sources, another 38 various other sources have been found that in some way address generativity. Not all particularly scholarly. But a meaning is a meaning, and shouldn't such be taken into account for the Conceptual Framework? And if so, in what way, to what extent? (p. 64)

In case you feel tempted to follow the trace of my sources of this foundational critical literature study, I included for you as an appendix the OD sources, the ancestor publications and the supplementary titles.

Big Bang

Considering that my April feedback sounded "Perfect, go on like this", the following half yearly meeting with Mark and the DPC director was a disappointment. I had delivered a lot of writing, but the first question to me was: "Where are you, considering the two year deadline for the certificate?" I had the impression they hadn't read my deliverables. "What about your revised PhD-proposal?" They should have seen it, but I showed them my print. "That is very brief." I reminded them of the two appendices. "Your future supervisor doesn't want to read all this." It was a short meeting. Later that day Mark surprised me with a few emails telling me that I needed to change my title into *A Conceptual Framework Generativity*. And: I should write my research journey in reverse order. I still felt supported and was very productive in July and August: all layers of my research came to completion and turned into proper writing.

End of August I heard that because of logistics, I would be getting a new mentor, and I would meet the old and the new on 5th September. My new mentor clearly hadn't seen my material, and her first question was: "Where in your manuscript do I find the overview of your research approach?" Following the orders I had recently replaced this part towards the end of the paper. "This is a lot of reading for a PhD supervisor, I wouldn't know anyone suitable for your case." I wondered whether she knew all 500 professors in Leiden University. She also asked something that I wasn't ready to absorb at that moment: "Why don't you just write a book?"

On the 18th September I remember having a constructive conversation with the DPC director, a bit dusty, but smart and kind person, and with a good sense for subtle humor. "Your proposed new mentor is not really willing to take you, but Mark feels fine to continue." Furthermore: "Your first chapter still needs significant revision to meet the academic standards." I thought that DPC asked me to only produce a PhD proposal. I had already written two chapters of my dissertation. Wouldn't the suggested standardizing better be a job between me and my future supervisor? Besides, I wanted to engage with a professor mostly on the basis of my seemingly perfect Chapter 0. "You are seeking a supervisor who is open to regular dialogues. But you know what? Professors don't really want to read your stuff or have cups of tea with you." When I asked him how big the statistical sample behind his statement was, he smiled and saw my point: "Of course I only know about the Leiden faculties." My last words were: "I am pretty sure that I will find a dialogic supervisor." This turned out to be a valid statement.

On 24th September I received an official email stating that my contract with the Dual PhD Center had been terminated.

Apotheosis

I didn't leave DPC with empty hands. I am grateful for their all-inclusive service offering. I was 125 source titles richer, and had actually discovered something with my data. As I see it now, I produced two genuine chapters of a possible dissertation, where I could have just produced a PhD proposal. With the advice of my mentor and the reflections of my fellow PhD candidates I had laid a firm foundation, which I presented on page 8 of my temporarily frozen DPC Chapter 1 in the following way:

> Since this research initially aimed for retrieving (more) meaning and less confusion regarding the phenomenon of generativity, and its more frequently used adjective generative, it may not be surprising that it presents its findings in the form of a user manual. The suggested set of 'rules and regulations' for a proper use of generativity and generative may be well regarded as a conceptual framework. And for the unconscious users, or for the ones fused with a certain preference around the two terms, it might as well serve as a conceptual unframework.
>
> See the table below for a first and brief encounter with the user manual on Generativity. It has been divided in six sections addressing different entities and how to associate these with generativity. Each section makes use of terms, data, analyses and conclusions derived from the literature study, and is enriched with logical reasoning and practical examples. The framework doesn't pretend to provide the truth. It is just a recipe, recommending a certain approach to a certain dish with generativity as its main ingredient. Whether this approach can be called generative, can be retrieved from reading the manual. Whether the conceptual framework Generativity will be called generative, only time can tell.

Conceptual Framework Generativity in Brief	
Perspective	Rules and Recommendations
Generativity as Such	Don't use it as (mostly incorrect) replacement of a more appropriate description. It only makes sense, and is recommended, to use generative when referring to three characteristics: (i) concern for future well-being; (ii) self-perpetuating and procreating; (iii) letting appear something unexpectedly new and appealing.
Generativity of Things	Things include: concrete material objects as well as sounds, flavors and scents. It is not only confusing but actually incorrect to call a thing generative. In specific cases, the process of perceiving a thing can be called generative, for which the description should be precisely formulated. Such a thing could then be called a generativity-contributor. Actually, each thing is potentially a generativity-contributor.
Generativity of Information	Information includes: the message, intended by, and/or understood from any textual or visual product. In general, it doesn't make sense to call information generative, because this mainly depends upon the way it is perceived. However, some extraordinary narratives are entitled to be called generative in the sense of self-perpetuating. Among these are famous quotes – 'winged pronunciations' - that outlived their sources, specific (research) methods and particular algorithms.
Generativity of People	In general do not speak of a generative person, unless: (i) he or she fits Erikson's socio-psychological life stage called generativity; (ii) the person fits and fulfills the role or mission that requires the intention and interventions to co-create and optimize conditions for a generative process to arise. Being generative in a role is temporary.
Generativity of Processes	Calling a process generative is relevant and justified, (i) when it includes human interchange and (ii) when something valuable is generated. The generative process itself is an intervention. The generativity of a process is of an immaterial kind and it can manifest itself in seven ways; we can speak of relational, transformative, disruptive, future-oriented, idea-giving, actionable and procreative generativity.
Generativity for a Purpose	When a phenomenon carries the possibility of becoming generative, it makes sense to add the adjective generative for the purpose of communicating a performative proposition, but only if articulated in an unmistakable context of 'wishful speaking'.

Quod erat demonstrandum. The framework has been derived from, and demonstrated in the four layers of my critical literature study. Moreover, this still too brief and abstract manual has been enriched with supporting evidence and practical illustrations. Find this elaboration - you may call it the celebration of language - in the respective appendix, included in this book part. After all, it can't be about the cold and brief results; it should be about the warm and full embracing of research findings to make a difference when it comes to improving one's future forming capabilities. And that starts with proper use of the language.

"If names are not correct, language is not in accordance with the truth of things. If language is not in accordance with the truth of things, affairs cannot be carried on to success. When affairs cannot be carried on to success, proprieties and music do not flourish." (Confucius, 551-479 B.C.)

GENARRATIVE

FIRST APPENDIX TO PART ONE

Extended guidelines for applying
the Conceptual Framework Generativity

The reader should be aware that speaking about the generativity of X implies that the speaker thinks that X is generative, and therefore also could speak of a generative X. When X possesses generativity, then X is generative; when X is generative, then X possesses generativity. This textual parallelism is fully included below, but for the sake of reader's efficiency sometimes only one of the two is mentioned.

[1.1] How to Use Generativity as Such? This first section addresses the pure, isolated use of the words generativity respectively generative. Three rules apply.

[1.1.1] Don't use the noun generativity when you actually intend to address (for example) productivity, creativity or generosity. In general don't use generativity when an appropriate and more clear alternative is available. When you have produced a lot of work, at your desk or in the factory, call that day productive or better: call yourself productive. If something really generative happened regarding you and your day, then formulate that precisely, after reading the rest of this manual.

[1.1.2] Don't use the adjective generative when it refers to a quality for which more appropriate descriptions are available. Such as: productive, creative, innovative, active, or: inspiring, motivating, enriching, mobilizing, changing, transforming. (Please refrain from using a phrase like "generative in a creative way"!)

[1.1.3] Consider to use the noun generativity (or the adjective generative) only when you want to address the following characteristics: (i) concern for future well-being; (ii) self-perpetuating and procreating; (iii) letting appear something unexpectedly new and appealing. The first option implies the presence of consciousness. The second implies the capability of creating offspring: the intention and possibility to bring a similar (generative) organism or entity to life.

The third implies both surprise and uncertainty: the absence of cause and effect, the lack of predictability or repeatability.

The consideration and suggestion to give preference to the adjective generative in these three cases, and better not use the explanatory description, is to be regarded as axiom in this conceptual framework; an axiom based on this study's main starting point: the word generative(ity) is valuable and meaningful, and should be used in a robust and sense making way. There is no intention, nor a good reason, to replace the word completely by its alternative descriptions, because of which the word might even disappear. The powerful, one-word alternative, especially as ethical and aesthetical as generative or generativity, deserves priority above extended descriptions. Furthermore, for the sake of proper research it was obviously not the intention to narrow generativity down to one single meaning. Therefore notice that, given this trifold of meanings, the exclamation "How generative this is!" still holds space for misunderstanding as long as the 'this' is not sufficiently clear. All can be attributed to Einstein: "Everything should be as simple as it can be, but not simpler."

[1.2] How to Use Generativity associated with Things? The second section addresses the use of the words generativity and generative associated with material (concrete, non-living) objects, as well as sounds, scents and flavors; phenomena that can be physically perceived: seen, touched, heard, smelled, tasted. Two rules apply.

[1.2.1] With regard to concrete objects, such as a chair, a stone, a pencil or a cloud: it doesn't make sense to call these things generative. They don't possess consciousness; they don't procreate; they don't let things happen. The only acceptable way to associate generativity with such things is described as such: "Watching that thing – or having a collision with it – suddenly generated a new idea in me."

It is actually the watching of it that may be addressed as generative, in the sense of letting new ideas appear. In that case the thing has contributed to generativity, which is not the same as being generative, and can only be determined afterwards. Besides, you won't be sure whether not watching that thing might have generated similar ideas; or whether watching that thing on another day might have generated different or no ideas. The thing itself has no idea. Don't call it a generative thing.

The material object that approaches generativity – in the sense of procreative - the closest is the 3D printer, since it can print (most of) the parts needed to construct a similar 3D printer. But it still can't reproduce itself completely. Therefore even a 3D printer can't be called a generative thing (yet). Nevertheless you will agree that observing a 3D printer can generate lots of new ideas in the mind of the observer.

[1.2.2] With regard to "media-things" such as sound, picture, scent or flavor: it doesn't make sense to call these things generative. The same arguments apply as used above for concrete objects.

Perceived media-things such as paintings, music and writings, can (too) easily be referred to as generative, in the sense that in perceiving them people can get carried away and encounter new ideas to act upon. The musical composition *Canto Ostinato*, by the Dutch composer Simeon ten Holt can be regarded as such: widely accepted as an highly inspirational piece of music. But it is also said to have caused – can that really be stated? - listeners to commit suicide (Gieling, Holt, Wieringa, & Haas, 2011), which rather be called de-generative. How influential for many people it may be; *Canto Ostinato* can't be regarded as generative in itself; it is a collection of sounds, inspiring for the one and annoying to the other. Whether or not generativity shall be in the air can only depend on the momentarily interplay between the music and the listener, and determined afterwards accordingly.

[1.3] How to Use Generativity Associated with Information? The third section addresses the use of the words generativity and generative associated with immaterial content, mostly textual, sometimes visual, containing a 'narrative'. Three extensive rules apply.

[1.3.1] With regard to questions, images, affirmative topics, metaphors and stories: under specific conditions it can make sense to call these narratives (inherently) generative, which needs special attention. According to earlier rules, the information-transporter (book, poster, mail message) should clearly not be referred to as generative. And although most of the articulated information shouldn't be graded as a token of generativity, qualifying the provided narrative as generative can sometimes make sense. This requires careful attention.

In the case of a (authentic) speech, in which the information-transporter is a person, the information can hardly be detached from the speaker. When the respective story would include a concern for future well-being, that can only be regarded as the speaker's concern. In such a case, please refer to the next section *How to Use Generativity Associated to People*. When people in the audience say that the speech moved them and gave them new ideas to act upon, the message itself still shouldn't be called generative, but the interchange between message and listener could include generativity. In such a case, please refer to the section *How to Use Generativity Associated to Processes*.

Nevertheless, some extraordinary narratives do deserve the adjective generative, in the sense of self-perpetuating, even procreative. The famous quote "I have a dream!" by Martin Luther King possesses clearly, even without being expressed, a concern for the future, although it can be defended that this represented of course King's concern. Still, somehow, the expression seems to have taken over this concern in itself. Besides, it also seems to possess the capability to procreate itself. Yes, obviously that procreation is supported by human transporters, who forward it. But who says that procreating takes place without the help of others? If so, only the female version of human species could be called generative, where we agreed that all humans are generative beings. The criterion is the inherent power to procreate and that seems mainly existent in the phrase itself, with *man* as a helper. Ghandi's famous proverb "Be the change you want to see in the world." possesses similar assumed generativity, for similar reasons. Notice that the ones who forward the messages, mostly also (try to) live the message, which supports the quality of generativity.

As such it might make sense to speak of generative messages, if and only if considered with care and understanding. Notice that time plays a role as an important assessment criterion, since the level of reproduction can only be determined over time. For obvious reasons, hypes are excluded from being generative.

Whether *The Bible* is to be considered a generative book, may better be left open for debate. It seems a definite yes in the sense of self-perpetuating, even more considering the fact that many opponents rather want to burn and bury it. Does it inherently contain a concern for future well-being? Being a book with substantial content, it will often have played a role as generativity-contributor in the interchange with its readers and researchers, but that shouldn't be called generative. *The Bible*; fully, partly, really generative? In the attempt to complete this category of content, messages and narratives, two examples from a different angle are given.

In *Gödel, Escher, Bach* you can find *Hofstadter's Law: It always takes longer than you expect, even when you take into account Hofstadter's Law.* (Hofstadter, 1999) Probably many people are tempted to call this a generative text. This self-referring, recursive sentence may have contributed to many creative moments among the readers (as will be the case for many other sentences by Hofstadter) but you will agree that this content-thing can't be called generative. Don't mix reproduction with repetition or self-reference.

Finally, a Zen Koan such as "What is it?" or "Who am I?" is supposed to be repeatedly questioned, with the purpose of bringing or keeping the beholder in doubt. Unlike the words by King or Ghandi, the number of candidate transporters to procreate this Koan, is very restricted. With all their due intentions these Koans, even the famous ones, don't inherently possess generativity.

[1.3.2] With regard to abstract (meta) information, such as a theory, a method or a science, first assess the word carefully and subsequently apply the most applicable rule of this user manual. (Thank you mister Hofstadter for hereby unexpectedly contributing to the newborn Law of Generativity: things can only be considered generative when they exist within the jurisdiction of the Law of Generativity.)

Notice that words being addressed in this section are exactly the ones that have been found in the literature study. They might serve as pars pro toto with regard to seemingly similar words, but such has to be determined by the user of this manual. Textual abstracts and meta-messages tend to be very fluid and need utmost attention when comparing and categorizing them.

[1.3.2.1] With regard to theory (or pattern, structure, model): calling these inherently generative doesn't make sense. This set of meta descriptions actually represents a generalization, a simplification of reality; it fixes or freezes or frames something and that is far from being inherently generative. The application of patterns and structures may create something that contains the same pattern or structure, but this can't be called self-perpetuating or procreative. With regard to theories and models: they carry the extra complexity that at some point in the future they might become refuted.

According to the trifold definition, even Einstein's famous formula $E=mc^2$, addressing huge energies, puzzling many scientists, and seemingly holding on, should better not be called generative. (Besides, it doesn't need it.) And yes, probably it is potentially a great generativity-contributor. And what about

Complexity Theory? Definitely to be considered a theory regarding generativity, especially in the sense of the uncertainty perspective. But better not to be called an inherent generative theory.

[1.3.2.2] With regard to an approach or a method: in some cases it can be justified to connect these with the adjective generative. When identified as a description - a written procedure or recipe - they should be addressed as a message, and treated accordingly in association with generativity. However, identified as the activity performed according to – or inspired by – the respective description, the method or the approach represents a process, which sometimes can be regarded as generative. For that, refer to the section *How to Use Generativity Associated to a Process*.

When Gergen (2015) suggests an alternative approach for research: "not mirroring, but making the world" in which upholding the inquiry seems more significant than collecting and analyzing the answers, two appropriate indicators apply for calling this generative research. The first addresses determination over time, after executing the respective approach; see also *How to Use Generativity Associated to a Process*. The second addresses the promising, wishful and purposeful nature, upfront contained by the phrase generative research; see *How to Use Generativity for a Purpose*.

One special occurrence of a method or approach is called algorithm: a script to be executed by a computer. In general, it doesn't make sense to call an algorithm generative. The computer does exactly what is asked of it; it reads and understands its "book" always in one specific way. Would you call such a book generative? Besides, forget about the so-called self-learning algorithm that actually instructs the computer to collect as much data as possible, in order to amplify the amount of possibilities for further calculative action; it follows constantly the same routine; only with more data.

Having said this, what if the algorithm has been written for the purpose of writing algorithms? In that case the algorithm, with the computer as its helper, represents the instruction to improve its own performance; for example by gathering (feedback) information on a performed task and rewriting its own code. That can very well be considered as procreative; it makes sense to call such an algorithm generative. Considering the development of autonomous weapons, highly based upon this type of algorithms, and for the sake of humanity, it is strongly recommended to speak of generative algorithms if and only if they also include a concern for future well-being.

[1.3.2.3] Associating the meta-abstract 'science' with the adjective generative is to be considered either pleonastic or intentionally. Science is not an opinion and not the absolute truth, it represents the interchange between the researcher(s) and the researched, and is therefore to be regarded as a process, perhaps even a living system, constantly procreating itself, frequently generating unexpected new ideas. Speaking of generative science would therefore be justified, but could for the same reason be regarded as a pleonasm. It makes more sense to reserve the phrase generative science to emphasize the hope or aspiration for that science to sustainably focus on future well-being. See for that the section How to Use Generativity for a Purpose?.

[1.4] How to Use Generativity associated with People? The fourth section addresses the use of the words generativity and generative associated with human beings, or perhaps better: human doings. Four rules apply.

[1.4.1] When referring to the biological nature of people (also animals, plants), calling them generative is to be regarded as a pleonasm. The actual animal or plant or any living species isn't normally called a thing. Since it is able to reproduce and therefore procreate, from a biological perspective all living species, including humans, are generative. Calling them generative would be pleonastic.

At the same time all creatures great and small do have an appearance, and/or make sounds and/or gestures, and perceiving these signals can be experienced as generative by the receiver. For that, they all are – like things – potentially a contributor to generativity. As clarified before, this is no reason for calling people and other creatures inherently generative.

[1.4.2] When a human being produces a high score in the *Loyola Generativity Scale* or the *Generativity Behavior Checklist*, it makes sense to call that person generative, be it to a certain extent, and under specific conditions. The two mentioned instruments (Foley Center, Northwestern University) are assessments, derived from the works of McAdams et al (McAdams & de St. Aubin, 1992; McAdams, Hart, & Maruna, 1998) These works build on the concept of (human) generativity, as introduced by psychologist Erikson to indicate "a concern for establishing and guiding the next generation" (Erikson, 1964). For the purpose of psychological research, the two assessments have been designed to 'measure' a person's level of generativity. Within that context, it would make sense to call (such) a human being generative; that is: to a certain extent.

Shouldn't it be justified to call someone generative if and only if he or she is always fully compliant to Erikson? Gauss' theory will support the assumption that only very few - if anyone – will score 100% on both scales at any time. What is being pointed out here, is the difference between being and doing generative. People with a fair rating on the two generativity scales, actually express a concern for future well-being; they take specific action to forward their life experience to others. Whether or not they *are* (completely) generative, they *do* often generative. The precise language would be: "That person is often behaving in a generative way." According to Erikson's theory, when the stage of human generativity arises, it will happen on average between 37 and 42 years of age. According to McAdams, this range should be extended until 60 years (McAdams et al., 1998). Taking this context into account, it makes sense to call a midlife person who is doing generative, a generative person; you can choose between slightly, quite, or highly generative.

[1.4.3] With regard to any person, in the sense of a relational being, don't use the adjective generative, although it sometimes makes sense to conclude that someone's behavior was generative. According to the literature study, and besides the biological and the Erikson perspectives, a person's assumed generativity has either effect on the self, or on others. The first includes the ability to adapt to change, to gain more self-knowledge, to produce or create something new; such a person could be called flexible, adaptive, creative or even able to reprogram him/her self, but preferably not generative. The second includes the capability to enable others to readjust and see things anew. Any possible generativity of that kind can only be present in the perceiving of actual behavior – one can't perceive someone's capability – because of which it can make sense to call that specific behavior, during or afterwards, generative.

Human behavior takes place over time; it is to be considered a process. Processes are entitled to be called generative. See the section *How to Use Generativity Associated with Processes*.

[1.4.4] A specific mission or role can require to be fulfilled by a generative person; not only capable, but consciously acting generatively with the intention to maximally contribute to generativity. Besides the (pleonastic) biological procreativity and the occasional (age and audit related) socio-psychological generativity, it doesn't make sense to speak of a generative person; only the process of perceiving that person's looks or words or actions sometimes can be called generative. Besides, are there no generative people to be found? Among so many ordinary people, there wouldn't exist anyone extraordinary genuinely generative? Indeed, not as such. The literature study however suggests a tiny clue about people being generative within the role they play; their generativity in that case is both intention and process related. The following represents a general example of such; a possibility, for further explication.

Some goals, whether simple or a bit more complicated, can well be achieved in solitude or through a rigid approach. But when challenges have to deal with uncertainty, and affect multiple stakeholders, complexity or even chaos are likely to enter the stage. In such a situation, the process to accomplish success will be characterized by a high level of communicative interaction. When it is even unclear what success looks like, a sensible approach includes: a concern for a better 'to be' than 'as is'; a learning process that keeps itself going; and the optimal circumstances for brilliant 'never thought of' ideas to pop up. In such a case, when generative conditions can contribute to success, the one in charge of that process (leader, initiator, facilitator) ideally is qualified as generative (with regard to the job). It then would make sense to have a recruitment message saying "generative facilitator wanted"; the ideal candidate being someone who really is and acts generatively in that role. "We consider Miriam a generative facilitator." That would be the nearest to calling a person generative.

Unlike the earlier mentioned situations in which people are not aware of their possibly generative behavior, exemplary Miriam is fulfilling her role with intention, consciously trying to (co)create a generative process, by providing 'generative' interventions. (Between quotes, because even the most generative Miriam cannot promise generativity in advance.) And with a bit of luck, her concern for future well-being will be contagious; the process will provide new, appealing ideas to act upon; ideally the process of dealing with the complex challenges will become self-perpetuating, and doesn't need Miriam any further.

(I dare to say that I "need" Miriam at my side, because she is my beautiful, spiritual, loving and beloved life companion, fellow AI practitioner, colorful painter, author of a dozen of books among which *Flourishing Together*, and my ever inspiring muse, enabling generativity all the time.)

This gives rise to time being considered again as indicator for generativity, but in an opposite way: when an assumed generative leader only sustains the success by staying in his job; just because of that he or she may not be entitled to be called a generative leader (anymore). If a generative person-with-a-mission exists, such can only be sustained for a restricted period, until expiration date. Do the leaders outlive their effects, or do the effects outlive their leader?

[1.5] How to Use Generativity associated with Processes? The statistics from the literature study make convincingly clear that the majority of associations with generativity refers to a process, i.e. an event over time in which something is happening. Actually, a process is synonymous with a change process. After all, when in a process nothing changes, it should be called a (static) situation. In a process, always something is generated but, as argued before, this as such is no reason to call processes generative. The findings of the literature study suggest narrowing down the use of generativity associated with processes. Three rules apply.

[1.5.1] Calling a process generative is relevant and justified, (i) when it includes human interchange (exchange, interplay, dynamics) and (ii) when something valuable (constructive, helpful, useful) is generated. Whether it be the encounter with an image, any image; whether it be the reflection of something in the eyes and mind of the beholder; whether it be the mindful group reflection on a poem or a piece of music; whether it be a dialogue about a way to improve; it takes the exchange of meaning to have a process that might turn out to be generative, and it takes one or more human beings to enable that exchange. We don't know when, or even if, a dynamic communicative process will show generativity, but when it does, people are partakers; all examples in the literature study point towards that condition. And also: when a new idea, a change of mood, an unexpected turn, a shared longing, or even a great confusion arises from the process dynamics; for a process to be called generative, these sudden, unexpected appearances will (at some point) be regarded as valuable for the process and for the intentions behind it.

[1.5.2] The generative process itself is the intervention. An intervention is often understood as that which makes the change. A 'kick in the butt' may definitely cause some kind of change, and perceiving the subsequent pain may even be called a generative process. The chances for such generativity to happen, may be less when the direct response to the kick (kick back) is an unconscious one, a reflex. There may be more sense in calling the kick – disputable example so far – only the catalyst of the process that follows, and calling that process the actual intervention, since it represents the change that one is undergoing. The literature study suggests that a process which has been experienced as generative, can be seen as the change (among the partakers) itself; it generates elements that in some way keeps the process going. Where a kick, a sudden crisis, or an opening question may be regarded as the (not further needed) catalyst of the process, the process itself can appear to be the actual change intervention. (Intervention = change.) Therefore it also makes sense to speak of a (possibly) generative intervention, be it only when referring to the process itself and not to the initiator of it. (Too much honor for the initiator.) As far as a relation exists between initiator and intervention, this would address the generative person in his/her specific role regarding – and during - the intervention. (Appreciation for the generative facilitator is justified.)

Perhaps similar reasoning is applicable for degenerative processes - they surely exist - however: (i) these seem to lack the orientation to future well-being; (ii) they have the implicit tendency to fade away (although it might take long), (iii) the literature study really focuses on generativity, that: is upward and forward, and (iv) the only instance in which the literature touches de-generativity is in the recommendation to embrace (not to ignore or fight) it when it appears, and use it for the purpose of generativity. Nevertheless, at least one potentially generative question remains open for further inquiry: "Is a process that cannot be regarded generative, automatically a degenerative process?" Is an intervention that is not generative, possibly a degenerative intervention? The answer to that stretches beyond the scope of this study.

[1.5.3] The generativity of a process is of an immaterial kind and it can manifest itself in seven ways. In more than 70% of the reviewed text fragments, generativity is associated with (dynamic, relational, communicative) processes. What (suddenly and unexpectedly) is being generated (if any), always appears to be immaterial: a mood, an intention, an idea, a longing. The rich amount of data regarding and describing processes being generative, gave rise to detect seven perspectives of process related generativity. They overlap and supplement each other. Notice that the seven manifestations also can be used for extra clarification in all aforementioned situations where something or someone is being called generative. Because of their ability to enable more understanding about the majority of generative events, together these seven perspectives represent the (beating) heart of the conceptual framework named Generativity.

[1.5.3.1] Relational Generativity. The process has a positive impact on stakeholder connectivity, human relationships and the time and attention spent for high quality conversations.

[1.5.3.2] Transformative Generativity. The process enables the experiencing of change, development and transformation among the ones involved.

[1.5.3.3] Disruptive Generativity. The process includes moments of disruption, contradiction and disequilibrium, experienced as valuable.

[1.5.3.4] Future-oriented Generativity. The process fuels feelings of hope and aspiration regarding future generations and their emergent well-being.

[1.5.3.5] Idea-giving Generativity. The process generates unexpected new ideas and stimulates special versions of seeing which challenge the status quo.

[1.5.3.6] Actionable Generativity. The process stimulates people to take action, to create different conversations, to start doing anew.

[1.5.3.7] Procreative Generativity. The process is contagious and self-perpetuating, self-replicating, procreating itself, even beyond its cata-lyzers and partakers.

[1.6] How to Use Generativity for a Higher Purpose?

Given the amount of data in the literature study, as well as the analyses and the variety of findings, the 'user manual' so far can be regarded highly complete in covering all possible variations in the use of the words generativity and generative. Comparing the rules and recommendations derived from the various publications, it seems that the authors of the sources must have made several mistakes in the way they mentioned generativity in their publications. However, trusting that all of these authors are educated scholars and professionals, it can't be true that they deliberately misused terms which seem to be so important for their work. (If not, these publications would not have been selected for this study.) So what else could be at stake here? In the application of the adjective generative, one angle seems to remain underexposed. Although still an assumption, it inspires to add a relevant and valuable rule to the framework.

When the author speaks of a generative question or image, a generative leader, generative change or generative research, he or she may have been aware of some linguistic or logical flaws; he or she may know that a question or image can't be (inherent) generative as such. But now, imagine that these authors share the intention and aspiration for future well-being. Could it be their intrinsic hope and concern for which they explicitly chose to use or include the word generative in their work? Such intentions seem to be even more present in the older sources, whilst the more contemporary and organizational publications tend to be a bit more concrete and conclusive in their language. Based on the whole of the documentary sources and the assumed generative intentions of their authors, and although based on not more than an academic hunch, this conceptual framework wouldn't be complete with the following rule.

[1.6.1] When a phenomenon carries the possibility of becoming generative, it makes sense to add the adjective for the purpose of communicating a performative proposition, but only when articulated in an unmistakable context of 'wishful speaking'. This rule should always be taken into account in addition to the application of all former rules.

GENARRATIVE

SECOND APPENDIX TO PART ONE

Threefold References

My Primary OD Sources

Avital, M., & van Osch, W. (2013). The generative archetypes of idea work. In D. Cooperrider, D. Zandee, L. Godwin, M. Avital, & B. Boland (Eds.), Organizational generativity: The Appreciative Inquiry summit and a scholarship of transformation (pp. 115–133). Emerald Group Publishing.

Bright, D. S., Powley, E. H., Fry, R. E., & Barrett, F. (2013). The generative potential of cynical conversations. In D. Cooperrider, D. Zandee, L. Godwin, M. Avital, & B. Boland (Eds.), Organizational generativity: The Appreciative Inquiry summit and a scholarship of transformation (pp. 135–157). Emerald Group Publishing.

Bushe, G. (2013). Generative process, generative outcome: The transformational potential of appreciative inquiry. In D. Cooperrider, D. Zandee, L. Godwin, M. Avital, & B. Boland (Eds.), Organizational generativity: The Appreciative Inquiry summit and a scholarship of transformation (pp. 89–113). Emerald Group Publishing.

Bushe, G. R., & Marshak, R. J. (2015a, August 6). Dialogic organization development: recapturing the Spirit of Inquiry [Presentation]. The First International Conference on Dialogic Organization Development, Vancouver, BC, Canada.

Bushe, G. R., & Marshak, R. J. (2018). The dialogic mindset for generative change. Submitted for the third edition of The change handbook: The definitive resource on today's best methods for engaging whole systems. Berret-Koehler.

Bushe, G. R., & Paranjpey, N. (2014). Comparing the Generativity of Problem Solving and Appreciative Inquiry: A Field Experiment. Journal of Applied Behavioral Science, 51(3), 309–335.

Bushe, G. R., & Storch, J. (2015). Generative image, sourcing novelty. In G. Bushe, & R. Marshak (Eds), Dialogic organization development: The theory and practice of transformational change (pp. 101–122). Berret-Koehle.

Carucci, R. A., & Epperson, J. J. (2008). Future in-formation: Choosing a generative organizational life. Outskirts Press.

Cooperrider, D. L., Zandee, D. P., Godwin, L. N., Avital, M., & Boland, B. (2013). Organizational generativity: The Appreciative Inquiry summit and a scholarship of transformation. Emerald Group Publishing.

Cooperrider, D. L. (2013). A contemporary commentary on Appreciative Inquiry in organizational life. In D. Cooperrider, D. Zandee, L. Godwin, M. Avital, & B. Boland (Eds.), Organizational generativity: The Appreciative Inquiry summit and a scholarship of transformation (pp. 3–67). Emerald Group Publishing.

Cooperrider, D. L., & Srivastva, S. (1987). Appreciative Inquiry in organizational life. In A. Shani, & D. Noumair (Eds.), Research in Organization Change and Development, Vol. 1 (pp. 129–169). Emerald Group Publishing.

Harquail, C. (2014). From generativity to generosity: What's at the core of these new business practices? Authentic Organizations. http://authenticorganizations.com/harquail/2014/10/02/from-generativity -to-generosity-whats-at-the-core-of-these-new-business-practices/#sthash.Fa RJjmaO.dpbs

Hoogendijk, C. (2015). Appreciative inquiries of the 3.0 kind: How do we connect, share and co-create for tomorrow's human wholeness? Utrecht NL: Society 3.0 Foundation.

Lichtenstein, B. B. (2014). Generative emergence: A new discipline of organizational, entrepreneurial and social innovation. OUP USA.

Marshak, R. J., & Bushe, G. R. (2018). Planned and generative change in organization development. OD Practitioner, 50(4), 9–15.

Morgan, G. (1997). Images of organization. Sage Publications.

Paranjpey, N. (2011). Appreciative Inquiry, generativity; Collective efficacy: Building the generative capacity of organizations. [Paper submitted to Academy of Management.]

Paranjpey, N. (2013). A field experiment examining the relationship between generativity and Appreciative Inquiry. [Unpublished doctoral dissertation]. Benedictine University.

Richley, B. A., & Cooperrider, D. L. (2013). The generative diffusion of innovation. In D. Cooperrider, D. Zandee, L. Godwin, M. Avital, & B. Boland (Eds.), Organizational generativity: The Appreciative Inquiry summit and a scholarship of transformation (pp. 361–376). Emerald Group Publishing.

Stacey, M. (2014). Generativity in Organizational Life. http://www.contextconsulting.com/generativity-in-organizational-life/

Thatchenkery, T., & Firbida, I. (2013). Appreciative Intelligence and generativity: A case study of Rocky Flats Nuclear Weapons Facility cleanup. In D. Cooperrider, D. Zandee, L. Godwin, M. Avital, & B. Boland (Eds.), Organizational generativity: The Appreciative Inquiry summit and a scholarship of transformation (pp. 409–432). Emerald Group Publishing.

Torres, C., Warner, T., Becker, K., Seitz, K., Robaina, M., & Pulliam, J. (2013). The Macon miracle: The magic of intergenerational design for the future of education. In D. Cooperrider, D. Zandee, L. Godwin, M. Avital, & B. Boland (Eds.), Organizational generativity: The Appreciative Inquiry summit and a scholarship of transformation (pp. 433–459). Emerald Group Publishing.

van den Nieuwenhof, R. (2013). The language of change: Generativity in dialogical process. In D. Cooperrider, D. Zandee, L. Godwin, M. Avital, & B. Boland (Eds.), Organizational generativity: The Appreciative Inquiry summit and a scholarship of transformation (pp. 159–188). Emerald Group Publishing.

VanQuickenborne, T. (2010). Exploring generative change. [Research project, The George L. Graiado School of Business and Management, Pepperdine University].

Veltrop, B. (1995). Discovering a generative path to organizational change. https://www.visionnest.com/btbc/cb/chapters/path.htm

Veltrop, B. (2002). Generative change. http://www.theinfinitegames.org/e03/05.php

Zandee, D. (2013). The process of generative inquiry. In D. Cooperrider, D. Zandee, L. Godwin, M. Avital, & B. Boland (Eds.), Organizational generativity: The Appreciative Inquiry summit and a scholarship of transformation (pp. 69–88). Emerald Group Publishing.

Zandee, D., & Vermaak, H. (2012). Designing Appreciative Inquiry as a generative process of organizational change. Paper delivered at 10th International Conference on Organizational Discourse, Amsterdam NL.

My Ancestor Sources

Ball, A. (2009). Toward a theory of generative change in culturally and linguistically complex classrooms. American Educational Research Journal, 46(1), 45–72.

Barrett, F. (1995). Creating appreciative learning cultures. Organizational Dynamics, 24(2), 36–49.

Bradley, C. (1997). Generativity–Stagnation: Development of a status model. Developmental Review, 17(3), 262–290.

Carich, M., & Spilman, K.(2004). Basic principles of intervention. The Family Journal, 12(4), 405–410.

Carlsen, A., & Dutton, J. E. (2011). Research alive: Exploring generative moments in doing qualitative research. Copenhagen Business School Press.

Chomsky, N. (1972). Language and mind. Harcourt.

Drazin, R., Glynn, M., & Kazanjian, R. (1999). Multilevel theorizing about creativity in organizations: A sensemaking perspective. Academy of Management Review, 24(2), 286–307.

Erikson, E. (1950). Childhood and society. Norton.

Erikson, E. (1963). Childhood and society (2nd ed.). Norton.

Erikson, E. (1964). Childhood and society (2nd ed., rev. and enl.). Norton.

Fredrickson, B. (2001). The role of positive emotions in positive psychology: The broaden-and-build theory of positive emotions. American Psychologist, 56(3), 218–226.

Gergen, K. J. (1978). Toward generative theory. Journal of Personality and Social Psychology, 36(11), 1344–1360.

Gergen, K.J. (1982). Toward transformation in social knowledge. Springer.

Gergen, K. J. (1994). Toward transformation in social knowledge (2nd ed.). Sage.

Gergen, K. J. (2009). Relational being: Beyond self and community. Oxford University Press.

Gergen, K. J., & Gergen, M. (2003). Social constructionism: A reader. Sage.

Jacobs, C., & Heracleous, L. (2005). Answers for questions to come: Reflective dialogue as an enabler of strategic innovation. Journal of Organizational Change Management, 18(4), 338–352.

Jaworski, J. (1996). Synchronicity: The inner path of leadership. Audio Literature.

Juarrero, A. (1999). Dynamics in action: Intentional behavior as a complex system. MIT Press.

Kotre, J. (1984). Outliving the self: Generativity and the interpretation of lives. Johns Hopkins University Press.

Kotter, J. P., & Heskett, J. L. (1992). Corporate culture and performance. Simon & Schuster.

Lane, D., & Maxfield, R. (1996). Strategy under complexity: Fostering generative relationships. Long Range Planning, 29(2), 215–231.

Ludema, J. (2003). The appreciative inquiry summit: A practitioner's guide for leading large-group change. Berrett-Koehler.

Malhotra, Y. (1996). Organizational learning and learning organizations: An overview. http://www.brint.com/papers/orglrng.htm

Mantel, M., & Ludema, J. (2004). Sustaining positive change: Inviting conversational convergence through appreciative leadership and organization design. In D.L. Cooperrider, and Avital, M. (Eds.), Constructive Discourse and Human Organization (Advances in Appreciative Inquiry, Vol. 1) (pp. 309–336). Emerald Group Publishing.

McAdams, D.P. & Hart, H. (Eds.). (1998). Generativity and adult development: How and why we care for the next generation. American Psychological Association.

McAdams, D. P., Hart, H. M., & Maruna, S. (1998). The anatomy of generativity. In D. P. McAdams & E. de St. Aubin (Eds.), Generativity and adult development: How and why we care for the next generation (p. 7–43). American Psychological Association.

McAdams, D. P., & St. Aubin, E. de (1992). A theory of generativity and its assessment through self-report, behavioral acts, and narrative themes in autobiography. Journal of Personality and Social Psychology, 62(6), 1003–1015.

Murphy, K. (1995). Generative coaching: a surprising learning odyssey. In S. Chawla, and J. Renesch (Eds.), Learning organizations: Developing cultures for tomorrow's workplace. Productivity Press.

Neilsen, E. H. (2007). Developing the positive organization from a secure base. In M. Avital, R. J. Boland, and D. L. Cooperrider (Eds.), Designing information and organizations with a positive lens, Vol. 2, Advances in Appreciative Inquiry (pp. 233–252). Emerald Group Publishing.

Schön, D. A. (1979). Generative metaphor: A perspective on problem-setting in social policy. In A. Ortony (Ed.), Metaphor and Thought (pp. 137–163). Cambridge University Press.

Wittrock, M. C. (1974). Learning as a generative process. Educational Psychologist, 11(2), 87–95.

The Supplementary Sources on Generativity

The Generativity Game. (2017).

generativity.eu – Generativity: manage it!

Bausch, K. C. (2000). Beyond Darwinism: Two new, strong, complementary theories of evolution.

Carkhuff, R. R. (n.d.). generativitylibrary

Carkhuff, R. R. (2010). Saving America : the generativity solution

Carmeli, A., Jones, C. D., & Binyamin, G. (2016). The power of caring and generativity in building strategic adaptability

Chiva, R., Grandío, A., & Alegre, J. (2008). Adaptive and Generative Learning: Implications from Complexity Theories.

Compton, K. (n.d.). Encyclopedia of Generativity.

Compton, K., & Mateas, M. (2017). A Generative Framework of Generativity.

Corballis, M. C. (1992). On the evolution of language and generativity.

Cossetta, A., & Cappelletti, P. (n.d.). Participation as a product of generativity Reflection on three case studies.

De St. Aubin, E., McAdams, D. P., & Kim, T. (2003). The generative society : caring for future generations.

Fabius, C. D. (2016). Toward an Integration of Narrative Identity, Generativity, and Storytelling in African American Elders.

Fiorella, L., & Mayer, R. E. (2015). Learning Strategies That Foster Generative Learning.

Förderer, J., Kude, T., Schütz, S., & Heinzl, A. (2014). Control versus Generativity: A Complex Adaptive Systems Perspective on Platforms.

Fujimura, M. (n.d.). On becoming generative.

Gilligan, S., & Dilts, R. (n.d.). INTERNATIONAL ASSOCIATION FOR GENERATIVE CHANGE. Retrieved from https://generative-change.com/

Giménez García-Conde, M., Marín, L., Ruiz de Maya, S., Giménez García-Conde, M., Marín, L., & Ruiz de Maya, S. (2016). The Role of Generativity in the Effects of Corporate Social Responsibility on Consumer Behavior

Grabowski, B. (n.d.). Generative learning: past. present and future.

Havey, E. A. (n.d.). What's Generativity and Why It's Good for You

Heiser, D. (n.d.). What is Generativity and Why Should I Care?

Kelly, K. (2010). Two Kinds of Generativity.

Klimek, K. J., Ritzenhein, E., & Sullivan, K. D. (2008). Generative leadership : shaping new futures for today's schools.

Lindsay, J. (2016). Generative Technology

Little, D. (2018). Understanding Society: Social generativity and complexity.

Lynn, A. (2017). Generativity: The Art and Science of Exceptional Achievement.

Magatti, M. (n.d.). Social generativity : a relational paradigm for social change. Routledge. McAdams, D. P., & Guo, J. (2015). Narrating the Generative Life.

Menon, S. (2011). Linking generativity and disruptive innovation to conceptualize ICTs.

Ogden, C. (2015). Networks for Change: Generosity is Key to Generativity : Interaction Institute for Social Change

Osborne, R. J., & Wittrock, M. C. (1983). Learning science: A generative process.

Priestly, D. (2015). The Art of 'Generativity.'

Pruitt, B. (n.d.). The Generative Change Community.

Romey, L. (2017). On generativity | Global Sisters Report.

Seligman, M. E. P. (2011). Flourish.

Smith, B., Peters, C., & Senge, N. (n.d.). The Way of Generativity: From separation to resonance

Spinelli, O. G. (2017). Generative Design and Evolution

Vaillant, G. E. (2007). Generativity: A Form of Unconditional Love. Warner, C. (n.d.). Generativity - Christ Church of Austin.

Weijer, B. van de. (2017). Hoe zelflerende robots al onze vooroordelen overnemen Wells, V. K., Taheri, B., Gregory-Smith, D., & Manika, D. (2016). The role of generativity and attitudes on employees home and workplace water and energy saving behaviours.

Zittrain, J. L. (2006). The Generative Internet

GENARRATIVE

PART TWO

02019 - 02021

Processual Generativity

Practice 2
To recognize, facilitate and accelerate
generative relational processes

"If our task is simply that of theorizing process, then there are many brilliant writers and thinkers in the recent past to turn to. But as I see it, these writers are mostly oriented toward helping us think about process 'from the outside', about processes that we merely observe as happening 'over there'. But if we are to rethink appropriate styles of empirical research, then we need a different form of engaged, responsive thinking, acting, and talking, that allows us to affect the flow of processes from within our living involvement with them."

These are the first lines by John Shotter in his article *Understanding Process From Within: An Argument for 'Withness'-Thinking.* I think it is completely different from the way processes are normally dealt with in organizational literature. At first, you may find it a complicated piece of writing, but perhaps it is closer to organizational reality than the abstracts we get presented most of the time in management books. Where Shotter makes the distinction between 'Aboutness-thinking' and 'Withness-thinking', this immediately resonated with my views on interventions versus innerventions, the difference between acting as a participant or a partaker, and managing versus co-creating.

Part Two of this book concentrates on processes. Thanks to a clear understanding of the word generativity as a firm basis, the chances are good that we grow our comprehension regarding the possible generativity of processes in organizations and communities, in such a way that this may benefit their futures.

Another two years of intense PhD work are waiting to be narrated. I learned new dimensions of scholarly practice, and made some great new friends. If I were to share my 'meta-data' - covering 150 journal pages, more than 600 emails, and not to forget three academic papers - you would be bored and overloaded. Since I rather like you to be partaker, I selected and compressed only the juicy parts of the story, trusting that your creativity will fill the gaps and smoothen the reading. Again we are heading for a valuable apotheosis as well as an unexpected even bigger big bang.

DIALOGIC TEAS WITH MY PROFESSOR

The only simplicity to be trusted is the simplicity to be found on the far side of complexity.

Alfred North Whitehead

By Dutch academic tradition, doctoral dissertations are supposed to include a list of theses; propositions that may have nothing to do with the content matter. Of course I couldn't help sometimes drifting away into my future and jotting draft ideas in my journal. In a moment of despair, really fed up with all protocols and restrictions regarding academic writing, I thought of the following thesis: "Since research merely has become Google search, and the format of an academic paper has been protocolized to the max, it won't take long before artificial intelligence takes over and will produce meticulous dissertations, without the need of human intervention." To support this, I can refer to the fact that a self-learning algorithm, after studying the works of Mozart, created a brand new composition in the same style. When an audience of musical experts was presented with a concert of Mozart pieces, including the artificial one, they didn't notice the fake. Just imagine: science as an automated process. Not so far from reality, because computers are already used to find out whether academic writings are genuine. Furthermore, students rather do elearning than attend classes, and the scholars that actually retrieve and read academic papers, do this in a very algorithmic way.

One proposition that I invented only now would sound like: "PhD supervisors who treat their candidates as important clients, including fast responses, constructive feedback and regular dialogic tea meetings, may not represent the majority, but they do exist." And Celeste is one of them: connective, responsive, energetic, full of life. On the 8th November 2019 we met each other over a cup of tea in the most central train station of The Netherlands. Coming from the east, she traveled more kilometers than me coming from the west. I felt blessed already by such a great demonstration of attention. Having fully read my DPC chapters and considering my first framework a real 'gem', she warmly invited me to join the circle of PhD candidates around her; at no charge. As a full professor she led CMOB: the Change Management and Organizational Behavior group within the University of Twente. Regarding me, she had a clear plan.

Finding Celeste was a matter of having a few good friends, and a clear picture about my future supervisor's profile. First it was my The Hague client-friend Rudmer who suggested a name. And yes, that professor was as responsive as polite: he liked my work but was too busy, and he gave me a new name. Again a quick response but a full agenda. The golden suggestion came from my friend Joep, fellow AI practitioner, fellow TAOS associate. On his own path toward a possible doctorate he met Celeste as a possible supervisor. She actually is a TAOS associate herself, and she even had invited David Cooperrider in the defenses of some of her PhD students. Celeste was the one I had been looking out for. And with just a few application letters I was back on track, or better: on a new promising track. UTwente is in The Netherlands known as the entrepreneurial university, famous for its startups where technology serves the human interest. When I completed my form in their PhD system called Hora Finita (!) Celeste told me to keep it simple - "just for the administration" - and to put the PhD due date for December 2021. Did I mention that Celeste is likely to be called a 'friendly firm achiever'? No pressure. Did I have to start my PhD from scratch again? One answer is: yes, because I was on the point of getting immersed in a completely new approach to PhDelivery. Another answer would be: it's all part of the emergence. Clarifying organizational generativity is a generative process of inquiry. Inspiration, transpiration, irritation, transformation. Two years ahead and awaiting.

A Welcome PhD Ceremony

As I would learn very soon, Dutch dissertations these days are in most cases a collection of published papers. After all, the highly learned peer-reviewers of the respective journals already gave their consent, thereby taking a part of the responsibility out of the hands of the final defense committee. As part of her natural welcoming gestures, Celeste invited me for another tea at her university, smartly organized on the day of a PhD defense of one of her students, which I therefore could attend as a guest. "Begin with the end in mind", she must have thought. It was my second occasion to join such a ceremony (and regarding a third chance: keep on reading). Wouter, a tall and handsome man, dressed in tuxedo, was going for his next doctorate, since he was already a medical doctor. He had completed his research on medical leadership, through an impressive series of articles, collected in a 400 page book. Reading that gave me a bit of the shivers - was I supposed to produce something alike? - besides a slight feeling of disappointment: so many surveys and interviews, so much data, all of it converging in a list of ten not very surprising medical leadership skills? None whatsoever about how these doctors were going to embrace and practice those skills; was this what science has to offer? Ten 'leadership behaviors', to be found for decades already in the average management job profile? Of course, I understood by then that the PhD is the proof for being a professional researcher, no guarantee for great Eureka's. But there is the process of research and the value of its results, I would say.

Wouter presented his lay talk for his family and friends gently and smoothly, whilst wearing a white doctor's coat with the typical stethoscope around his collar. When he addressed his children in the audience, I drifted melancholically away to the possible moment where I would be standing before my own six kids, all nicely independent social entrepreneurial beings, equipped with the latest 21st century skills, not too impressed by decorum, but most of them in for a party with their father...

Change of scenery. The white coat was replaced by the tuxedo again, the highly learned 'opponents' took their places, and suddenly we were presented with a new order of discourse. The play had begun. I don't remember most of it, but three comments from the committee members drew my attention. Three instances that made me appreciate the respective professors for their practical wisdom - and note their names for future purposes. Professor Severs regarded leadership not so much as a set of skills, but merely as an 'in-between process'. Check. Professor Van Egmont wondered how to regard leadership when the employee involved is not so much a consumer anymore, but to be developed into a "prosumer'. Check. One comment I remember, not sure by whom, was a bit wicked when suggesting that there might be an important eleventh medical leadership skill being overlooked. This remark surprised and confused Wouter highly, and the professor had to rescue him out of his eloquent but overcomplicated arguments. The eleventh management skill should have been "Having a cup of coffee with one's co-workers." I loved that comment. Wouter graduated with a cum laude.

The engaging encounters with Celeste and her entourage made me feel comfortable in this faculty. And when asked, a few months later, I was very happy to do some reciprocity favors, by giving classes in the CMOB masters on leadership and cross cultural behavior. Of course, I didn't lecture; I invited these bright and eager students to practice Appreciative Inquiry.

My biggest takeaway - I still memorize it whenever I can - was co-created with the Italian born assistant professor and program manager Lara. She asked me about AI. I first gave her my spontaneous example of not-AI: "So you are an Italian. You probably like pasta." This kind of thinking happens to a lot of us. "You are from Asia; they have a culture of shyness and shame." And actually, Lara confirmed that lots of lectures in the cross-cultural master included indications and explanations for cultural differences. Which may exist on average, but not necessarily on the individual level. So I asked Lara a genuine AI (energy) question: "Hi Lara, what would you consider your favorite dish?" She said: "Bread with peanut butter." (Of course I don't dare to call this a typical Dutch meal.) We laughed. We connected. And we decided that this would be the format for my CCB class: bring the students - a variety of nationalities - into appreciative inquiry interviews and let them find out about similarities and differences, unbiased by theories. These classes have become a success, according to the evaluations that Lara always happily shares with me. I may not be Celeste's PhD student anymore, but I still regard Lara and others as dear colleagues, and as long as I can, and they will have me, I will continue to give those classes.

A Seemingly Simple PhD Plan

"Will that be a rewrite or a remake?", I asked Celeste two days after our first tea in the train station. At that moment she already suggested that I could turn my DPC Chapter 1 into an Academy of Management 2020 Conference paper; deadline for submission 15th January 2020. Although I knew vaguely of this famous yearly event, I wasn't aware that it counts more than 10.000 participants - half of AoM's registered members - and receives thousands of submitted papers. According to Celeste, it would be an opportunity to enter the academic network at large, and my wife and I already envisioned a holiday in the surroundings of Vancouver where AoM2020 was to be held. I got enthusiastic and accepted Celeste's advice. This would need a shrink from my earlier 80 pages to 30. "Yes, a remake. Preferably in the format of a rigorous literature review. And after that paper you might build a training curriculum around your framework, and we would ask some managers and professionals to reflect on that. But okay, one step at a time." She had just outlined a new PhD route, but I wasn't yet aware of that. In my journal of 8th November I jotted a big YES. By the time I really freed my agenda to get started with my AoM paper, I had one month left before submission, and some other surprising elements of the "Celeste approach" were waiting for me.

THE DRILL OF PRAGADEMIC WRITING

You can define a free person precisely as someone whose fate is not centrally or directly dependent on peer assessment.

Nassim Nicholas Taleb

Reminding myself that the book you are reading is supposed to reach scholars and practitioners, and if you would belong to the latter, it occurred to me that you may have seen the term PhD too many times already, and ask yourself whether you should be concerned about not having or not aspiring those three letters behind your name. Relax. Let me share my emerging view on becoming a philosophical doctor or not.

The perspective is hopeful: different from car driving on the public road, for which you need to be able to show your driver's license, you are warmly welcome to do scientific research of any kind, without the diploma called PhD. You can self-publish your findings and may attract an audience. If you wish, you can try to publish your work in an academic journal, which needs the approval of peer-reviewers. You'll be surprised. All this is possible without the corresponding 'license'.

To be honest, when I entered the Leiden Dual PhD Center, I came with the romantic idea of creating my 'masterpiece', and you may have had a similar idea of a dissertation. Although the various academic courses included plenty of reality checks, it needed a new university, in particular 'a Celeste' to help me out of my dreams: "What it takes to get your PhD certificate is three scholarly articles in proper journals, well-introduced and completed by appendices, research-data and references." There you are. We are not talking Einstein brains nor a Ken Follett pen. A PhD is the proof of being able to perform proper research, according to the rules and regulations that go with it. It may even happen that you are granted to go for your PhD, mainly on the basis of previous articles that you managed to get published as an 'amateur'.

A PhD refers to a specific skill. A truck driver's license gives you access to a transportation job, and doesn't say so much about your conversational skills; with a PhD you can apply for a job at a university or high school, and again: no guarantees that you are also a great teacher. So, the good news for the practitioner-reader is that you can start a research on a topic that triggers you; you can co-create - even publish - with 'real' scholars, or figure the skill out yourself; you can be invited to give guest lectures on a topic from your practice. Academic life, if you want, is closer than you think, and no license is needed.

Of course there is a flip-side, and if I didn't find out about that already in Leiden, it became perfectly clear in Twente. Doing research these days is synonymous to publishing papers. Academic workers have even a target for that. Writing and publishing an article in a peer-reviewed journal is time-consuming, not necessarily rewarding, hard work also, and at times even boring. Like any other job, it must fit you. Please don't consider the PhD as 'the highest achievable' in life. Research - and teaching about it - is as valuable and as necessary as many other jobs in society. The one job needs IQ, the other EQ or SQ - there seem to be ten of these - and I don't even know the abbreviations properly. You can do research as a hobby, and take all the time you need, without 'peer-pressure'. Somehow, the idea occurs to me that I am approaching a third audience: that of PhD students, not fully aware yet of what they are to encounter. I think this book is for them a plea to move on with their good work, ánd to reflect on job-fitness.

By the time I am writing these lines - July 2022 - the Organization Development Journal accepted 'my' article for publication. How does that feel? The fact that I am writing the book you're reading, and not struggling with my next scholarly article, may give you a bit of a clue. In Dutch they call it 'mustard after the dish', meaning: okay, fine, but a bit out of momentum. At the same time I feel happy and relieved, especially for my two co-authors who are expected to publish regularly, and without whom there hadn't been such an article at all. I also feel confident and yes, perhaps a little bit proud, because having that article provides this book with 'scientific support'. Finally, since I now can refer to the article, I can save you as reader some time, stick to the relevant experiences in the corresponding research journey and focus on the intentions and skills that could enrich your future behavior.

One thing has become crystal clear: for a deep understanding of organizational and societal life we should look at the processes going on, and not just at the outputs of those processes. So let me update you on this second part in my journey, rightly to be called a (pragmatic + academical =) pragademic episode. Two years of being supported and guided by skilled scholars who became real friends, of seeming imbalance between format and content, of dreaming about dialogue with the anonymous peer reviewers, of killing my darlings or at least put them in the freezer, and also years of chewing (with 'long teeth') so much on my old stuff, that unexpected new flavors appeared on my tongue. Let me take you along the marvelous dr. Celeste, my forbidden Eureka, no-nonsense dr. Jeff, the crucial difference between generativity 'in' and 'of' organizations, digging up darlings, the rise of engaged scholarship and making scientific sense of processual generativity. Future forming practices ahead.

Running for AoM Paper Presentation

Revision. Re-vision. Isn't that a kind of looking at the same thing with new eyes, as Marcel Proust once said? Exactly on time - 15th January 2020 - I submitted my AoM conference paper called *From Review to Framework: Conceptualizing Generativity for Organization Development*. It survived the peer review and was accepted six weeks later as document number #16701. Suddenly this whole PhD thing seemed relatively easy. Finally, I was in the game. The only thing I didn't know was in which league I was playing.

I had a great coach, not to say meticulous and demanding. If you are still thinking that supervisors are hard to reach, and respond in riddles, meet Celeste. Just imagine. This is her deal: "When you deliver your writing before 5pm, I can print it at the office and take it home. I will revise it manually in the early morning, and I will put it in the scanner first thing at the office. So you will have it back before 10am the next day." I can't remember if she ever failed to meet this service level agreement. Chapeau! And apparently I was not her only PhD candidate; she had an average of ten to fifteen papers in her workload. Okay, there's a flip-side. After three weeks of co-working like this, I felt nervous and insecure. It seemed like my texts were never good enough. I asked myself if I could still call myself a genuine author. Furthermore, I noticed that she would read my rewrites everytime with fresh eyes, not necessarily aware of her earlier comments. (Impossible of course, when you are editing fifteen papers at the same time.) It could happen that she revised something back to what it earlier had been. I felt frustrated and asked for a meeting. What I concluded from her listening ear and constructive reflections is that she admired my research findings, and really wanted the paper to be a success, which needed her long time experience in writing, editing, reviewing and publishing academic papers. And no, it really was still my paper; no need to add her name as a second author. I was back on track again. So far our process of co-creation, and although I don't have much data for comparison, I think she is unique in her way of working.

Structure plays a major part in academic writing, and size restrictions increase the challenge. A proper paper should contain an Abstract, an Introduction with a clear positioning of the research, a referenced description of the Method, and of course the Findings, elaborated by the so-called Discussion section. Tables are very important, because they summarize the essences in an even more structured format. The list of References should be presented in one of the many existing citation styles, in my case often APA6 or APA7. Every journal has its own conditions for addressing relevant audiences, size, number of tables, character of the discussion and style guide. With all these boundaries you could easily forget what it was you actually had been researching, and for what purpose. There is a chance that, for each journal, you are telling your story starting from a completely new rationale, to an unexpected new audience, with new findings to present, and using different arguments in your discussion; just to get your work published. Poor scholars for whom publishing is part of the job contract.

Compared to the 80 pages I took with me from Leiden, my remake for AoM was surprisingly familiar, at the same time immensely different. It included an abstract of exactly 100 words, eight tables, 25 pages of body text and five pages of references. The title page completes it up to 40. In four weeks of intense writing and rewriting, quite a lot had happened. Re-vision and re-make, re-member?

First and foremost, as the title of my newborn AoM paper suggests, there's a conceptual framework to be admired. The former one, about the proper use of the word generativity, had to be degraded to an intermediate finding to make space for a new one, proudly introduced as *Conceptual Framework of Organizational Generativity*. Spoiler alert! Here comes my text that lifted my CFOG on the AoM stage:

> Having extensively reviewed and analyzed the use of the term generative/ity in OD literature, and after deriving pragmatic suggestions for proper use of the term in written and spoken language, we now combine our findings to propose a robust framework regarding the term generativity. The framework is constituted of five foundational concepts that emerged from our reflections: Intentionality, Processuality, Serendipity, Performativity and Procreativity.

This one paragraph covers quite a quantum leap, from reframing the word generativity to identifying organizational generativity in five factors. I will call it the fivefold, and let it rest for now, because this very fivefold would be facing severe criticism only a few months later and be put out of favor. Part Three of this book will take care of its rehabilitation.

Although the AoM paper may have jumped too far or too fast in its conclusion, it did present a compact and still fairly complete overview of my research itinerary. It needed just one table to systematically present the subsequent steps. To enjoy this compact view, I share this one here.

Nr.	Step	Criteria	Intermediate Result
-1	Become intrigued by the term organizational generativity	Academic relevance	Starting the research
0	Search possible relevant sources addressing the term	Search string 'generativity OR generative'	± 20 million Google hits
1	Dictionaries' definition of the term	Keyword generative	± 25 descriptions of and synonyms for generative
2	Search sources that include the term in their titles	Search string: 'allintitle: generativity OR generative'	± 500000 Google hits
3	Building a database on generative/ity in OD by selecting publications that address the term within the OD domain	Search string: variations on 'generative and organization'; term addressed in title, abstract or keywords; term 'as closely as possible connected with OD'; term used prominently. Also: iterative exclusion of non-relevant domains such as biology, linguistics, information technology etcetera	27 publications (18 primary authors)
4	Extract from the selected publications all text fragments that include or address the term one way or another	Exclude duplicates/repetitions when in the same publication	157 Text fragments, ina traceable way stored in a spread-sheet, including cited references

Nr.	Step	Criteria	Intermediate Result
5	Examine the dataset of 157 fragments on its validity for rigorous literature review	Enough variety of authors; enough spread over time; any bias?	A data set showing a fair distribution of valuable and relevant content
6	Review Level 1: explore the accuracy of the way the term is used	Focus on the syntax of noting the term in the texts	Four categories of noting: as Definition, as Adjective, as Condition, as Result
7	Review Level 2: explore possible meanings and interpretations of the term	Focus on the semantics of noting the term; coding each text fragment related to the object of the terms	Three subsets of fragments using the term as a quality of a Thing, a Human, or a Process
8	Review Level 3: in-depth exploration of meanings or interpretations in the fragments that relate the term to Processes	Focus on the text fragments coded as Processual Generative	Seven subsets of fragments referring to process characteristics: Relational, Continuous change, Disruptive, Future oriented, Idea giving, Actionable and Procreative
9	Review Level 4: explore 90 references, as part of the 157 text fragments	Exploring 45 secondary sources by 30 authors to underpinning the term; selecting most cited and relevant ones	Insights of most influential secondary authors that enrich the findings so far
10	Analytical reflection of the findings so far	How to clarify proper use of the term?	Recommendations for proper use, plus theoretical sampling
11	Towards a conceptual framework	Considerations for clear understanding and application of the term	Conclusions, discussion and propositions

Within its tight boundaries, the paper not only provides an accurate overview of the research; compared to Leiden even new ideas were added.

First, my research journey became underpinned with a referenced methodological foundation, described as: "a rigorous literature review (Wolfswinkel, Furtmueller, & Wilderom: 2013) into a conceptual framework (Jabareen: 2009)". Although it felt a bit strange to add the methodology after the research, the AoM paper was fairly consistent with the work I had done.

Second, we felt the need and reserved the space for "actionable suggestions". These made the paper reach beyond linguistics and touch the original research goal of contributing to organization development. One of the main practical suggestions sounds: "Build a curriculum for organizing generativity". Of course, this was the suggestion from Celeste to myself, our idea for the next step in my PhD.

There was even room left for positioning the idea of a 'generative organization' between other qualifiers. This to show that 'generativity' was really in the need of clarity, where other concepts such as learning (organizations), healthy, adaptive, sustainable, excellent, lean, and agile already had been fairly documented. Even the virtuous, the flourishing, the dialogical and the teal organization had their sources. Quite a strong argument for the importance of generativity to be clarified, yes? The twelve presented in one table create the notion that 'generativity' belongs to a professional list, and that OD practitioners couldn't leave it aside. That is, if OD practitioners exist who are up to date with more than a few concepts. Have you ever seen these twelve together in one table? Food for OD practitioners.

Top-12 OD Relevant Qualifiers 1: Frequency, Clarity and Performativity

Nr.	As an adjective: (before the word organization(s) or organizing)	As a noun: (after the word organizational)	Clearly Defined[2]	Relevant Source
1	learning	learning	yes	(Senge, 1994)
2	healthy	health	yes	(de Smet A. et al., 2014)
3	adaptive	adaptivity	yes	(Consortium for Service Innovation, 1992)
4	sustainable	sustainability	yes	Since 1991 included in Dow Jones Sustainability Indices
5	excellent	excellence	yes	As defined in 1998 by European Foundation for Quality Management
6	lean	'lean-ness'	yes	(Krafcik, 1988)
7	agile	agility	yes	Derived from *Manifesto for Agile Software Development*
8	generative	generativity	no	(Cooperrider et al., 2013)
9	virtuous	virtuousness	yes	(Arjoon, 2000)
10	flourishing	flourishing	yes	Introduced in 2017 by Aim2flourish.com
11	dialogical	'dialogic-ness'	yes	(Bushe & Marshak, 2015)
12	teal	'teal-ness'	yes	(Laloux, 2014)

[1] Based on the number of hits in Google Scholar (end 2019). The chance of hitting the first six qualifiers is 10 to 20 times higher than hitting one of the last six qualifiers.

[2] In the sense of: extensively and fairly, uniformly described and accepted or used accordingly.

Small is beautiful? Is a lang walk in a pine forest with thousands of pine trees more nourishing than standing next to one pine tree? There is a reason for academic papers to be as short as possible: they represent just one tree in an overloaded forest; they better not be a forest themselves. And besides, it is possible to write a paper of 25 pages about a whole forest as well as about one seed. It's a matter of choice. As nature does, science lets you find your own way through. What can be said is that the one month exercise, leading to my first academic coming out in the form of a conference paper, brought many benefits. It is good to have the story 'out there', enabling others to respond and reflect or build on it. The tight document restrictions are both a guidance and a challenge, and that helps to focus. The remake for AoM urged me to revisit my earlier retrieved data; this review gave me new insights and brought my findings a bit further. I think I delivered more substance in less pages. (Of course with less supporting arguments, references and examples, the things that peer-reviewers like so much.)

Celeste provided a profound lesson in efficient academic writing. The whole exercise helped me to reshape and sharpen the way my PhD trajectory would look like. In one month! Good enough to copy bits and pieces for you in this book, without any chance of plagiarism. I liked, and still like that first official piece of AoM paper.

Being in the shrinking mode I managed to turn my tiny paper into an even tinier five minutes video presentation. This was needed to make sure that my "in person" AoM conference speech would stay within the time limits. Let me be brief about my minutes of fame: the conference had to be converted into a digital one for reasons of Covid-19; my audience consisted of a friendly host, four fellow-presenters and six participants. On the AoM site you will only find the abstract of my paper, together with my email address to request the full copy. I never got such a request.

I don't think a conference paper, even peer-reviewed, will do for a dissertation. Although, there was this email, shortly after the conference, from an unknown journal, offering to publish my paper. Celeste considered the journal not high enough in the ratings and suggested not to follow up. Besides, this happened in the same period that we submitted a full article to the (A-rated) Journal of Applied Behavioral Science (JABS), which attempt was a bit of a nightmare.

Muddling Through JABS Journalism

Different from writing a full dissertation, a kind of a continuous labor I thought I was doing in Leiden, the PhD-through-articles-strategy brings you in situations of waiting. The time between submitting the AoM paper and presenting it at the corresponding conference was eight months. A self-respecting academic journal takes normally three to six months to give you a clue about the publishability of your manuscript (and don't you dare to 'shop' with it in the meantime). AoM needed ten weeks for the review of all their paper submissions. Being self employed, I do have the responsibility to look after my income regularly, so the gap after 15th January was easily filled with more earthly activities, like finding and serving clients to get humanized - not a sign yet about Covid-19 sneaking round the corner. Celeste granted me a 'well deserved rest' - another good side of her professionality - but I had got the taste of it, and asked myself what would be a proper next step. At such moments I always start conversations. If not with others, I converse easily with myself and my journal. According to my notes I spoke to Celeste only six weeks later, in Twente, to give lectures and enjoy tea with my supervisor. (If you are a reader as well as a PhD supervisor, please check whether you have sufficient conversations with your students, will you? They will love you for it.) Before the tea meeting I sought contact with my old friend Gervase, the dialogic OD and generative image professor who had most probably already published three or four new articles since the last time I met him. I found him focusing on Generative Leadership, and I have forgotten whether I generously approved the title of his new topic as correct language according to my first conceptual framework on generativity. After all, leadership is to be considered a process. He was quite appreciative about the AoM paper I showed him, and suggested that I amplify it into a genuine journal article; he mentioned the *Journal for Applied Behavioral Science* (JABS). A journal on applied behavior?, I must have thought, but I took note of it and would ask Celeste for her expert opinion.

It occurred to me that by far the most of my journal pages in that period addressed my growing concerns about the spooky kind of leap between my research findings and the five factors of Organizational Generativity. I apparently suspected that real peer reviewers of real journals wouldn't let me go free with a recursive excuse like "it was generativity that made me come up with factors of generativity". I had to find a solution, and I must agree: I came close.

End of March, the AoM paper was officially accepted, a good reason to officially move on. Celeste directly said yes to JABS, because publishing in a top rated journal would make me famous. Although she first suggested that this could be my second paper, regarding the OG curriculum, we soon came to the conclusion that we better improve and strengthen the AoM paper, to set and settle the necessary foundations. JABS provided the luxury of 40 pages main text, and by the end of April I presented my first draft to Celeste, who switched to her speedy meticulous response modus. To cut it short: it took me nine months and nine major revisions, besides numerous minor ones, to co-create an article that met Celeste's standards in such a way that she was confident about the upcoming peer-review. I almost insisted, and she agreed, that she would be mentioned as the second author. The article seemed very robust to me as well, and the clue for the five factor Eureka leap had become 'retrospective analysis': a way of afterwards making it plausible that new insights make sense.

It made me think of Martin Seligman, the happiness professor who was so courageous to criticize his earlier book *Authentic Happiness* by publishing a new theory in his book *Flourish*. Already in the first pages he introduces the acronym PERMA (Positive Emotion, Engagement, Positive Relationships, Meaning and Accomplishments annex Achievements). I asked myself: where did he get these five? PERMA just falls out of heaven, and Seligman elaborates on it in the rest of the book. Celeste told me that once you are a famous professor, you can introduce what you like and publishers will publish. That simply meant that my five factors - with three P's, one I and one S not even close to a nice acronym - would not be accepted easily. Besides my own doubts, that is.

By mid October 2020 we submitted to JABS our 49 pages of manuscript under the title *Generativity Reviewed, Five Drivers for Life-Giving Organization Development*. We didn't kill the darling in the very last paragraph, called Endnote & Andnote, where I introduced the new word *genarrative*. We set our alarm clock for mid January 2021, when the verdict was to be expected. This created another pause in the PhD process, which turned out to be very well spent, the fruits of it to be found in Part Three of this book. Of course I didn't know that by then, nor that all kinds of dramatic turns were waiting to cross my path.

Exactly three months later we got the response from JABS. The two peer reviewers were partly appreciative and partly not-amused. For one, surprisingly, my statistics were a no-go. How on earth could I state that 157 text fragments were not biased by too many Appreciative Inquiry related authors? Being a mathematician, I actually had made the effort to show that my dataset was representative. Of course this included partly qualitative, language related arguments, and no tables with five significant numbers behind the comma. (Everytime I see a non-bèta article, based on fifteen unique interviews, presenting tables with H0 and H1 hypothesis, normal distributions and statistics that do not correspond with the qualitative nature of the data, I tend to vomit, but the journals love these tables and call them scientific proof.) Perhaps I'd have had a better chance if I simply had skipped the data validity part; perhaps no one would have missed it. I don't see much data validation done in qualitative studies, because... qualitative. The other peer reviewer had - rightly - concerns about my spooky emergent leap toward the fivefold OG factors, and no retroperspective reasoning was going to help me out of that sink hole. One of the peer reviewers suggested changing the research method to something more convincing, which I didn't consider a very scholarly advice.

Celeste didn't mirror my disappointment, was actually very optimistic, because having a peer-review means being taken seriously. She already started revising the manuscript before I had a chance to let it all sink in. For her this was business as usual, so it seemed. And for me? I could only think of the weirdness of peer reviewers being anonymous people, even with partly conflicting comments, where to me dialogue should be the way to bring science further. I will not bother you with my fourteen pages of a desired dialogue with the reviewers, in which I added my reflections to their comments , in the sincere expectation that I could have an email exchange with them. These notes were never sent. A no go; she made that perfectly clear. I thought I had written an essay, but they seemed to expect a legal defense. I should be glad and honored with having a 're-submit' on my first article; the revision was up to us. I wasn't sure that Celeste's energetic corrections were going to make a difference; after all we had done the best we could. When I suggested that we might benefit from a third author, she liked the idea and suggested one of her former PhD students, dr. Jeffrey Hicks. He saved us. But we wouldn't know that until July 2022, after which the attempt to turn the AoM paper into an accepted article had taken two and a half years.

Jeff lives with his family in Texas and teaches Organizational Behavior at the state university. His job demands him to publish or co-publish regularly, which made our request also an opportunity for him. We only met in email and Zoom and I never saw him without an old baseball cap on his head. He is the friend you want to have. He reads good books like *Shop Class as a SoulCraft*, one of his great recommendations. I am sure he repairs his own motorcycle. His vocabulary can differ from straight forward no bullshit yankee slang, including some decent cursing, to a refined choice of academic words and smooth sentences. He is gifted with the linguistic sensibility to craft complicated things into understandable reading, and when he is focused, he is right on it, to deliver. What an amazing guy. Celeste and Jeff, what a great pair of co-authors you are.

Digging Up the Darling

By the start of April 2021, Jeff was on board. In the beginning he was still a bit modest: "I am very happy to help you out a bit, to look at the peer-reviews with fresh eyes and to suggest some alternative texts." But soon, he became the driving co-maker of our re-submittance. He came up with a new rationale, to position the article better in the scientific debate. In numbering his revisions, he called the drafts consistently Phoenix, and by the time we re-submitted, we had reached Phoenix_ version_45_CW_CH.

Slowly and gently Jeff started asking me why I had stepped so easily over what he considered my main research findings: the seven manifestations of processual generativity. In the meantime it had occurred to me, thanks to the peer-reviews, that I may have been too focused on the organizational meta level alone, almost forgetting that many things also happen inside organizations. In practice I was aware of generativity IN organizations besides generativity OF organizations, but in my theoretical approach I had clung on too long on one of them, where both views at least are interrelated if not mutually entangled. Only later I found in my archive an article about a theory by Giddens, making sense of the mutual influencing relationships between parts and the whole in a social system. This Structuration Theory describes quite accurately what is going on between processual and organizational generativity. Nevertheless, we decided to be sensible and reshape the article around my most tangible findings. And therefore it had to be that the seven manifestations of generative processes, already present since Leiden, finally became the protagonist of the article, reducing the spooky fivefold to a possible perspective in the last paragraph of the discussion called Future Research.

All made sense. Three is a company. We tackled the peer-reviews in a joint effort, and showed our ability to change perspective. The article had become more consistent than ever before. The seven processual manifestations now determined my new framework and got the full podium. We reduced the number of tables to create more space for Discussion. Both the theoretical implications and the practical implications looked profound, as you soon will come to know. Mid June 2021, we re-submitted our genuine remake, and were convinced in praising and pleasing the peer reviewers. The new title being *Clarifying Organizational Generativity: A Generative Process of Inquiry*. Very processual. No promises. Just proper research. Another three months of hopeful waiting started.

On the 1st of August, without any further explanation, JABS declined our article for publication. Jeff was silent and sincere. Celeste instantly suggested alternative journals and started to revise the manuscript again, as if JABS simply was one of plenty. And I?

I resided in the small Spanish village of Viladrau, joining my wife in one of her contemplative retreats. From my monastic room with a simple desk and wooden chair I watched a wise and silent mountain top and reconsidered my aspirations. I felt annoyed by the idea of having spent more than a year on what seemed minor textual changes to research findings that were there already in the first place.

Then my co-supervisor called: "Hi Cees, I will be co-authoring your second article. All will be fine with your first. When do we start?" I thought my PhD purpose was doing research, not writing articles. And I wrote in my diary: I AM A PRACTITIONER! It was the moment that I decided to let go of my PhD diploma aspiration and its conditioned publishing demands. I didn't want to belong to the scholarly family and their rules, but wanted to properly relate to them. I was still eager to pursue what I was up to, although from a less academic angle, and started to focus on my professional life as an OD practitioner. I would need a better proposition, a better story and in particular a better website to bring my aspirations to where I want them to be: in organizational life, and its inhabitants. I wrote the utmost sincere and appreciative letter to Celeste and Jeff, explaining my tough and liberating decision. And I resumed my retreat as a free man. The search would continue, including some unexpected surprises. After all, Celeste and Jeff had become my friends.

Knowledgeable Co-creators

In a few pages from here you will get the chance to learn about inter-relational processes and how to understand their generativity: their potential to contribute to flourishing futures for all partakers and stakeholders of organizations and communities. Was it just about writing a JABS article in the past 18 months? There's something good about waiting after having submitted. The manuscript is kept in a sort of safe, completely out of your hands. A great opportunity for you to move on, because research is always creating new research. A conceptual framework is after all only a stepping stone for practical application. In this case, the aim was to create a kind of curriculum for leaders and professionals, to enrich their skills. And since the baker shouldn't test his own bread, I shouldn't be the one to test my own thesis. The method of *Engaged Scholarship*, as introduced by Andrew van de Ven, inspired me to turn the next phase of my research into a wider co-creation. The necessary knowledge, wisdom and experience needed to come from others than my biased self.

A conceptual framework can be compared with certain assumed features of unknown territory. If you want to facilitate adventurers to move safely across that area, they need guidance. Jeff quoted the term 'unknown unknowns' in the context of facing unexpected futures. To put the signing poles out there, it needs an expedition of experienced hikers, who may not be completely familiar with all features and dangers on the way, but who can be trusted to understand them when they see them, and to deal with it. I called these engaged researchers my Knowledgeable Co-creators, and they would be the ones to make the 'unknown unknowns' of the territory a bit more known to new visitors.

So I spent my first JABS waiting intermezzo to discuss ideal profiles of such fellow travelers, with the ones I already had in my inner circle. Through recommendations, constructive conversations, proper recruitment and genuine intake sessions, I was able to gather a diverse and powerful group of KC's, willing and able to join me on this next adventure. They would be the ones to find actors in organizations to interview about elements of my Conceptual Framework Organizational Generativity. The five factors, remember? I was aware that it had an Eureka character, but a concept is a concept, isn't it? And the 'engaged scholarship' approach was exactly the way to get the concept underpinned. Or not. Whether it would end up in a curriculum? That's the beauty of future forming research, and this was exactly what the KC's were going to do.

The integrity committee of Twente granted me officially her fiat for my corresponding research proposal, including method, instruments, and proper care for safety and privacy of the interviewees. Everything was in place to use Appreciative Inquiry in this second stage of my research journey, both in one-on-one interviews as in group reflections. Later on when awaiting a JABS response for the second time, the KC's came into action, with me as their coach and coordinator. I interviewed them; they interviewed their self-chosen candidates and we built all together a substantial 'data set' containing experiences, discoveries, visions of 'organizational actors' on the possible existence of organizational generativity in their contexts. This could have become that article with my co-supervisor a.k.a. co-author, which did not appear. The data was nevertheless very useful to shape Part Three of this book, and the KC's are automatically designated as my co-creators in that. And you will be my peer-reviewers. Or a KC yourself.

Published At Last

I really appreciate Jeff and Celeste for showing such constructive energy and professional attitude. They found a way to accept my resignation and still keep me engaged in finding an outlet for the manuscript. They deserved a return on their investment, and after a while we found ourselves tracking possible other journals. All of these had different conditions for style and size and character of discussion, and Jeff surprised us from time to time with an unexpected rewrite: "Would this be working for that journal?" We weren't very successful, often got rejected already on technical conditions, and it needed a conversation with my esteemed friend Ronald Fry, constructive OD professor at Case Western Reserve University, to get the golden tip. For me he is the personification of Appreciative Inquiry. His responses to my questions are wise, comforting and constructive. When we zoomed, in the spring of 2022, he reflected on good old time's full dissertations versus contemporary article-PhD's, and in between he humbly suggested that a book still might be a good way to present my ideas. He also thought that the *Organization Development Journal* (ODJ) could be interested in our manuscript.

Celeste agreed. Jeff went for it, narrowed the text down to all-in 28 pages and I thought it was a crisp reading. The nature of ODJ asked for practical implications, if not suggestions, and we managed to fit these in the tight boundaries. I found it actually fun again to work on the manuscript. We submitted it on 15th February, and by 27th of May we had our positive response: with only a few minor revisions, especially regarding the practicals, it could be published. I felt inspired to really give it a shot, and refined and enriched the set of guidelines for practitioners as far as my experience could supply. On July 3rd we re-submitted. On July 21 we were asked to correct a few typos, perform a last alignment with APA7, and replace the word 'processuality' because this was not to be found (!) in the *Oxford Dictionary*. All set and delivered by the 28th of July, formally accepted in August 2022, and - after adding page numbers everywhere we quote from the 157 fragments - finally published in the May 2023 ODJ issue.

Tracing back from its earliest conception in 2018, my emerging text has been presented under about 30 different titles. It is August 2022. The latest - final? - title has become *Clarifying Organizational Generativity: A Future Forming Perspective for OD Practitioners and Researchers* (ODJ issue May 2023).

HOW TO ASSESS
A GENERATIVE PROCESS

If we don't know what it is, we call it a system.
If we don't know how it works, we call it a process.

Anonymous professor, to be said sharing this wisdom like a comedian, with his finger pointing upwards and speaking with a funny accent.

This chapter goes with scientific underpinning. And since the ODJ article represents the most profound version of clear language, I feel very comfortable quoting the relevant parts from it. My second conceptual framework Processual Generativity describes seven manifestations of processes to be called generative. How did they come to existence? The answer is: by coding, which is a regular thing to do when analyzing qualitative data.

It started with the selection of 157 text fragments that somehow referred to the noun generativity or the adjective generative. In my first attempts to distill meaning, I discovered, or better: it must have been my logical linguistic reasoning of that moment discovering that generativity is not so much the inherent quality of a person or a thing, but seems significantly connected to what goes on amongst and between people, in general to be called processes. Almost 87% of the text fragments pointed that way. So, I found myself looking at 136 processual text fragments, such a number that one unconsciously starts to categorize. This is not a one way road, as grounded theorists will tell you. Going over and over the fragments made me disclose a first idea of labels, like "these ones address the relational nature of processes" or "those ones typically include an orientation toward future". What happened next is building a grid, or a spreadsheet, with all 136 fragments as lines, and a slowly growing number of columns for the labels. The moment a new label-column appeared in the dialogue with my data, I checked all 136 for possible matches. What matters is that a new label should be connected with at least a significant number of fragments, and if not, discharged. Note that text fragments can have more than one label; the description may very well refer to Relational as well as Future oriented. By endlessly repeating this procedure the coding came to a clear end: no more new labels to detect; all fragments coded.

It actually didn't feel like *my* discovery since there had been an interactive - generative? - process going on, with me extracting insights from the data, and the data providing me feedback on logic and relevancy, and my reflective reasoning in between. My spreadsheet finally showed seven coding columns and corresponding labels, representing specific manifestations of processes, by their various authors referred to as generative. I mentioned them in my first CFG, but didn't make much fuss about it. I mostly ignored them for a long time, in my urge to clarify generativity on the organizational level. It needed peer-reviewers and co-authors to make me aware that these seven were to be considered major research findings. Can you believe that? It took me a while.

Now they are there, the question is: do they resonate with your experience? Can you imagine that a new way of looking 'into' processes might reveal new perspectives of which organizations and communities can benefit? They might prefer the more generative processes to be happening, if possible. For that, these specific processes need to be identified, recognized and appreciated as such. Are you willing to study, to take my findings further? This is what genarrativity is meant to be. Future forming practices for building better legacies. You may find yourself a process expert already. Are you ready to look at the same phenomena with new eyes? Will I succeed in providing you with the right set of spectacles? Shall we find out? This is what science is about. How far can we get? Please be the change you want to see in the world. Would the Abstract of the ODJ article be a good start? Here it is.

As the catastrophic consequences of the COVID-19 pandemic have made clear, both the practice and research of organizational development (OD) are in urgent need of alternative pathways to the future. Organizational generativity (OG) offers one such promising alternative. While much of OD practice and research are focused on enabling organizations to better prepare for an unknown future, OG accommodates new ways for organizations to proactively create their own future. As a nascent field of inquiry, however, research on OG is under-developed, and characterized by a lack of clarity. The purpose of this paper, therefore, is to clarify the construct of organizational generativity, so as to be more actionable by OD practitioners, researchers and managers alike. Using grounded theory, we review and critique the literature on generativity, from the "ancestral" writers in psychology to current OD authors. Through successive rounds of inquiry, we reveal the syntax, the semantics and the inherent processual nature of organizational generativity. We then derive a conceptual framework describing seven manifestations of generative organizational processes: relational, transformational, disruptive, future-focused, idea-giving, actionable and procreative. Finally, we discuss implications for OD practice, and opportunities for future research.

The following paragraph contains some more citations from my ODJ article. In a proper journal article these should be surrounded by quotes and references, but we have permission of the author ...

Apotheosis: Conceptual Framework of Generative Processes in Organizations

This is how the second framework got its first official presentation, in the ODJ article:

If our research into organizational generativity is directly associated with processes in organizations, how can practitioners recognize these processes as being generative? How do they manifest themselves? If asked by a practitioner to describe a generative process, what would be our response? Focusing on the 136 processual fragments, we coded that data to arrive at a **Conceptual framework of seven qualities - or manifestations - of generative processes in organizations.**

Relational
Generative processes are manifested as inherently relational, that is, they are "lived within the context of relationships". People relate and communicate, and thereby enact relational processes within organizations. To experience a generative relational process, from the inside, is to experience "high-quality connections" in inquiry and dialogue with colleagues. A generative relational process "catalyzes [that] connectivity" between and among people. Acting relationally can be manifested as remembering, even amidst a busy work schedule, to "make time to gather and share".

Transformational

Generative organizational processes are manifested as transformational. Generative, transformational processes emphasize "bottom-up experiments and learning as you go" and shift the norms of the entire organization. Transformation can also be very personal - that is, transformational processes can either initiate, or result in significant inner, personal change, which may or may not be apparent to others.

Disruptive

Generative organizational processes are manifested as disruptive. Any interactive process includes moments of disruption, contradiction and disequilibrium which are unexpected, but could be experienced as valuable. One has to respond to disruption to make it valuable, which gives this manifestation a stronger or more visible push for actual change than the Transformational manifestation. Disruptive processes can be generative, because they have the "capacity to reunite seeming opposites (theory-practice; secular-sacred)".

Future-focused

Generative organizational processes are future-focused. They fuel, and are fueled by, feelings of hope and aspiration for future generations and their emergent wellbeing; they "pass on what has been learned" [18]. Although perhaps not in a physical sense, this manifestation or quality of a generative process suggests a certain direction in which the organization needs to go, also taking into account the widest possible circle of stakeholders.

Idea-Giving

Generative organizational processes are idea-giving. They generate, or better yet, they are experienced as the generating of new ideas. Generative, idea-giving processes "rejuvenate, reframe"; they stimulate "special versions of seeing" and seeing "old things in new ways" - including ways that challenge the status quo. More than simply "intention" or "orientation," idea-giving organizational processes also bring actual content to the table, such as plans. And not plans necessarily "ordered by top-management" but created by whomever is involved, according to their sense for what the present circumstances are really asking for.

Actionable

Generative organizational processes are actionable. They stimulate people to act - including in novel ways and sometimes with unpredictable results. Actionable generative processes create different conversations about starting anew. Practitioners are not "stuck;" there's less "analysis paralysis." Actionable processes provide a sense of what to do, of what comes next. Actionability encourages moving beyond just producing plans, to enacting them, living them. This manifestation of generativity in the context of an organization refers to the pure act of dynamically organizing something deemed of value.

Procreative

Generative organizational processes are procreative, and encourage stories that "tell it as it may become". They produce desirable action or are "conducive to producing in abundance," meaning growth-oriented action. Procreativity self-perpetuates and self-replicates, procreating even itself, beyond its catalyzers and partakers. Procreative, generative processes can be manifested as future-forming. In comparison with procreativity, the familiar notion of "sustainability" begins to seem replicative of the past, and even defensive toward the future. Perhaps somewhat counter-intuitively, procreativity is also about leaving behind, and focusing instead on that which better serves future situations/generations.

Now is the Time for Your Own Journaling

You just have been reading about seven concepts, manifestations, qualities, appearances of a process. What did that tell you? Now, do you have 30 minutes left for a reflective exercise? If not, you might consider closing the book or tablet, or just re-view the previous paragraph one more time and then stop reading. This is a good moment.

And if you're back or still here, ready for a deep reading, please take a stable sitting position, both feet connected to earth, shoulders relaxed so to support a comfortable stance of your neck and head. What follows is a series of questions from me to you, a kind of appreciative inquiry interview, inviting you to view seemingly familiar phenomena with new eyes. Feel free to make notes, either in real or in your mind.

You have been informed that processes when said to be generative, include qualities such as Relational, Transformative, Disruptive, Future-focused, Idea-giving, Actionable and Procreative. If this new information made you curious to learn more about it, enlightenment may happen when you reflect on the following questions.

1. Do you recall a moment in your life that you felt really curious about something? It could have been about a certain expectation or hope, but perhaps it was genuine curiosity in the sense that you were aware that there was more to know, and that you really would like to know more. Think about that personal experience of being curious. When did it take place? What was the object or phenomenon that triggered your curiosity in the first place? How did it feel to be curious? Did you come to know what you wanted to know, and what did you learn? How did it work, satisfying your curiosity? Did you apply in some way your newly gained knowledge? What makes this experience valuable for you?

2. Choose the context you prefer: either your community, neighborhood, sports club, extended family, or the organization you are working in or with. Think of something being produced in or by that community or organization. That could be a cake, a dish, a party; think of the ones that provide it; think of the ones that benefit or literally consume it. In the context of organizations lots of things are being produced, like concrete products (a toothbrush), a (dental or public) service, and even good advice or a good meeting is 'produced'. Think of something familiar to you - keep it small - and consider all activities and actors that contribute to its production process. Play with your inner imagination. Do you see the ones involved in the process? What are they doing? What made them go into action? What does their 'product' look like and to whom is it delivered? How does it benefit the receiver? Try to oversee the whole process. Does it have a clear beginning? A clear ending? What would be a good name or title for that process? You may need more than one word, perhaps even a sentence. Give it a try. This is the process you are exploring. Hold on to your mental picture of it.

3. Although I can't read your mind - oh if I only could - I guess that there's a lot to be seen when you are imagining 'your' process. Considering the whole process, or parts of it, do you see elements that you would describe as relational? Please move slowly back and forth in the process, and across all players involved, and their activities. Stay realistic, the process is what it is for now. Do you see transformative or disruptive qualities appear? Do you sense future-focus, the creation of new ideas, the will to act upon, to realize ideas? Does the process leave something behind that stretches beyond the product or service delivery? Thank you for fulfilling this reflective exercise. What was for you the most valuable discovery?

4. Perhaps your thought experiment so far showed you already some generative qualities of the process you have been envisioning. You may have developed a bit more clarity about the possible generativity of processes: their capability to give life and shape futures beyond the here and now. Let me now invite you to dream about that same process. Picture it in its most generative version. Yes, dream. Imagine you are in the near future, you are experiencing the process that you remember from the past, and it seems to be ideal to you. Now, what do you see happening? What makes you happy about it? Which three of the seven generative qualities are really flourishing? How do they manifest themselves? What is the difference with the original process you were watching in the past? What must have happened to make that glorious change from then to now?

5. Thank you for co-creating this mental experiment with me. What did you appreciate the most? What do you consider a take-away that you can already use in daily practice? What about your curiosity? How would you describe your feeling of the moment?

Thank You Again, for Your Kind Attention

Of course, it is in my hopes and imagination that you have been doing - not just reading - the previous exercise. Jane Watson, one of the founding mothers of Appreciative Inquiry, wrote the book *Change With The Speed of Imagination*. So, you have read or answered the five questions. Are you experiencing a certain change in your world-view? Do you perhaps see more or different processes than before? Do you sense a bit of generativity in the ones you put your attention to?

Do you see these processes in their full generative potential? I can only wonder how you are doing. Now I am the one to be curious!

To be honest, I started "thinking processually" 30 years ago. Perhaps I was already wired for seeing the flow rather than the finals. In the nineties of the last century I designed a management school containing a complete module regarding process thinking, designing and improving. Parts of it are included in my 2017 book *Organize Your Processes (and you never have to reorganize again)*. And not to forget my five past years of processual research. I can imagine that I am a little ahead of you. I am at least ahead of most of my participants, when they engage in one of my *Process Improvement* workshops. To give you an idea: I always ask them to take a pen and a white sheet of paper, and to make a drawing of what they imagine to be a process. The illustration below shows the average of responses. Do I need to say more? When it comes to processes - how common this term may be - there seem to be multiple realities. I prefer the view that stays the closest to something that flows...

You may agree that it's not very easy to see a process the way I am suggesting so far. Perhaps you appreciate some examples from my part, and some guidelines to help you further, hopefully saving you my decennia of stumbling and falling.

Sampling Processual Generativity

Let's start small. Organizations and communities can - as you will find out later - be considered processes in itself. At the same time, they hold - or are constituted by - countless smaller processes. Having a phone call with your old aunt is a process. Helping out a colleague is a process. Having a coffee at the machine is a process. For the purpose of practice, try to keep your samples small.

What could be a typical Relational process? Perhaps it is easier to think of processes that are non-relational: no interaction with or between people involved.

Think of a machine. Very non-relational, agree? Think also: operating that machine. Perhaps only needed when it breaks down; perhaps it needs proper monitoring to prevent breaking-down. If that monitoring would be done by a human operator, we can already speak of a relational element in making that specific 'machine product'. And if the machine would be a more complex one, requiring two operators, they might have conversations about what they are seeing and doing. Increased relationality in the process. You might not expect so much relational activity in machine manufacturing, but seeing it from a slightly wider angle, generativity may appear. For example in the form of a creative discussion between the operators on how to increase the speed or the safety of their machine. As long as they are not forbidden to have such conversations - who would dare? - the dialogue could develop into ideas, actions, sustainable improvement, and also about the question whether the end product actually contributes to a better world. Wow, I got drifted away. I tried to give just a simple example with only one generative feature - Relational - and my example almost reached Procreation. Perhaps it also gave you to think about the possibility of this men-machine process being de-generative. This raises the question whether the Relational quality is enough for generativity. Taking this question further: are all seven manifestations needed for a process to be called generative? The answer is: I don't know yet. My research followed an opposite direction, concluding that a generative process at least must qualify as relational.

What about Transformation? I am not thinking about a press in a factory, squeezing and folding a sheet of metal in the shape of a car door being manufactured. I merely think of an artist who is creating a sculpture in (out?) a piece of stone. Everytime he or she reshapes the stone with the chisel, the stone 'provides' new information on how to proceed. What happens could be seen as both Relational and Transformational, would you agree? To drift a bit further, various disruptions could happen: the stone turns out to have a crystal core, which suddenly reveals itself after a hit with the chisel; and this event might - and probably will - disrupt the thought process of the sculptor. Disruption is a strange phenomenon in our conceptual framework. It is not so much that Disruption is possible; it is above all about how to deal with it, to start with recognizing and embracing the disruption. So many group processes are unconscious of valuable disruptions that could have made the generativity so much better...

To stay with our sculptor, I would say that Future-focus is not so much about how the sculpture looks when it is ready, but a way of thinking that stretches much further in time and space. Future-focus in this example could be about changing the destination of the stone, about the essence of being an artist and how others could gain from your talent, or about how possible earnings could be spent on good purposes. How far do your intentions reach, in the now, in your personal life, at your work? Are you allowed - do you allow yourself - to include a future beyond your imagination? One that will come, if not in your lifetime, perhaps a few generations further? Isn't there always future to take care of? Why not care for it now? How can your actions in the now serve an unknown future? How good is the ancestor in you?

Feel free to proceed with this way of sampling: choose one of the seven manifestations and think of a process that may show such quality. Allow yourself to drift away; in itself a generative process. Besides, let me give you some real exemplary case studies, that I consider generative in some way, and in which you might identify one or more of the seven qualities. My apologies when reading this book is starting to feel like work. I am afraid this is inevitable if you consider becoming a Genarrator.

More Examples of Generative Processes

In the mid nineties I spent a week at Bang & Olufsen headquarters in Denmark, to do a feasibility study on a sales performance program. I became impressed by their attention to high quality sound and vision, and their personal eye and ear for the customer. The way they organized creativity seemed to me quite revolutionary. They constantly sent out engineers and marketers to all parts of the world to find out where novelties could be detected; they would share their findings in the secret B&O Vision Room, only to be entered through a special elevator and by selected people. What I found astonishing - a profound illustration of generativity - was a story being told about a period when business was not going well. (I can't retrieve when this has been - even the book *Flexible Firm* by Jakob Krause-Jensen doesn't mention it - but my memory places the story in the 60's or 70's.) Not less than 500 staff had to be fired to save the company's poor economic situation. From what I remember being told, the 500 were selected with the utmost attention for their ability to overcome. Moreover, the employees that could stay in their jobs, took care of their unemployed colleagues. This lasted for almost two years after which the fired ones became the first to get a job again. How would you assess the generativity of that process of necessary reorganization, with your present knowledge?

Earlier in this book I shared openly about being fired three times at DHL Express. I would call exploring my task at least transformational, with disruptive elements. To what extent would you consider it generative? After all, this job somehow triggered me to take up a PhD, and made me decide to become self-employed, being very responsible for creating my own future...

Transformational is what I surely would call the dialogic process *The Circle Way*, in which I once have been certified. *A Leader in Every Chair* is the subtitle of the corresponding book by Christina Baldwin and Ann Linnea. Derived from the ancient campfire meetings, one of the main principles of this talking stick dialogue is that one speaks intentionally, not to someone specific in the circle, but on behalf and for the well-being of the group as a whole. The silence caused by intentional listening appears to me as a highly transformational experience. Isn't a well performed open dialogue, built on such intentions, per definition to be called generative?

Seats2meet is a community around co-working places which came to flourish in the start of the 21st century. If you were open to share your knowledge, you were very welcome to take a 'seat' - a workplace with free wifi, free coffee, free lunch, and the wisdom of the other co-workers around you. If you represented a company, and wanted a place to meet with your team, you would pay for the room and the fact that all knowledge should stay inside. The ultimate idea was to join the open space co-workers with the rented team meetings and exchange even more creativity. Founder Ronald van den Hoff introduced the sharing *Society 3.0* with principles such as creative commons, asynchronous reciprocity, and the disruptive bypass: the way to create alternatives for suffocating bureaucracies. Surf to TheSerendipityMachine.com and you will find more. Disruptive? Sure. Procreative as well, I would say, because anyone who wants to start a new Seats2meet community or location can do so without difficult franchise constructions. Right to Copy.

If there is anything among organizational interventions that can be called both future focused as well as procreative, it'll be my concept of the in-house academy. Call it the training department of a school, a hospital or another organization, but then more integrated, more aligned with the constantly evolving learning needs, more in support of the organization's vision, and more co-owned by the employees than any other internal department. The concept includes multiple levels of maturity of the academy, compared to the maturity of the surrounding organization, as well as clear criteria and strategies for bringing the academy to the next level. A few (Dutch) books appeared around this 'power source of organization learning' in which the metaphor of building a cathedral is used to explain the essence: one doesn't build an academy nor an organization: you are contributing to the development of an academy and its mother organization. Both actually develop each other. Academy building, a generative process? Time will tell. Cathedral builders normally didn't live long enough to see the result of their work.

The Appreciative Inquiry summit is a whole system, constructive co-inquiry event and I designed and facilitated more than hundred of these. One of these stands out, and demonstrates the idea-giving and actionable manifestations of this undoubtedly generative AI process. In my own city of The Hague, the children vaccination had decreased below the critical point of 95%. (It was July 2019 and the word vaccination didn't have anything to do with Covid.) In brief: the city councilor for public health approved the organization of an AI summit to generate ideas around the question: What does it need to get child vaccination safely and sustainably beyond 95%? More than 100 citizens attended the two day event: civil servants, general practitioners, parents, health coordinators and so on. The four D process - Discovering what works, Dreaming the sublime, Designing options for action and Delivering results - was not only big fun and warmly connective; at the end of the second day, the counselor welcomed the fantastic pragmatic and partly already proven options for action. She promised to take the ideas to the city council for further decision making. The summit participants smiled and thought: "You decide what you like, but we already started today".

To my strong, certainly biased, but also repeatedly underpinned opinion, the Appreciative Inquiry summit, if well designed, is a generative process to the max: relational, transformational, disruptive, future-focused, idea-giving, actionable and procreative. Once you have been touched by an AI experience, you want to become an AI practitioner yourself. How procreative is that?

ODJ Requested More Guidelines

Our ODJ article - *Clarifying Organizational Generativity: A Future Forming Perspective for OD Practitioners and Researchers* - contains not only a peer-reviewers approved version of the framework we are so intensely studying here; it also is fairly clear in its presentation. When the editor asked for a minor revision, in particular to elaborate more on guidelines for practitioners, I was happy to put more effort in that, especially because I already was writing this book. Every increase of knowledge and information would be most welcome for the purpose of engaging candidate-Genarrators, be it practitioners, academics or PhD candidates.

To complete this Part Two, I copy-paste those extended guidelines just as they are to provide you the fullest possible 'processual understanding' for now. Yes, it may still be understanding, even deep understanding, perhaps not an internalized skill-set yet; that will be something to re-visit in Part Four. There we go; quoting myself (and my two honorable co-authors) from our ODJ approved article:

"[...] Below, we provide guidelines for putting the framework into practice, and then close out the paper with suggestions for future research. [...]"

Putting Organizational Generativity into Action - Practical Guidelines. So how can OD practitioners, managers, and consultants add the idea of generativity to their practice? How can they use and improve the framework we have developed to assess the generativity of their current processes, and to create new ones? Below, we offer a kind of recipe for practitioner "cooks" to use, based on the assumptions that the cooks are aware of their intentions and beliefs regarding organizational generativity as a future-forming capacity. A moment of self-reflection on personal purpose could therefore be regarded as a proper preparation before taking up the guidelines in practice.

Be Aware of Intangibility. To begin, an important disclaimer needs to be made. First, our paper offers an alternative to traditional/historical OD practice. And our central topic, generativity, has significant implications (if not complications) for concreteness and measurability, when compared with more established theories and methods alike. With generativity, the (im)material we are craftily holding and molding here is that of human interactivity itself, the effects of which (successful or otherwise) are to be fully measured only in the future. Even if we replace the word "concrete" by "specific," we will face the limits of language, and of those using it. When observing relational processes, any concreteness about their generativity might be found in dialogically obtained consensus among participants, or "partakers" - and with this dialogue itself influencing the process. What one could report, in the most specific way, is this: "our process appears to be generative, in the sense of showing certain manifestations at a certain moment." Besides reporting on more tangible deliverables so far, we should report and reflect about the potential of future delivery. In the realm of generativity, we are dealing with moving targets.

Try Raising Managerial Tolerance for "Processual Generativity" or "Organizing Generatively". Forming the future - like most innovative practices - implies risk and uncertainty, and the tolerance for such activity will vary according to many factors, including managers' risk appetite, organizational culture, and of course financial and economic conditions, micro and macro. In addition, generative processes are just that - they are processual, and by definition, never ending, and are often characterized by a certain "ongoing-ness," all of which runs counter to the prevailing idea of processes (and managerial practice in general) as having discrete and finite endpoints or outcomes. When speaking with those unaware of or perhaps even skeptical of generativity, better to begin those (generative) conversations now - as Margaret Wheatly reminds us: "Even great and famous change initiatives begin this way, with the actions of just a few people, when some friends and I started talking" (2009, p. 145). Continue having these conversations as long as needed.

Observe the Process Itself. This may sound obvious, but in practice we often see processes being assessed only by the (end or interim) results, products or deliverables, instead of by looking at the process itself. Edgar Schein writes: "The emphasis is on 'process' because I believe that how things are done between people and in groups is as - or more important than - what is done" (Schein, 1999, p. 3). Relatedly, and particularly for external/internal OD consultants, beware of the focus shifting away from the process, toward persons and/or things.

Find the Right Processes. Organizations are crowded with (relational) processes (Hoogendijk, 2017/2021). Every organizational actor is involved in multiple processes, but may not be highly aware of such. It is not obvious where to start when trying to find a process to assess its possible generativity. Insofar as an organization has made the effort of describing processes, by which we mean further than job and task descriptions, or org charts, these process descriptions contain some clues where to start the search.

Processes are supposed to deliver something. So, try to find the point where products or services are expected. The receiver of that can be - will mostly be - an internal client, waiting for a report, an advice, a newsletter, a promotion, a change, etcetera; or an external client waiting for what has been promised. From that point of delivery, trace back among the people involved in co-producing that (internal/external) service or product. They may represent a department, a team, or just a more random bunch of people. Observe their conversations, their interactions. The fact that the processes as we address them in this paper sometimes are so hard to find, is because organizational life generally has been designed around functional or hierarchical structures through which processes flow.

Observe from Within the Process. We recommend practitioners to sense or experience the process from within, as a participant or partaker. This is a profound assignment, as John Shotter (2006) explains:

> We have here, then, a process of inquiry in which practitioners become co-researchers and researchers become co-practitioners, as each articulates what they have been 'struck by' in the unfolding process. It is a process in which both researchers and practitioners alike are engaged in creating with each other an 'action guiding' sense from within their lived and living experience of their shared circumstances (p. 601).

Because generative processes are relational, they cannot be fully assessed with only external measures or snapshots. A brainstorming process may fill the walls with hundreds of Post-It® notes, but that doesn't mean it was experienced as generative, or resulted in new ideas. Conversely, a period of inactivity or collective silence during a creative process might appear unproductive, but can just as likely contribute significantly to generativity and the envisioning of new perspectives. Otto Sharmer and Katrin Kaeufer, for example, in the *SAGE Handbook of Action Research* (2015), speak of "catching social reality creation in flight" (p. 199). The implicit knowing of taking part in a generative process seems the most significant. Making this knowledge explicit needs to be done with utmost care, if it should be done at all.

Start with What is Already There. Before attempting to initiate generative processes, first find out if and where in your environment self-sustaining, self-improving, or self-organizing processes already exist and how viable they are. Rather than the processes as a whole, assess these specific qualities - the sustaining, the improving or the organizing - intuitively on possible manifestations of processual generativity. Such assessments will contribute to further understanding and, perhaps with some generative OD guidance, shed light on ways to even strengthen the generativity of the respective processes. In other words: leave the gap analysis in the toolbox. What we focus on appreciates, or grows, in value (Stavros et al, 2016).

Use Questions as Instruments of Inquiry. In qualitative research, questions are the most common instrument of inquiry. To find out whether process manifestations adhere to our sevenfold conceptual framework (see Table 5), we need to ask questions. The most basic form would be like "Is this process relational?", "Is it transformational?" and so on. We can make the questions more specific if we inquire into the behaviors of the partakers. Let us illustrate this by presenting one question for each manifestation. Take into consideration that every question can be asked to yourself as well as others involved in the process.

- *Relational.* Do the partakers stay connected, and keep the conversation going, even when the "leader" (facilitator, chair, etc.) is no longer present?
- *Transformational.* If the partakers kept a journal of their behavior and opinions, would their notes show changes over time?
- *Future-focused.* Do the conversations and considerations in any way show explicit attention for an (ever changing) future?
- *Disruptive.* Do the partakers memorize unexpected events in the process?
- *Idea-giving.* Are new ideas (options for action) created and considered regularly?

- *Actionable.* Are new ideas carried out or tested in practice, and is even the slightest attempt to contribute to process improvement appreciated?
- *Procreative.* Does the process also create deliverables that are beneficiary to its future partakers or stakeholders?

Practice, Practice, Practice - Generativity Requires Craftsmanship. Recognizing generativity involves observing phenomena one might have overlooked before. It can only take place in contact with the process to be observed. This is a craft that may benefit from practical advice or support, and includes becoming (more) sensitive to the phenomena of non-generative or even degenerative processes. Re-framing is useful, as are "What if?" questions, and asking not only "What's next?" but also "What's possible from here? What opportunities does our current situation (and our various re-framings of it) afford?" Recognizing generativity can be aided by remembering the characteristics of non- or de-generative processes or situations: detachment, apathy, resistance, tunnel-vision, unsafe, domination, indecisiveness, stagnation, alienation, incivility, and protectionism. The practical advice would be: if you detect such or similar manifestations of non-generativity, just be aware, don't focus on them, but on new, more generative narratives.

Whether we should call these skills new or necessary, the fact is that they can be regarded as advanced. Be it Scharmer's (2009) fourth level of listening: *generative listening*; be it an excerpt of the *Inner Development Goals*, as presented by Ekskäret Foundation (2022); be it Appreciative Inquiry, not the method but the internalized way of being. Becoming actionable in OG requires purpose, practice, deep understanding and learning, not necessarily in this order, and there are no exams.

What are your thoughts now about processes and their possible generativity? Different from before? How different would you say?

Not so Big a Bang anymore: message from Viladrau

To my PhD supervisor Celeste Wilderom, and our co-author Jeffrey Hicks

Viladrau, 4th August 2021

My dear and honorable academic friends,

"We know more than we can tell." (Michael Polanyi)

It took me four days of meditative silence, combined with deep reflection on the question "What am I here for?", to finally realize and decide that I will fully dedicate my time, experience and energy to my 'genarrative' work for the benefit of organizations and (candidate) organizational actors. I therefore will not continue my journey towards the achievement of a PhD degree. I hope that you will accept and understand my decision.

Thank you, especially Celeste, for accompanying me in valuable parts of my journey that started by coincidence in 2004 at the UvH, and resumed in 2017 at RUL. I appreciate highly that, during my two years at UTwente, new words and meanings have been given to my work as an OD practitioner. I consider this a rich outcome of my inquiries so far, and a sound foundation to build upon in my ongoing practice.

Thank you also for unconsciously contributing to making myself clear that I am a practitioner after all; I see myself relating and contributing, but not belonging to the academic community. Feeling grateful for your invitations to share my Appreciative Inquiries with your students, I would like you to offer my unconditional availability for providing these classes on the long term.

Regarding our 'JABS' article, I support your intentions and actions to find alternative journals, and will be stand-by for necessary co-creations in that respect. Furthermore, I will continue my phase 2 inquiries, be it with the aim of processing change rather than papers. If anyone would be scholarly interested in adopting the corresponding research plan, I am happy to give the transition support needed.

Looking back with gratefulness, and looking forward with curiosity, trusting that all of us share the best possible intentionality, starting the second half of my week of silence now,

Faithfully yours,
Cees

In March 2022 I visited UTwente again for my yearly lectures, and of course Celeste invited me for a coffee. Our conversation lasted more than four hours; we both needed to cancel appointments. Celeste showed her full understanding of my 'resignation' and loved me to stay within the neighborhood of her team, and co-create practical-scholarly new ideas. Thank you Celeste, for your energy, your expertise, your positivity, your friendship.

GENARRATIVE

PART THREE
02019-02020-02021-02022

Organizational Generativity

Practice 3
To understand, appreciate, see and enhance the generativity of organizations and other kinds of communities.

"In a sense, generative theorizing is a form of poetic activism. That is, it asks us to take a risk with words, to shake up the conventions, to create new ways of understanding and new images of possibility."

I thought that the title of Ken Gergen's prize winning essay was a question: "What about research, not as a mirroring but as a making of the world?" However, the printed 2014 version here on my desk is actually named *From Mirroring to World Making: Research as Future Forming*. Apparently my research is not so much mirroring or world-making; more like making up. Moreover, when I quoted from this essay in my JABS manuscript, I referred to a 2015 version, published as an article. The JABS reviewers weren't already that happy with me. I'm glad they didn't see this big citation error; almost a criminal act. What must have happened? I must say that I still prefer the title-as-a-question. Assuming that I was so impressed by that simple line "what about research as world-making?", I must have connected the quote about poetic activism, the one at the top of this page, with that particular 2015 article. Quite wrongly, because these poetic lines about generative theorizing are from a book, also by Gergen, also published in 2015, titled *An Invitation to Social Construction*, which I never read. Not the essay, but this book should have been the "2015a" in the List of References in the JABS manuscript. Are you still following this? Surely the peer-reviewers will. At least this mistake has been corrected now. I still like the poetic activist in me.

GETTING INTO PART THREE

Science may be described as the art of systematic over-simplification.

Karl Popper

Would you believe that I prepared this upcoming Part Three even more scrupulously than the previous book parts? I hope you won't notice it too much, in which case it would have become more of an article than a book chapter. Perhaps I took the extra effort because, unlike Part Two, I have to do Part Three without the official support of a peer-reviewed article. Perhaps because I thought, and still think, that Generativity is not complete until we associate it also to organizations as a whole, which is an abstraction quite difficult to grab and explain, and therefore needs extra care. Perhaps because of a certain 'proudness' that wants me to show to the world that I can produce a proper piece of research work, even though I don't aspire to the official license for that. I don't know. What I do know is that I prepared Part Three "walking on eggs and on the top of my toes" (typical Dutch sayings), and this intention probably goes for the further writing as well.

The thesis - or hypothesis - here is that Organizational Generativity, for the purpose of understanding, recognizing and promoting, breaks down into five factors: Intentionality, Processuality, Performativity, Serendipity and Procreativity. We could call this the Conceptual Framework Organizational Generativity, third in row after the foundational Conceptual Framework on Generativity, and the Conceptual Framework on Processual Generativity. Compared to the first and the second, which are firmly underpinned and acknowledged, also peer reviewed, the third may only exist as an axiom - a presumption - like "0+1=1", the axiom on which the huge body of mathematics has been built, but never has been proved to be true itself.

What mathematicians do, whilst enriching their knowledge, is to constantly be aware and transparent about what has been proved already, and what is still to be taken as an axiom. I am not sure whether Organization Studies is treated in such a meticulous way, or ever has produced a proof of something. In math however a thesis, for centuries bound to be an axiom, can get its proof after all. A beautiful example is Fermat's Theorem: the equation $x^n + y^n = z^n$ has no solution for n>2. 'Fermat' happened to be my topic for graduation in mathematics in 1985, and by then we didn't think his thesis would ever be proven, because great mathematicians had worked on it for 300 years already without result. Furthermore 'there ain't no computer big enough' for a proof that needs to include infinity. And yet, the brilliant Andrew Wiley managed to prove Fermat's Theorem in 1995. The exciting book about it by Simon Singh is a breathtaking must read.

What I am arguing here is that at some point in time, my 'axiom under construction' with its five OG factors may be falsified, or improved, or perhaps even be accepted as helpful. I don't expect my 'fivefold' ever to be considered as officially true; the content is much too qualitative for that. What I also suggest is that it will always be others who take the effort to 'test' the thesis. So, please accept my warm invitation to further my generative theorizing and subsequent poetical activism, for which the knowledgeable co-creators provided valuable ingredients. Perhaps you will detect and identify organizational generativity in your own environment. You may find ways to promote, strengthen or even unleash OG. That's what this book was made for. That's what this part is focusing on.

Although still chronological - after all it's a memoir - the story in Part Three has a fragmentary character: my OG Eureka moment originated from 2019, the co-creators have been gathered in 2020, the research method was accepted in 2021, when also the data collection took place, and the actual analysis of that was realized in 2022.

Somehow it feels like my framework was always around, and that's why you don't have to wait for it anymore. The following chapters are meant to present subsequently the five presumed qualities of organizational generativity in brief, the attempts to underpin the framework they make, the engaged research to 'test' and 'substantialize' the five OG factors, the findings from that, and finally a proper Discussion; as if all this were an extensive manuscript for to become a journal article. You'll never know. And you will be surprised.

CONCEPTUAL FRAMEWORK ORGANIZATIONAL GENERATIVITY

Truth is what your contemporaries let you get away with.
Truth is what is better for us to believe.

Richard Rorty

You already saw how the five factors appeared in the AoM2020 conference paper. By the time I presented the fivefold in my first JABS manuscript, I had given it much more consideration, resulting in the following upgrade:

Conception of a Framework called Organizational Generativity

Having extensively analyzed, or to some extent "philosophically investigated," the (proper) use of the term generativity in OD literature, it now feels both safe and appropriate to consider the interaction between the researching and the researched as a generative process in itself, with induction and Eureka! as its main heuristics. From our inquiries into the topics discussed above, a better description of the word generativity in OD contexts emerged. We propose that the term is composed of five fundamental qualities: Intentionality, Processuality, Performativity, Serendipity, and Procreativity.

In Table 10, the five connected phenomena are presented as a conceptual framework of organizational generativity, and depicted from three different perspectives: foundational, OD practitioner-oriented, and organizational. From the foundational point of view, we provide descriptions in an abstract way, which is the closest to the nature of our foregoing literature review. From the OD practitioner's viewpoint, we may derive a certain behavioral repertoire associated with each of the five fundamental generative qualities. In the organizational viewpoint, we present the five qualities in conjunction with manifestations at the generic organizational level.

The respective Table 10, shown below, contains a basic description of the five factors, still compact, and in fairly abstract language.

Table 10. *Three Perspectives on the Five Qualities of Organizational Generativity*

Organizational Generativity	1. Foundational	2. OD practitioner	3. Organizational
Intentionality	There is hope and concern for the well-being of future generations.	Conscious behavior, fueled by the will to benefit future generations of employees within an organization, through the actions of today and tomorrow.	Existence and application of corporate policies and ways of decision making that incorporate the needs of future generations.
Processuality	Organizations and other societies are constantly under construction.	Full comprehension and recognition of the process flow character of organization and all its components and events.	Corporate OD strategies and interventions that acknowledge and empower relevant and valuable on-going change.
Performativity	Narratives and language in general carry the potential to produce human action.	Deliberate practice and growing proficiency in crafting questions, high quality conversation and generative listening.	Scrutinous, artisanal, impactful Corporate expression of organizational and managerial (change) language.
Serendipity	Potentially valuable ideas can appear by chance and better be recognized.	Acknowledge, identify and embrace occurrences of chance, coincidence or fortuity.	A culture of unleashing and embracing all stakeholders' intuition and creative potential.
Procreativity	There is transfer of intentions, ideas and behavior to one's successors or stakeholders.	Create the freedom, delegate responsibility and transfer the knowledge for others to grow.	Distributed leadership, implicit trust, co-ownership, mentoring, and appropriate self-organization.

Re-reading this 2020 breakdown of my thinking feels fine, and also makes me clear that these kinds of concepts need extensive elaboration to come to life;

elaborations - dissertations so to say - for which the average academic journal doesn't really provide the space.

As you know, JABS didn't like the Eureka-nature of my framework. And I must have sensed that already before submitting. My journal notes in March 2020 show concerns about the validity of my invention. It made me review my data analysis on the one hand, and search for underpinning 'after the act' on the other hand. So I made for my first JABS manuscript a substantial plea to defend my 'generative' findings. Of course, the word 'emergence' played a major role in my defense.

Retroperspective Structurization

Where the AoM conference paper brought me some experience about being peer-reviewed, I surely expected the *Journal for Applied Behavior Science* to be more scrupulous. So for my JABS manuscript, I did all possible effort to make my case plausible. See below how I formulated my plea. It starts with a convincing quote about emergence. Sharing this piece of text here is mainly meant for encouraging researchers and practitioners to embrace their gut feelings. Perhaps it makes clear that abduction - besides induction and deduction - is a respected way of reasoning, perhaps even the one most likely to bring novelty; maybe the most generative one? The best way to underpin an 'abducted hypothesis' is through testing, for which time and future research will be the judge. The second best, to finish and submit the paper before the due date, was Retrospective Analysis. My well intended attempt reads like this:

> *"Emergence results in the creation of novelty, and this novelty is often qualitatively different from the phenomenon out of which it emerged."* (Capra, 2002, p. 117)

It would be unproductive to ask how the emergence from our research to our results took place, since emergence generally suggests an unclear relationship between what emerged, and what it emerged from, to be compared with the fact that, on the one hand, water molecules are not wet, while water is. Two years of continuous interaction between the data and the first author generated (in his mind) the five respective concepts as the most obvious conceptual outcome. What now follows is a retrospective analysis with the intention of showing that the outcome of this study can be regarded as plausible.

First, we need to point out that the 'we' in this paper refers to the first author in co-creation with his surrounding stakeholders, the latter acting as expert informer, as lay reflector, as professional English editor, or as academic mentor and thinking (or text-crafting) partner. These co-creators have been included in our 'we' as a logical and justified token of gratitude and acknowledgment. However, when it comes to the thin ice of inductive, emerging, and even serendipitous framework creation, the first author takes full responsibility for the results given, possible flaws, biases, or misconceptions in this study.

Second, how plausible are the five concepts that arose as a result of our research process? The labeling of the seven processual manifestations must have had substantial impact, not only on the appearance of Processuality as one of the five qualities in the framework, but also on the conception of the other four qualities. The underlying intentions of the OD authors (on which we based the analyses) must have played an important role, because their publications clearly express an organizational striving for stakeholders' sustainable health and well-being. Applying reverse engineering on emergence is too much to ask, but to strengthen the plausibility of our findings, we did a retrospective analysis of each of the five concepts, as summarized in Table 11.

Table 11. *Retrospective Analysis: Associations Between Research Findings and What Emerged*

OG quality	Associations to the seven process manifestations	Strength of associations to the OD authors and ancestors	Strength of associations to the findings in the analytical reflections
Intentionality	Transformative, Disruptive and Future-focused	Strong	Light
Processuality	Associated with all seven manifestations	Light	Light
Performativity	Relational, Idea-giving and Actionable	Light	Strong
Serendipity	Disruptive and Idea-giving	Moderate	Light
Procreativity	Future-focused, Actionable and Procreative	Moderate	Light

Third, the question remains how the five qualities of organizational generativity arose. This question brings the researcher himself - and subsequently the research limitations - into the dialectical playground. Through the image of the fivefold organizational generativity qualities, one may see not only the first author's understanding of the reviewed textual content (as a talent for interpreting, combining, and redesigning language utterances), but also his practical experience as manager and dialogic OD professional (with a conception of complexity and emergence), and also his professional longing for contributing to healthy, flourishing, life-giving organizing. We must acknowledge, then, that this researcher's specific actions may represent bias. However, without his intellectual efforts the results suggested may have been less convincing, or may never have come to existence. What remains is the question: would the data contain perhaps a sixth concept, comparable and complementary to the five already given, and overlooked by the researchers? Therefore, others are invited to review the same data for that purpose; the database with 157 text fragments and corresponding analytics is available for anyone upon email request.

Was't that convincing? Apparently not for the JABS reviewers. I'll spare you the details of their comments, and will respectfully summarize these as "We need three reliable sources, to which you can refer." Perhaps I should have included Michael Polanyi, and cite from his book *The Tacit Dimension*: "it is impossible to represent the organizing principles of a higher level by the laws governing its isolated participants" and: "While the machinery of scientific institutions severely suppresses contributions, because they contradict the currently accepted view about the nature of things, the same scientific authorities pay their highest homage to ideas which sharply modify these accepted views."

Okay, let's accept and appreciate that mirroring still seems to be mainstream science, and quickly jump to how we 'normalized' all this in the second manuscript, when the framework around the seven processual manifestations came to the fore. Consequently, the fivefold was brought to the background, turned into a humble suggestion, be it with the interesting Giddens in the middle. Cited below is the last paragraph of our JABS re-submission. I think it represents the logical invitation to proceed with the inquiries as executed in this third part of the book.

Future Research on Organizational Generativity

Our inquiry made us see that organizational generativity is a processual phenomenon taking place on the level of (social-interactive) processes in organizations - for which our conceptual framework [about the seven that is] provides guidance. The same term, OG, also gives rise to the question: "What about the generativity of organizations - that is, generativity at the organizational level, i.e., generativity as a quality of the organization as a whole?" We posed this question at the very outset of our inquiry, and we return now to it here. The generative organization - which by now can be understood as an overall process itself - forms the context for generative processes within, and not in a passive, background way, but in active and mutually constitutive or co-constructive ways. Employing Giddens' theory of structuration (1984), we could say that generative processes in the organization create - or at least influence - generativity of the organization; and that organization, in turn, can then influence which generative processes occur. According to Giddens, the interplay between the parts and the whole can best be described as emergent, in the sense that we can't say that one always causes the other. This in turn leads to the question: How does generativity manifest itself on the organizational level?

To complete our inquiries to clarify OG, and for the sake of fueling possible future research, we propose that generativity on the organizational level manifests itself (to both internal and external stakeholders) through a "fivefold" of factors: intentionality, processuality, performativity, serendipity, and procreativity. Legitimizing this proposition, Giddens' theory holds that such constituting cannot be achieved by direct derivation. Instead, we first envision which organizational characteristics could contribute to the generativity of its processes. In this "structurative interplay" between the "sevenfold" on the process level and the "fivefold" on the organizational level, some (seemingly mundane) conversations may take a generative turn, perhaps aided e.g. by an OD practitioner who is skilled in stimulating or conditioning these social changes.

When relating the "sevenfold" to the "fivefold," one may associate the processual qualities Transformative and Future-Focused to an organizational context of Intentionality through which the overall system shows what it stands for. We relate process-level Relational and Actionable with Performativity at the organizational level, i.e., the organizational ability to communicate in such a way that it affects stakeholders' understanding. We see Transformative and Relational as mutually influencing Processuality: the collective awareness that the organization is a constant flux of relational activities that needs constant managerial attention. We connect Idea-Giving and Disruptive with the organizational alertness for Serendipity: to not miss unexpected surprises, even turn them into benefits. We link Future-Focused and Procreative generative processes with Procreativity: an inherent future-creating driver on the OG level. The subsequent research question now could be: How to bring the proposed fivefold to life? Perhaps future-forming research within and between organizations is the best way to find out.

What if purposeful and passionate visions supplied the source of inquiry? Given a valued vision of the possible, the challenge for research would be to explore how such a possibility could be realized. The aim of research would not be to illuminate what is, but to create what is to become (Gergen, at page 7 of his world-making essay).

The old school manager could have demanded to skip all the previous and come to the point, preferably in five (or less) bullets. The mainstream scholar prefers to be satisfied with sufficient evidence from the past, building upon firm foundations of knowledge. I think it's time to look ahead, to move forward, to let the likeliness of my framework find itself in the future.

Not that we don't look back; OD authors and their ancestors have shown to be of importance in our path unwinding, but they can't be expected to have known how it will further enroll. The only way to find out what OG has to offer is to continue our journey. We better stop trying to verify our roadmap, since it is a map of the road behind us. Let's create a map of what we are going to explore, only to be achieved by exploring. That map might become what we used to call "a curriculum to understand and develop organizational generativity". Curriculum literally means "the course of life". In this case: the life that's awaiting us. Let's gather the explorers and start our appreciative inquiry into five possible drivers for organizational generativity.

Are you aware that I am deliberately including you, esteemed reader, as a co-explorer of what needs to be inquired into? I hope you appreciate it. I hope that you like the idea of 'not just being fed with facts' but really being a co-creator of the insights that are waiting to be revealed. This scholarly co-production of new knowledge asked for a suitable and plausible approach, in itself a product of co-creation, and it is laid out for you in the next chapter.

FUTURE FORMING INQUIRY,
A WELCOME RESEARCH PRACTICE

Pragmatically, the effectiveness of a research approach should be judged in terms of how well it addresses the research question for which it was intended (Dewey 1938). [...] The primary motivation of engaged scholars for undertaking research is to understand this complex world, rather than to get published and promoted. The latter is a by-product of the former.

Andrew H. Van de Ven

My task now is to tell you about the method: the process in which the five factors of organizational generativity are to be studied; words that would suit the early paragraphs of a wannabe journal article. The extra challenge here is inviting you to step into that process, to become partaker of our inquiries, and to join us in the corresponding future forming practice. I'd like you to consider taking up the role of Knowledgeable Cocreator yourself.

I am serious: the design of this upcoming research in itself may be co-creative and engaged, it's still in line with the existing academic integrity principles. Besides the "go" by my supervisor, and the inspiration I found in Van de Ven's book *Engaged Scholarship: A Guide for Organizational and Social Research*, my research proposal has been officially approved by the ethical commission within the University of Twente, as you can read below; all accounted for.

UNIVERSITY OF TWENTE.

APPROVED BMS EC RESEARCH PROJECT REQUEST

Dear researcher,

This is a notification from the BMS Ethics Committee concerning the web application form for the ethical review of research projects.

Requestnr. :	210142
Title :	An Appreciative Inquiry into the Engaged Structuration of Organizational Generativity
Date of application :	2021-02-20
Researcher :	Hoogendijk, C.J.
Supervisor :	Wilderom, C.P.M.
Commission :	Visser, M. de
Usage of SONA :	N

Your research has been approved by the Ethics Committee.

Since we now separated the seven processual manifestations, finally acknowledged in the ODJ publication, from the five factors on the organizational level, we regained the freedom to study the latter independently, leaving room for possible 'structurized' reunion in a later stage. In other words, we leave critical literature review and textual analyses behind, and embrace a new approach, starting with an "abductive hypothesis" and characterized by (not inductive, nor deductive, but) "pro-ductive" future forming inquiry, also known as Appreciative Inquiry.

My research proposal wouldn't have been supported by my supervisor or the ethical commission, if it hadn't been encapsulated in a clear research question and goal, thorough considerations about the nature of the study, relevant literature on the benefits and pitfalls of AI as a research method, an underpinned plan and subsequent planning. It covers eighteen pages and I decided not to add it here, not even as an appendix, since it is purely food for PhD-supervisors. It will rather come to you in bits and pieces, materialized in concrete actions that address my fellow researchers-practitioners. The following brief 'roadmap' serves as a first impression, to give you an overview of the research process, partly accomplished, waiting for you to become engaged in yourself.

1. The first step was to turn the basic research question into an appropriate 'affirmative topic' as a starting point for an Appreciative Inquiry. This included - as suggested by Celeste - my own preliminary interpretation of the five concepts.

2. Very important are the so-called Knowledgeable Cocreators (KC's), my 'extended arm' researchers. They needed to meet a certain pre-designed profile, which I created thanks to conversations with early adopting KC's. They were all invited for an intake conversation, including their own reflections on the five factors - to be considered as research data - and asked for their consent regarding their role and task.

3. With the KC's as sounding board I designed a structured AI interview protocol, to be used for interviewing so-called Organizational Actors (OA's), for which each KC would need to find two candidates: working in or with an organization, being in the position to oversee and to influence policy and strategy.

4. On the basis of the AI protocol, and after having their consent, each OA is interviewed by their KC. The recordings provide additional research data. The OA can stay anonymous if desired.

5. The next step includes a meeting with the KC's, to share their findings in a two step AI process: Discovery of relevant insights, and Dream about possible areas of opportunity, where it comes to identifying, understanding and promoting the five OG factors; the findings to be draftly reported by me for further use.

6. Ideally, the KC's would contact their OA's again, as far as they are interested, to reflect on the specific areas of opportunity, and make them more robust; this Design step to be reported back to me.

7. Finally, I would decharge the KC's and get back to my desk to study, analyze and merge all the collected data into a draft description of findings. This

would preferably be a set of 'options for action', a kind of backbone of an OG curriculum.

8. This backbone should finally be further developed into a draft set of interventions and innerventions, ready to be applied in a real organization, among real organizational actors, inviting them to engage in the new paradigm of Organizational Generativity. This would represent the third phase of the intended PhD journey. Hopefully this book ignites among its readers a lot of 'applicational' experiments...

Quite a future forming research process, would you agree? Likely to be generative, also on process level? (We should be able to appreciate this question by now.) To my surprise, the realization of this research plan had gotten further than I assumed. When I browsed my emails and folders again, I counted nine active KC's who reflected on the five factors and processed my questionnaires, together providing the recordings of twelve OA-interviews.

As I am writing this, I am at the point of opening those files and starting to observe all research data. Of course, I first reached out again to the KC's - it had been a year or so since our last contact - to reconfirm their earlier consent, and that of their OA's. All very well.

I can't wait. Perhaps I am in the most unbiased state to study the data. I will report back to you in a later chapter. But not before I try, in the coming paragraphs, to turn you into a KC yourself, and make you consider performing (parts of) the inquiry. By this, you will surely enrich the findings I am going to deliver.

Imagine Yourself a Knowledgeable Cocreator

Now, let me treat you as a genuine KC, or at least as a potential candidate. For this, I present to you the following humble request, and a questionnaire, to start our co-creation.

February 20, 2021 [to be replaced by your own present date]

Dear (potential) knowledgeable co-creator (KC),

May I ask you to read this piece and answer the questions in the document? As soon as I get them back from you we will make an appointment to discuss your answers. Consider this as the preparation for our final research process. I will try to make things as clear as possible below.

Thank you very much in advance,
Cees

The intended research in a nutshell
Generativity is posited here as a desirable quality of and in "healthy" organizations. The Conceptual Framework Organizational Generativity (CFOG) describes generativity in/of organization as a composite of five qualities: Intentionality, Processuality, Performativity, Serendipity and Procreativity. Through a so-called 'future-forming study' we want to describe the best conceivable 'information, inspiration and instructions' that enable the influential actors within an organization to understand, promote and make visible the five OG qualities. To this end, we are organizing an Appreciative Inquiry, with the guiding question ('affirmative topic') being: "What is the best way to make the five OG qualities visible at the organizational level?" The complete AI process includes the following main steps:
1. A 'pre-inquiry' with and among the KCs (inner circle) to 'equip' them as well as possible and (thus) to make the inquiry as successful as possible.
2. Each KC holds - based on the script agreed upon at the time - an AI interview with two or three 'organizational actors' (collectively called the outer circle) whom they have selected based on the relevant profile.
3. The KCs participate together in a 'half' AI summit, consisting of the AI steps Discovery and Dream respectively, and therein arrive at so-called Opportunity Themes concerning the research question.

4. The KCs coordinate the promising themes with 'their' contacts in the outer circle, in preparation for the second half of the AI-summit, with Design and Delivery as steps that are expected to result in the best conceivable action proposals in relation to the research question.
5. The action proposals will be compiled by Cees into a practical and accessible "OG Guide" that will be submitted to the outer circle for comments.
6. Finally, the inner circle will be asked to comment on the formal research report to be written by Cees, of which the OG Handbook will be an appendix.

The above process will ideally take place between February and June 2021. Each step will be prepared by Cees, 'scripted' and facilitated where necessary.

PRE-INQUIRY

The Pre-Inquiry takes place with the members of the inner circle (the KCs) and has the following goals:
- careful contracting of the KC's
- Adequate and jointly endorsed organization of the research
- to optimally equip the KCs for their crucial role in the execution of the research.

In order to realize these goals, each KC is asked:
- complete the questionnaire below and return it to Cees
- discuss the answers with Cees afterwards
- agree or not with the 'protocol' Cees will provide.

1 Please include your name, any titles (as you wish to be officially listed), and primary contact information here: ...

You are going to participate in a scientific study. By doing so you implicitly conform to the applicable core principles of Honesty, Carefulness, Transparency, Independence and Responsibility. You can download the Netherlands Code of Conduct for Research Integrity via https://tinyurl.com/6d344m83. By giving your approval or signature here, you essentially declare that you will participate (economically) selflessly in this research. With regard to sharing research data with third parties, you should follow the guidelines of Cees, who himself is also bound by the core principles mentioned above.

If you prefer not to be mentioned by name in the research reports, this is the place to report this. You will use the same care as described above towards those (outer circle) that you will involve in the research process.

2 Would you please state below whether and to what extent you agree, and which questions remain?

3 The nature of the research question and corresponding context requires a particular profile of the Knowledgeable Co-creator. Currently, the profile reads as follows: "The KCs are professionals who are aware of their environment, their own relevant knowledge, their being; people who understand organizations and organizing, who share the underlying mission of 'making organizations more beautiful', who have sufficient language and empathy to further interpret and explore the five OG qualities, perhaps know how to bring them from implicit to explicit, and also understand the multilayeredness (recursion) of the process they are stepping into, in order to contribute to the fact that in the future others can learn from the insights gained."

Please let us know concisely below to what extent you recognize yourself in the profile, and whether you would add any elements to the profile, with a view to the quality of the research?

4 Apart from your profile, it is of course also about 'meaning': to feel like it; to find it meaningful....

Could you briefly tell us what attracts you most to this 'job' at the moment? And also: what do you foresee that this path could bring you ideally?

5 Crucial in this research - and thus for the abstraction of the KC - is that we start from and think about qualities that are manifested at the organizational level, and that are not necessarily a resultant, sum or average of individual qualities within the organization.

(Cees sometimes cites the metaphor of the 'non-wet water molecules' and the 'wet water'. Or the obvious misconception that 'healthy employees' together bring about a 'healthy organization'. Or - more to the point - the 'rafting' where one paddler sometimes has to paddle against - or not - the other to contribute to the correct course of the raft as a whole).

Would you produce from your own mind an example showing that you can see and explain such a distinction between organizational level and individual level?

Your answers to questions 6 through 10 are valuable in two ways.
- They contribute to the further interpretation of the 5 OG qualities in relation to our research question.
- They can be helpful in the accessible formulation of the interview questions we will ask the 'outside circle'.

Now, forget for a moment how Cees interprets[4] the five qualities…

6a What do you see when you think of Intentionality at the organizational level?
- do you think you have seen it before (in some way)?
- which organization and which year are you talking about?
- what did you see that organization doing in this regard?

6b Imagine … a super Intentional organization. What do you see happening?
- note down your top 3 please

7a What do you see when you think of Processuality at the organizational level?
- do you think you have seen it before (in some way)?
- which organization and which year are you talking about?
- what did you see that organization doing in this regard?

7b Imagine … a super Processual organization. What do you see happening?
- note down your top 3 please

8a What do you see when you think of Performativity at the organizational level?
- do you think you have seen it before (in some way)?
- which organization and which year are you talking about?
- what did you see that organization doing in this regard?

8b Imagine … a super Performative organization. What do you see happening?
- note down your top 3 please

9a What do you see when you think about (optimally responding to) Serendipity at the organizational level?
- do you think you have seen it before (in some way)?
- which organization and which year are you talking about?
- what did you see that organization doing in this regard?

9b Imagine … a super Serendipity-responsive organization. What do you see happening?
- note down your top 3 please

---

[4] The KC's received my personal interpretation of the five factors along with this questionnaire. In the present situation I rather have you browsing the questions without any pre-information from my side. However, you will find it in the next paragraph.

10a What do you see when you think of Procreativity at the organizational level?
- do you think you have seen it before (in some way)?
- which organization and which year are you talking about?
- what did you see that organization doing in this regard?

10b Imagine ... a super Procreative organization. What do you see happening?
- note down your top 3 please

---

11 We are going to design the best conceivable questions for an AI interview that you as KC will conduct with 'organizational actors' who meet the following profile. "They work in (belong to / are members of) an organization; they have (through their position, role or skill) above average influence on their organizational context; they are aware of the contribution they make to the organization of which they are 'members'; they can express their thoughts well in words; they share the vision that an organization should flourish in order to perform permanently; they are basically interested in the concept of 'generativity of organization'."
If you have people of this profile on your mind, would you please describe them in advance below? (Name is not important in this context).

---

12 We are on our way to that AI interview of yours, with that 'organization actor'. (You're supposed to record the interview, so Zoom, for example, might come in handy for that.) Think about the end goal of our research: an accessible OG curriculum, intended for the target audience of 'influential organization actors.
Without needing to be complete.... What language would you like/could you use in that interview?
- What terms might be better avoided?
- What could be an energy question, to put the person in the realms of 'thriving'?
- What could be a discovery question, to retrieve a relevant powerful experience from the other person?
- With which question - or attitude - do you get the other person to dream about ideal situations? And how do you help the other to become practical again?

Finally: how do you prepare yourself to ask non-judging questions, to merely listen, and to let the other person be his/her own?

Thank you, thank you, for any form of consideration for this questionnaire on your part. What about Intentionality, Processuality, Performativity, Serendipity and Procreativity as five factors driving organizational generativity? Do you experience more clarity or more confusion?

Now, let me bring you in the same information position as the KC's were at this point.

"Cees, how do you see the five factors yourself?"

Considering that the average KC would ask me for my own view, I provided them - and now you also - with the following additional information:

Dear Knowledgeable Cocreator, here is my attempt at an answer, which immediately forms an inseparable part of our 'affirmative topic'.

About the whole and the parts

Let me make clear that this research focuses on generativity as a quality of the organization as a whole. One could still speak of generativity in organizations, in the sense of 'it hangs in the air'. Because organization is quite an abstraction, or a complex phenomenon, the linguistic difference between 'of' and 'in' may be small. But let's not rule out yet that there may be a big difference. Let us stay 'at the reading of organization level', and not descend to parts, groups or individuals.

It is tempting at this point to move on to my view of the five OG factors, as if they were separate entities. I should emphasize (again) that each of the five have been derived from a higher phenomenon and form a bond through that common relationship. If generativity were a human face, then the OG qualities form its 'traits'. The traits you could possibly refer to as eyes, nose, mouth, chin, skin, and the like. With the human face we have come to the point that we (think we) know quite well which features 'determine the face'. If my preparatory study has been done correctly then you can at least say that 'if there is generativity then there must be the five OG qualities'. If the study had been carried out completely, we could perhaps even say that 'if there is presence of the five OG qualities then there is presence of OG'. I would not dare to say the latter. I would like to use the former as a starting point, which is why I also call the five OG qualities factors (all of which must be greater than zero if they are to be greater than zero together).

Why this exposé? Because I am concerned with bringing about generative organizations. If we could do that with less than those five OG qualities, then we don't necessarily need to include them all in our research. The starting point that they are all necessary and must be visible in the organization in order to speak of generativity, ensures that we actually have to take all five OG qualities into account in this research.

Having said this, I now dare to present my views on each of the five OG qualities.

"Cees, what do you see when you speak about Generativity of Organization?"

Moved by this imaginary question, I pretend that I am already in the process of an 'appreciative inquiry', in which the interviewer asks me to tell about OG and the five qualities, both in a discovering and dreaming way. I think I can put anything in my answer, ranging from relevant sources I've found about the phenomenon, powerful examples I've once experienced in practice, and thoughts about how one might also or even ideally look at it. Please consider my answers to the five questions in this imaginary perspective.

"Cees, in the context of organizational generativity: what do you see when you speak of Intentionality at the organizational level?"

To me, intentionality is more than 'having an intention'; even more than behaving according to an intention. For me, the intention that we're studying here is by definition a "good intention". I wonder whether one can even speak of 'bad intention'. Wouldn't that be a contradiction? In my view, intentionality stands for something deep. In the context of generativity I associate this with profoundness. This reminds me of the AI concept of positive core, promoted by the famous Dutch author Rutger Bregman in his book *Humankind*, suggesting that most people are intrinsically good. Thinking carefully about - and being aware of - intentionality leads to the consideration that 'good intention' is to be taken as a pleonasm. That means that organizational intentionality represents a state of being immersed by good intentions. When an organization has good intentions, it must have them towards all its stakeholders. Consequently, the (good) intentionality 'runs' the behavior of the organization. The effect of this could be measured by the degree of appreciation that the organization brings about in all its different stakeholders. With the emphasis on "all", because its stakeholders also include for example: "humanity", "nature", and "future generations". If an organization cares for the well-being of all these stakeholders, then it truly demonstrates intentionality.

As is the case with most 'quality criteria', there are two ways to measure: 'internal' and 'external'. The internal measurements are often predictors of the external. Regarding a call center, for example, think of internal measurements such as 'wait time' and 'call duration'; and for external, 'number of cases resolved' and 'customer satisfaction'.

The effect of the desired intentionality could be measured (externally) by asking the respective stakeholders, which requires adequate representatives to the non-speaking stakeholders (such as 'nature'). How do we measure the appreciation of the next generation? Be it complicated, this can still be done or at least simulated. Can we also measure intentionality inside the organization? Then we might want to find out whether everyone in the organization knows or can know what the organization wants to be 'valued' for; and if everyone experiences the freedom to intervene if they think it is 'not going in the right direction'. This behavior could be based on clearly defined principles like: 'This is what we do it for' and 'Everyone acts accordingly' and 'If you think you see someone who does not act according to our intentionality, you speak to him/her about it, and you speak to the organization about it; the organization will respond immediately'. Such a system of instructions and agreements and the corresponding behavior can very well be 'measured'. Once demonstrated, I believe there is (good, proper) intentionality at the organizational level. This measuring must, of course, be done systematically. I think I gave an idea about how an organization could measure and promote their intentionality. I would dare to say that we can organize Intentionality.

Intentionality at the organizational level is not the sum of individual intentions. It's an agreement with individuals to live by the principles of intentionality at the organizational level. We can be very spiritual about that, but what each individual does behind the curtains doesn't really matter. (This is the irony that Richard Rorty points to in his treatise on private and public action in his book *Contingency, Irony and Solidarity*.) If you find yourself in a quandary between your individual intentions and the intentionality of the organization, there should be a principle of action for that; in itself it should not immediately lead to dismissal since an employee is also a stakeholder.

Now one could say: if we manage intentionality that way, the organization will be perfectly fine. But if we build organizations solely on intentionality - and I happen to know a few - the continuity is at stake; forget about thriving. It takes more than Intentionality to be Organizationally Generative.

Finally, the academic context. What in the OD literature comes closest to intentionality at the organizational level, and which sources are relevant in this context? The closest concept seems *Organizational Virtuousness* (OV). Bright & Fry (2013) opened a JABS special with the article *Building Ethical, Virtuous Organizations*; it is a certain plea. In *Exploring the Relationships between Organizational Virtuousness and Performance*, (2004) Cameron and Bright associate OV with Moral Goodness, Human Being and Social Betterment. What their study aimed for and found out is that organizations showing more OV also demonstrate better (economic) performance. Further back in time we find the concept of 'phronesis', introduced by Aristotle, which means 'being aware that you are doing the right thing'. Perhaps the survey done by Cameron and Bright is useful to measure stakeholder perception, but I am not sure yet whether they surveyed 'all' stakeholders, as I outlined above. Perhaps another interesting source to reflect on Intentionality is *Six Characteristics of Virtuous Organizations* by Kent Rhodes (2015), being (i) clarity in its mission as a family, not just as a business, (ii) a strong sense of responsibility to give back, (iii) high commitment to employees' health and well being, (iv) giving and philanthropic involvement that is not politically centered, (v) the maintenance of a long-term, generational view, and (vi) few (if any) overt references to themselves as ethical or virtuous. So far my elaboration of Intentionality.

"Cees, in the context of organizational generativity: what do you see when you talk about Processuality at the organizational level?"

The complication here is that we all have an idea about the word process. We shouldn't make it too difficult, as long as we are open to alternative views. I could refer to Whitehead (*Process and Reality*, 1957), to Resher (*Process philosophy: a survey of basic issues*, 2000) or more recently to Shotter (*Understanding Process From Within: An Argument for 'Withness'-Thinking*, 2006). What they come up with is the difference between "talking about processes" and "talking from within the process".

What matters to me is the possibility - or the necessity - to see organization as something constantly in motion. Organizations are made up of events and interactions between people, and this goes on and on. Trying to 'solidify' this in an organizational chart, or in texts that describe actions (which nobody exactly keeps to) is a hopeless task, and it doesn't do justice to the inherent process nature of organization. In his book *Images of Organization* (1997), Morgan mentions eight different ways to look at organization. The dominant way still is the idea of organization as a machine that delivers exactly what it is constructed for, and in which you can replace the worn parts (read: people). We should understand by now that a machine cannot be called or made 'agile'. Many of Morgan's other perspectives, such as Flux and Organism, refer to movement or even 'life', which bring us back to the process-view. I still think that all this is a bit too philosophical, and even a bit pleonastic. If one denies that an organization produces services and products - a process in itself - and is continuously developing itself to that end - also a process - then that one must have been living under a stone.

Regarding processuality as a quality of organization, I go beyond the insight, which by now has become established, that an organization comprises all kinds of processes. For me processuality is associated with concepts like craftsmanship and mastery, whereby 'contact with the material' and 'doing things well just for the sake of it' (Sennett, *The*

Craftsman) are the essential ingredients of good quality. (In my 2017 book *Organize your processes, then you'll never have to reorganize again*, process thinking and process improvement go together). Crafting pottery - with care and attention - makes you better at crafting pottery, playing the guitar makes you better at playing the guitar. So in my opinion, the processuality of organization lies mainly in the ability of continuously keeping a finger on the pulse of the process of organizing, which is no more and no less than doing all the necessary to produce the intended services and products. High processuality of and in the organization is for me equal to continuously knowing what you are doing (*metis* in Greek); which only is possible 'in contact with the context'. The Findhorn Community in Scotland - a socially constructive process going on for decades - calls it: 'Work is Love in Action'.

When we say process, we also say time. Chronos. A process runs over time. Teleological. It goes from somewhere to somewhere. Processuality is a quality related to time spans. Organization today is different from organization yesterday. When I think of processuality of organization, we have to move from a safe pleonastic quality "an sich" - organizations simply are processual - to more courageous speaking of less or more inherent processuality, which requires "measures".

If you ask me, processuality is the most difficult of the five OG qualities, in terms of "understanding from within". At the organizational level it requires 'knowing what you're doing, knowing what you're making, and immediately reacting/adjusting 'in the process'. The potter knows what kind of vase he has in mind, yet he is also guided by the material that moves between his hands. The ideal process thinker in my definition is someone who has built quality control into their own actions. You can only control when you measure reality against desirability, and for that you need to be aware of what you are doing. My own process model applies to all aggregation levels in and of organization. The primary question being: what is being produced here? I also argue that management is a process: together, managers produce organization (or better: organizing). So processuality here is about producing organization - or organizing - according to the rules of craftsmanship: knowing what is being produced, keeping in contact with the co-workers, and continuously adjusting.

Processuality of organization is the degree of quality or adaptability in which the organization (re)produces itself, in order to become and stay the best organization for its intended purpose. High processuality equals continuous improvement; not of the products and services, but of the organization itself, as a whole. The organization as a whole needs to be continuously polished, and the polishers are those who together *form* the organization; in my view these are the people jointly responsible for the process (in the old way of thinking still called 'management'). The more process-oriented the organization, the more it is tilted from vertical to horizontal thinking and acting.

If a reorganization is necessary, then leadership has been asleep... Perhaps a bit provocative? It's all about adaptability and speed in organizing. Do you want to call that agile? Fine. Agile is actually a software manifesto; if you adjust one statement in a computer program, you have to test everything again. In that respect, an organization is much more potentially agile than software code, if certain conditions are met. In my process book I give my definition of the ideal organization: every employee knows and does what is the best thing to do, and does that all the time. How do you organize that? With solidified structures and job/task descriptions? Or with something else? The Dutch change professor Thijs Homan found out that organizations change despite their (change) managers. So, fortunately, not everyone does exactly what they are told to do; a very processual aspect of organizing.

"Cees, in the context of organizational generativity: what do you see when you talk about Performativity at the organizational level?"

Out of the five qualities, I think that the concept of Performativity has been studied the most; in the linguistic domain that is. The theory behind performative language is beautiful and still such an abstraction that it can be transposed perfectly well to the organizational level. But since language takes place between people, performativity is essentially about the ability of transferring words and sentences that generate a certain impact on another person; language not as just an utterance, but an utterance immediately representing an act. The theory is called *Speech-Act-Theory* and was introduced by J.W. Austin in his book *How to do things with words* (1962). For example, the little sentence "I promise you..."is an act in itself. To reveal the theory a little more: in relation to performativity, the speaker can use illocutionary, locutionary and perlocutionary expressions. The last category represents language that really 'touches' the other. I admit that this takes place at the individual level. I am not sure that we can speak of a performative person. Perhaps it is better to speak of someone who knows how performativity works, probably a person with language skills. Or better, referring to Confucius, someone who uses language well, so that as few misunderstandings as possible arise and thus the right things happen. This also addresses authority. For example, think of the person who utters the words: "I hereby declare you to be united in marriage." For that statement to be perlocutionary, the speaker must hold the proper 'license', or nothing will happen.

I also relate performativity to congruence or 'practice what you preach'. From this point of view you are a much better role model when you whisper "please be silent" to your noisy children, than when you would shout "BE QUIET!!!". For me this reveals a difference between short and long-term effects of proper communication. The manager may immediately get something done with tough, powerful coercive words, but the question remains whether the employees will stay with him for long.

So what can be said of Performativity as an organizational quality? The organization as being performative? Or: communicating in a performative way? In particular I think of the quality of the organization's language, and to what extent the inside messages are congruent with its outbound messages. Simply stated: how effectively does the organization communicate? Inbound and outbound? What about clarity, about the consistency between the messages and the messengers or media? Plenty of surveys are in use to measure the quality of communication, but I wonder if they also measure whether - through that communication - things happen as they were intended. Could we move toward an organizational Speech-Act Monitor?

Relating the quality of Performativity to "corporate or internal communication" implies a certain degree of goal-action orientation; not just at the message level, as most communication advisors aim to do, but considering the whole of the messages that are expressed within or on behalf of the organization. This makes organizational Performativity perhaps an easy phenomenon to discuss, but very difficult to 'organize'. Firstly because the 'perlocutionality' is partly determined by the receiver; secondly because everything from and in the organization, including the behavior of every employee, contributes to organizational performativity.

Is organizational language being used properly? This exhibits relationships with Intentionality (how could it not) and with Processuality (of course) but it is also complementary to those two, for it directly calls attention to the quality of the actual language expressed. The promotion of this lies with everyone who communicates with influence or authority, which suggests a relation between individual and organizational performativity. Most elusive is the opinion of the 'receiver', of the 'audience'.

The academic context of performativity may be primarily of a linguistic, individual nature. However, Gond, Cabantous, Harding et al (2006) actually address the concept in relation to Organization & Management Theory (OMT), according to their article *What Do We Mean by Performativity in Organizational and Management Theory? The Uses and Abuses of Performativity*. Admitted, they focus on how performativity is used in OMT from an academic stance. But their research also notes the following and I quote: "It also reveals the lack of both organizational conceptualizations of performativity and analysis of how performativity is organized."

"Cees, in the context of organizational generativity: what do you see when you speak of Serendipity at the organizational level?"
What makes serendipity different from the other four is that it doesn't represent a capability; serendipity is a phenomenon that you may deal with in a certain way, when it appears. So, this fourth OG quality should be understood as "how the organization responds to serendipity", or even: "how the organization embraces the existence and value of serendipity and makes the best possible use of it".

Perhaps it is useful to treat Serendipity in relation to my conception of Processuality as a kind of high-quality craftsmanship, in which the organization always knows where it wants to be, and can quickly adjust accordingly when deviations occur. (Think of the potter and his spinning clay.) Whereas Processuality has a strong Chronos component, in the case of Serendipity I think of Kairos, the demigod of 'seizing the moment as it presents itself'. Whereas with Processuality one always measures against a certain goal - even though that can change - in the case of Serendipity a situation arises unexpectedly, and either it is not seen or not appreciated and passes by, or it is embraced as an opportunity, whereby in that serendipical moment in fact a new goal is created: "Hey, we can do something with this." I think everyone knows the creation of the Post-It at 3M in this respect.

We could see serendipity as a special variety of processuality, namely "the process of keeping in touch with the unexpected coincidence that can turn out to be very valuable".

Would we want to "organize" serendipity - or handle it well - then this asks for making and 'playing' scenarios for mobilizing the eyes and ears in the organization to be open to various coincidences; protocols for organizational listening to every crazy idea that is put forward, in particular the fourth level of Otto Scharmer's levels of listening: Generative Listening. The habit of being open to unexpected opportunities can be organized along the lines of Appreciative Inquiry, a skill also seen at the organizational level in the format of AI-summits.

There is a lot of literature on Serendipity as a phenomenon, mostly fairy tale-like (*The Princess of Serendip*, where the name comes from.) For random events, we should take note of the work of N.N. Taleb (*The Black Swan, Antifragile, Skin in the Game*) who in turn is the great inspiration of Bert Zwart (TUE) who studies extreme unexpected events where big data does not provide a solution, but 'common sense' does.

This treatise was a bit chaotic, but perhaps organizing a collective provisional response to unexpected events, and then taking advantage of that, needs a certain chaos. It looks a bit like risk management, but handling serendipity it is much more than that.

Wait a moment. Speaking of Serendipity, and interrupting my reflections for a moment, did you notice something strange when reading the so-called French Title Page of this book? Something that looked a bit weird, but you put aside, expecting that it would be clarified? Something that you understood and made you smile? Perhaps you simply missed it, or already forgot about it. Let me help you.

The subtitle on the *cover* of the book says:
Future Forming Practices for Building Better Legacies

The subtitle *inside* the book says:
Super Cali Fragilis tic Expli Cali Docious

If you didn't notice yet, speak both lines out loud, one after the other. Future Forming Practices for Building Better Legacies. Super Cali Fragilis tic Expli Cali Docious. You might 'hear' or 'sense' that they contain a similarity, not in content, but in rhythm, and perhaps even in rhyme or in the tone of the spoken words. Got it? That was my moment of serendipity. What happened? As usual, it took me a while - and multiple versions - before I was happy with my official subtitle. For me such text crafting is not only about content, but also about how words and sentences look, feel and sound. Shortly after I agreed with myself on "Future Forming Practices for Building Better Legacies", the famous magic spell of Mary Poppins appeared in my mind. Apparently a very old memory, deep down in my brain, suddenly connected with a sentence I had just created. I saw the opportunity, and used it just for the sake of it. Now you know. Might there be some potential serendipity for you as well in this story?

"Cees, in the context of organizational generativity: what do you see when you speak of Procreativity at the organizational level?"
Of course I immediately think of procreation. In a biological sense, we procreate primarily when we are fertile and preferably we have that

arranged before we die, otherwise our species will face the end of its existence. Dying organizations we can see often, but I dare to say that organizations can stretch their life and thus their fertility quite well if they would demonstrate a high degree of Intentionality, Processuality, Performativity and Serendipity.

At the organizational level, Procreativity is not directly a quality for survival, in the sense of the popular word *resilience*. However, it is inextricably linked to the concept of the Generative Organization as the ability to help itself into the future, to even create that future, and thus to connect with the stakeholders of the future. This brings us full circle and back to the Intentionality of serving future stakeholders well. Procreativity is in my opinion the perfect quality to operationalize that good intention, to make it happen.

Because we simply cannot project biology to organizational life, Procreativity may be the one OG quality easiest to understand from an organization perspective.

So what do I see in an organization with a high degree of procreativity? I see an organization engaged in "leaving itself well behind". I see an organization with actionable principles like: "Celebrate successes considering succession", "Make decisions with an eye to the interests of the generations to come", "Teach your successor to do it himself", and "Make yourself redundant". (More of these can be found in *The Good Ancestor* by Roman Krznaric.)

A possible "Procreativity Dashboard" can only measure what is done in the here and now, where only 'time can tell' if that was the right thing to do. But let's not rule out the still very practical *EFQM Excellence Model* by the European Foundation for Quality Management. Admittedly, the EFQM assessment cycle spans only a few years but it definitely holds a procreative principle: 'enablers before results'.

The five answers above include the best I could deliver at that moment. And when I read and revised them for this book, they still show a high degree of theorizing. At the same time, the majority of my views on organization development originated from decades of work in real businesses and institutions, so there must be something realistic in my reflections. Besides, my views only represent the start of the future forming inquiry, performed by my Knowledgeable Cocreators. They created the 'research data', first in their personal reflections, then through interviewing 'living' organizational actors, creating the possibility to make more sense of my hypothetical OG framework and its five factors, as a starting point to actually bring those factors alive... of which you will be updated in the next chapter.

But first...

Would You Perhaps Consider Interviewing an OA Yourself?

Let's keep in mind that this chapter is describing the approach, the design, and the main questionnaires of the research that - at that point in time - still was ahead of me. And since I warmly welcome you to imagine yourself in the role of Knowledgeable Cocreator, you may feel invited to do a bit of the research yourself, for the sake of 'grabbing' the corresponding substance matter. Perhaps you actually completed the KC-questionnaire, or may want to do so now? I really think that answering questions will deepen the understanding of the abstracts I am sharing here; it might also make "processing" this book more fun.

The next logical question to you is who would be the influential organizational actor in your netwerk, to approach for the interview that has been done twelve times by your fellow KC's. Doing this would probably strengthen your growing understanding of what I am trying to propose. You and your interviewee would be actually working and practicing with the OG matter, and in that you would also act as Genarrator: my appreciated ambassador of organizational generativity, planting seeds in new audiences.

If this appeals to you, let me then equip you now with the letter of invitation for OA candidates, and subsequently with the full protocol for having that generative interview.

No pressure. You don't need to actually use all this. By just reading the following information, you will get a good picture of how to do an appreciative inquiry in order to clarify and materialize the five OG factors. That already is sufficient preparation for going into the next chapter, where my findings from the KC and OA questionnaires will be presented. Reading the interview script, and this chapter in general, might also inspire you to design and do a similar future forming study on a different topic.

Okay, let me start with the draft letter to inform the (or your) Organizational Actor candidates about their upcoming interview. If you consider using it, feel free to personalize your letter before sending..

The Generative Organization
What do we recognize it by, and how do we promote it?
May 2021: information for those who are going to be interviewed

In the search for what makes an organization flourish (= to continue to develop and perform healthily, even in socio-economic ups and downs) the qualification 'generative' seems a promising term. Because the concept of 'generativity' is used in the context of organizations but is hardly explained, Cees Hoogendijk conducted an in-depth literature study to better interpret the concept of the 'generative organization'. This led him to the hypothesis that generativity at the organizational level comprises five qualities: intentionality, processuality, performativity, serendipity and procreativity. Admittedly: still very abstract concepts, (because) referring to behavior of the organization as a whole. You may forget them again for now.

Cees' ambition has always been practical; he is looking for how 'interventions' can best contribute to something like a generative organization. His current research revolves around the question of whether and how those five aforementioned organizational qualities can be recognized and promoted; a question that is put to 'influential organizational actors'.

Thank you for your willingness to make your knowledge and experience available in a forthcoming interview. The reason that this interview is not done by Cees himself has to do with preconditions of a purely scientific nature, intended to make the research as objective as possible.

What exactly is asked of you?

1. To participate in an (online) interview of maximum 60 minutes, based on Appreciative Inquiry*, conducted by the person who invited you for the interview, and based on a questionnaire provided by Cees Hoogendijk. (Planning: between mid-May and mid-June 2021).
2. Agree to have the online conversation recorded, under the strict condition (in accordance with the Ethics Committee for Scientific Research at the University of Twente) that:

---

a. your statements will only be used for the purpose of this research;
b. In the research report, any quotes from your statements will be anonymized, so the source cannot be traced;
c. you can choose not to have your name mentioned in the research report;
d. you will be given access to the parts of the report that concern your contributions;
e. you may withdraw from the study at any time without explanation.
3. Participate in a second round of oral or written interviews. (Ideally in July 2021.)
4. Optional: reading and commenting on the practical-content portions of the research report. (Expected from September 2021).
5. Confirming willingness described above in the first step of the online (recorded) interview.

(*) Appreciative Inquiry is not a problem focused but a possibility oriented approach. The research process is not looking for objective facts or 'the truth', but gathers a diversity of relevant powerful personal experiences via guiding questions, on the basis of which the people involved together picture a desirable future. This type of research is also called 'future forming', in which the research process actually includes a change intervention.

Once the OA has given his or her consent, and the date has been set for the interview, the instructions and interview questions below are to be followed by the KC. The reason why I share it here, and not in a scholarly appendix, is that the interview script contains a lot of performative language to discover. Will you give it a go?

The Generative Organization
What do we recognize it in, and how do we promote it?
Future forming inquiry script for the appreciative inquiry interview with an 'influential organizational actor'.

Preparation
- You have (received) a Zoom-connection, with the possibility of 'recording'.

- In addition to this script, make sure you have the document 'information for the interviewee' at hand.
- Limit the 'catching up' as much as possible; before you know it, you're already into the content...

The interview
(60 minutes maximum, less is allowed)

1. Thank you for participating and so on ...; first a few formalities.
a. In the preliminary information you have read the conditions under which you participate in this interview. Have you read them? Shall we go through them again? Do you agree?
b. Now I will turn on the Record button. Do you see that Zoom is recording?
c. For the sake of completeness and accuracy of the investigation, would you please state your name?
d. Are you familiar with the terms and conditions of this survey, as stated in the preliminary information?
e. Do you agree to these terms and conditions?
f. Thank you. Here we go. Today is <date> and my name is <my name>.

2. I'm going to try to put you in the right frame of mind with the following words. Our core concept in this conversation is "the generative organization." This concept is associated with the image - or wishful thinking - of an organization that thrives; that is able to continue to evolve and perform in times of ups and downs; an organization with healthy vitality, which is different from the ability to survive. An organization thriving through a variety of possible unknown circumstances. The assumption under our conversation is that you are interested in such life-sustaining organizations and that you would like to contribute to these if possible. Is that right? Do you have any wording of your own that might help describe such a desired organizational quality?

3. Okay, imagine the organization as a whole. As a body, or organism that provides services or products and is in contact with all kinds of stakeholders to do so. You look at organization, or an organization, as if it were one whole. Preferably you position yourself as an external stakeholder - e.g.

customer, supplier, observer - who experiences the organization from the outside, by having certain interactions with it. Perhaps you even have a specific organization in mind which may give you an even better idea of what you are observing. Try to look at the behavior that the organization exhibits. Behavior in quotes, because we usually attribute that word to individual people. In this case, you are beholding or experiencing the behavior of that organization as a whole. Got it? Remember, you observe that organization - even if it's yours - from the outside.

4. Additionally, you can move to a position within the organization, and from there experience the behavior of the organization around you - as a whole. Perhaps in this perspective it would be helpful if not necessary to take your own organization, where you work now, or where you once worked, as a frame of reference. Either way, in this perspective you are looking at, and experiencing, the organization from the inside, and you are trying to form a picture of how that organization organizes itself. Do you get the picture? Be careful. Don't descend to the level of individual behavior, to behavior of employees in the organization, but rather see the organization, or your organization, as a whole. Sorry for this extensive discourse so far. Let's dive into the subject matter. In the following questions I will take you through the five qualities that Cees Hoogendijk suggested as components of organizational generativity. One more thing: in this interview we are trying to recognize, or imagine, certain characteristics of organizations purely and simply. The question of how you could bring about or promote desirable characteristics at the organizational level is certainly going to be asked, but not yet today. For now, we are limiting ourselves to questions like "Have you ever seen this?" and "What would it ideally look like?". We're building it up slowly. Here come the substantive research questions.

5. Considering an organization - as a whole - have you ever seen or experienced, or perhaps sensed, its good intentions? And by that I mean that the organization radiated its good intentions to as many different external stakeholders as possible.

a. How did those intentions manifest themselves? How did they come across to you? What feeling did they bring about? What did you most appreciate or value in the externally perceived intentions of that organization or organizations?

b. Have you also experienced such good intentions up close, or possibly even literally witnessed them, from the inside, whilst working in that organization? How exactly did those organizational intentions manifest around you?

c. Building on the ability of an organization - as a whole - to act intentionally towards its external and internal stakeholders; what would you like to see when such an organization is at its best in terms of intentionality?

6. If you think about it, you could consider an organization not as something static, but as continuously moving, changing, developing. In a more abstract way one could say that organization has a process character. If you look at the organization as a whole you could say "the organization organizes itself". The organization flows, keeps on flowing, and is constantly changing into a slightly different state. The organization is in fact a process in itself. Here are the questions.

a. Have you ever experienced, from the point of view I just sketched, that an organization is, as it were, aware of the fact that it lives, flows, develops? That the organization understands that it is continuously changing?

b. How did you experience this? From the outside, or seen from the inside? This is a tricky question. A glimpse of recognition or a small example is already valuable.

c. And if you look ahead into the future, imagining the ideal forward-living organization, which has its finger on the pulse of its own continuous development ... In what aspects does this best version process-organization excel? What would you really notice when working in it? What would the outside world notice?

7. Take a deep breath and relax for a minute. We have tried to form an image - through possible recognition or by fantasizing - of organizations with good intentions, of organizations that are conscious of being in flux. Now I ask you to focus on how the organization as a whole communicates with its stakeholders, its outsiders and employees, and what effect that has.

a. As an external stakeholder of an organization, have you ever experienced an organization's communication to the outside world has caused a certain transformation in you? Or in others as far as you can tell?

b. In fact, communication encompasses all behaviors of that organization, and we're looking for situations where stakeholders experienced impact. To be precise: a healthy impact, in line with the intentions. Does an example come to mind?

c. And, being an employee of an organization, have you experienced constructive effects of the internal communication, of the behavior of your organization as a whole?

d. Regarding communication between individuals, the concept of performativity indicates that words can lead to actions. Imagine that an organization in all aspects would excel in communicating messages that create an optimal constructive effect? What do you see? How does that organization ideally "behave" (in quotation marks) toward its stakeholders?

8. The term serendipity refers to a random, unexpected event; something you didn't take into account or weren't waiting for; but which could be beneficial in some way. The most famous example in the organizational context is the PostIt, once created when someone wanted to invent a good glue and was annoyed that the piece of paper didn't fully stick. Then someone else saw that 'pulling it off again' could actually be very useful. Serendipity always goes with a smart, creative response to that unexpected situation. So it's all about the ability to take advantage of seemingly unwanted surprises. If we don't do anything with them, the opportunity will pass by.

a. Have you, as an outsider, experienced that an organization was able to see an unknown situation as an opportunity, and even took advantage of it? Or, do you know of 'hearsay' examples?

b. Do you know of examples where your own organization - or part of it - showed to be prepared for pleasant or unpleasant surprises, and managed to turn them into opportunities?

c. Imagine an ideal organization that is completely ready and open to serendipity. Can you name three aspects that demonstrate this?

9. We have arrived at the - according to one Cees Hoogendijk - fifth component of generativity at the organizational level, which is the quality of doing the right things in the Now, so that the organization will still be running well in the Future. Procreation in biology is maintaining the species by providing healthy offspring. In car driving we call it anticipation. Many athletes visualize their success before the match. In organizations, success in the future might be thought of as: properly arranging succession in the present. Who will take over the estafette stick? Here are the questions.

a. As an external stakeholder, have you ever experienced an organization consciously taking into account its future existence? What is your best example?

b. As an employee, have you experienced that your organization was aware of its future and taking action on it in the present? What actions were these?

c. Now think of the ultimate procreative organization... What do you see that organization doing; from the outside, from the inside?

10. One more question left, in which we consider all five aspects as one whole. Imagine. We are five years from now. You wake up on a sunny day, and you go to work in this completely and totally generative organization. Five years ago you suggested that this organization still had a lot to gain in terms of generativity ... By now, it apparently has created a dashboard - or something alike that fits generativity - on which all five factors are reported, and not only that: they show high scores. Daydreaming is allowed in that five-year-from-now organization. And you daydream about the next generation - our children - and you are so proud and happy about what this organization already has been able to achieve for them - perhaps even with them. The organization is actually ready to pass over the steering wheel to the next generation, with confidence. Do you have the picture?

a. Name three aspects of that five-years-further organization that make you the most proud and happy and that seemed impossible five years before...

Thank you so much. Do you want to add to everything you've shared so far? If so, I'll now press the Record button on Stop.

Needless to say that my original KC's proved to be committed and crafted co-creators of the script you just read. Thanks to their comments I was able to refine it, and they were able to internalize it before entering the actual interviews. So again, don't feel obliged, but if a colleague or client would come to mind as a willing candidate for this interview, you as an additional KC would be in good company. The interview itself is the intervention. It may make this book for you a bit more concrete. No need for a recording, or reports. And if you would like to share, you're always welcome to leave your experience at genarrativity.org; highly appreciated.

Future Forming Inquiry Accomplished? Well ...

Mission completed? Well, from a research perspective, I hoped for twenty KC-OA recordings. I got twelve, and I'm about to process them to prepare for the next chapter. You are now in the midst of research! Compared to my initial roadmap, there may be unfinished work, like having a group conversation with the KC's, and follow-up on the KC-AO conversations. Let's see what still can be done. What I didn't know when mapping the research road, was the possibility of having multiple readers, spectators, perhaps even co-makers of the emerging research, which compensates a lot.

Besides, history counts many more unfinished works, probably a lot more famous than mine. What to think of *The Neverending Story* by Michael Ende (what's in the name?), a story about a book that comes to life. Charles Dickens died halfway writing *The Mystery of Edwin Drood* and the good news is that others created multiple endings; how socially constructive is that? *Die Unvollendete* has been called the 8th symphony of Franz Schubert, although it was chronologically his seventh. Schubert created nine symphonies and why he didn't finish the previous is still a mystery. Classical music counts at least ten more unfinished pieces. And what about the Sagrada Familia in Barcelona? Will it ever reach completion? Perhaps there will be - or has been - a date for the last brick, but should we call that completed?

So, by leaving some loose threads for you, dear reader, practitioner, manager, PhD student, we all find ourselves in good company. Don't bother about finishing. Let's first find out what the twelve organizational actors answered in the respective interviews.

ORGANIZATIONAL GENERATIVITY PLAUSIBLE? DISCOVER AND DREAM

It is July 18, 1955. The official opening of the first Disneyland is a celebration. The twenty attractions are overwhelming. The pink castle radiates joy, mystery, excitement. Mickey Mouse is busy shaking the hands of every kid. A journalist says to one of Walt Disney's grandsons: "What a pity your grandfather can't see this." To which the grandson replies: "If my grandfather hadn't seen this already, it wouldn't have been there."

Consider Disney's plan for an attraction park as a formula, like $E=mc^2$ represents the formula created by Einstein. I wouldn't dare to compare myself with these guys, but I do see some 'processual' similarity between their formulas and mine: OG $\cong$ It x Ps x Pf x Sd x Pc, where the symbol $\cong$ stands for "is congruent with". I think it is an educated guess that the ideas behind these formulas must have suddenly appeared in the minds of their creators, constructed from a mixture of knowledge and experience, and driven by the will to make the world a better place. Logically, none of the three formulas could be underpinned by referring to earlier sources. Some references might be appreciated as inspirational, but the respective ancestors didn't have a clue that their thoughts would inspire their reader to such novelty. At the same time, the formula - the hypothesis, the blueprint before the real thing - must have been sufficiently attractive or tempting for others to make (more) sense of it, or even substance, like a genuine Disneyland. We may frown when thinking of some materializations of Einstein's formula, and we might need to put less sugar in Disney's candies, but their successors brought the formulas to life. Exactly what I am attempting here with the presumed five factors of organizational generativity.

Just imagine that with OG we are on a path to enable organizations to be healthier and more flourishing in the long run. The only way to find out whether we are moving in the right direction, is to animate and vitalize the five abstracts as far as we can, starting with the questions: Did we see glimpses of them already? and How would they look when ideal? From there we can start to design possible bricks to actually construct generativity; what would these building blocks, and the constructing, look like? Oh, if only we could bring in the generous and delightful mrs. Poppins, to apply her magic formula ...

Well, it's been a month, I did the work, and will tell you about it in a not too scholarly way. Where did we come from? A linguistic analysis brought clarity about the do's and don'ts in using the term generativity; the rigorous literature review ended up in seven manifestations of generative processes in organizations, and a set of guidelines to comprehend this new way of thinking and seeing. And what has just been done, in the past four weeks, is to grasp and analyze the engaged dialogical inquiry into the five factors, in order to make more sense of the emerging hypothesis of generativity as a collective organizational behavior. Although I made notes in my still existing diaries, I kept them brief, knowing that they wouldn't have to wait long for being transferred to this memoir - my ultimate notebook. Ity may feel like you are holding my pen. The next paragraphs will show you how things have been inquired into, and I can tell you that the preliminary findings are promising.

Processing the Interviews

It took me a while before I actually put on my headset and started playing the first KC-OA interview. Maybe I felt a bit like eavesdropping when stepping in the intimacy of a conversation I didn't attend. Perhaps the idea of at least twelve hours of focused listening made me procrastinate. Since I know the KC's in person, monitoring their interviewing style feels like putting myself in the examiner's seat. The only way however to stop procrastination is to get going. I pushed the play button, and started listening and writing. Doing that left no time for concerns about my role. Doing one or two a day seemed plenty. One hour of conversation uncovers a lot of content, and to keep an objective stance in my note taking can be exhausting, so I experienced. To focus even better on pure registration, I decided to play the recordings at one and a half times the normal speed. Strangely enough, the language then gets more crisp and seemingly better to follow, and any remaining room for additional thoughts vanishes.

From my second interview on, I typed my notes directly in a spreadsheet. I set up columns for name and date and research agreement, a column to register the interviewee's first associations with organizational generativity, ten columns to register the discovery and dream responses for each of the five factors, and a final column to fill with the integral dream. It was actually fun to do. I wanted it all done, waiting for the moment to really go through the 'data'. Yeah.

I'd like to thank and appreciate my seven KC's Gert, Geert, Joep, Gerard, Barbara, Erica and Lars, who together produced the twelve recordings. A few of you turned my structured interview into an inquisitive dialogue that generated the answers. Most of you followed my script to the letter. I was often pleased to be the witness of your high quality interviewing and corresponding deep listening. What beautiful silences I 'heard'; you really created the space - often associated with Appreciative Inquiry - for generativity.

Adding Latara and Peter to these seven makes the nine that completed the KC questionnaire. Since this was structured along the same line of discovery and dream, I could add their responses to my spreadsheet, counting up to nineteen sets of interview data, in total almost 7000 words. Before entering the next step of further structuring this data set, let me share some glimpses of discoveries among the various responses.

Volvo Company for example was mentioned for showing great Intentionality when they decided to keep all their 1000 suppliers alive when Covid caused a crash in sales and production. For one and a half years Volvo kept investing in the relationships, by taking up design projects and providing training for their employees. A Dutch institution for mental care supported their employees to do the utmost on behalf of the patient's well-being, even when sometimes rules and procedures need to be 'bent' for this; governmental regulations can be complicated and sometimes ineffective.

Discovering or experiencing Processuality, especially as an external observer, wasn't so easy. One respondent compared processuality like a meandering river that can overflow without harm in the wetlands, for more space to flow. However, in organizational reality it is more like a canal, with dams and narrow parts, and quays between which one has to stay. That organizations are aware of their own processuality, is not shown very often, although they definitely are processual. We will come to that later. The question inspired someone to quote Bruce Lee: "to change with change is the changeless state".

Performativity, and the experience of being transformed by organizational behavior, gave a lot of associations, both positive and negative. Some messages produced by companies were experienced as outright suspicious, and didn't cause so much of a personal transformation. A biological grocery did have such an effect on a respondent, not just by promoting and selling the goods, but by really informing the customer about what happens in the supply chain before reaching the shop. Another remembered a banking organization that consciously invested in green developments, and invited their clients to visit these places that benefited from the interest on their money; an example of performativity "without words".

We can never be sure to what extent Serendipity and creativity overlap. The more "unreal" the initiative, the more it seems that the organization is really enabling the space for people to be responsive to unexpected events. Like the start-up that transported to their client a shipload of notebooks, which unfortunately were robbed during the shipping. When the provider turned the loss into a story and started communicating about "hunting the stolen notebooks" this raised a lot of publicity and actual support. The client decided to stay client, even without the delivery. And in the end, the notebooks have been found. The essence in most of the examples is that people can be creative and come up with "stupid ideas" when needed; however, what really helps is an organizational atmosphere of "there are no stupid ideas".

Discoveries regarding Procreativity vary from family businesses who really think "next generation", Joe Biden who already appoints Kamala Harris as future president, and the Dutch farmer Bart, fourth generation successor, who placed his - now ecological and circular - farming business out of time to envision it still flourishing after 1000 years. At the same time our respondents still see too many 'short term gain' strategies, where the future makers form the minority. Today - 15 September 2022 - I read about a superb example of procreativity in yesterday's The New York Times:

Billionaire No More: Patagonia Founder Gives Away the Company

A half century after founding the outdoor apparel maker Patagonia, Yvon Chouinard, the eccentric rock climber who became a reluctant billionaire with his unconventional spin on capitalism, has given the company away.

Rather than selling the company or taking it public, Mr. Chouinard, his wife and two adult children have transferred their ownership of Patagonia, valued at about $3 billion, to a specially designed trust and a nonprofit organization. They were created to preserve the company's independence and ensure that all of its profits - some $100 million a year - are used to combat climate change and protect undeveloped land around the globe.

The unusual move comes at a moment of growing scrutiny for billionaires and corporations, whose rhetoric about making the world a better place is often overshadowed by their contributions to the very problems they claim to want to solve.

At the same time, Mr. Chouinard's relinquishment of the family fortune is in keeping with his longstanding disregard for business norms, and his lifelong love for the environment.

Did I say glimpses? Yes. We can't call organizational generativity mainstream yet. That's where AI starts her strengthening journey. AI is not sugar coating. It accepts reality. This is made beautifully clear in David Cooperrider's article *Appreciative Inquiry in a Broken World* (2020, free on the internet). I selected for you two promising 'utterances':

> Instead of "problems to be solved," human systems are "universes of strengths." In a real way - when you think about how the appreciable world is so much larger than our appreciative eye - human organizations are the offspring of the life-giving miracle of human interaction and imagination, our cooperative relatedness, and the remarkable story of civilization itself. The more we study "what gives life" versus "what's

wrong," the more we can move in the direction of or become what we study. Instead of studying low morale, for example, we should, if indeed we want to accelerate the future we desire, study times and enablers of human flourishing in the workplace "because human systems move in the direction of what they study."

The simple act of observation in a human system changes the phenomenon itself. In another realm, in physics, for example, this concept has been called the Heisenberg observer effect. But in human systems, the result is even more powerful. Inquiry and change are not separate moments. Inquiry intervenes. Let's say we do 200 in-depth interviews in an organization into the times, the conditions, and the enablers of flourishing. Change, in this instance, is already happening. The attention of people has shifted. The stories they are learning from have shifted. People's sense of the possible has, just through the act of asking questions, shifted. Even their dreams and hopes for a better future are shifting. In marketing, it is called "the mere measurement effect," but honestly, there is nothing small about it. When we look at how inquiry-is-change - how inquiry-and-change is a simultaneous moment in human systems - we start seeing the power of it. It is something I've called "the exponential inquiry effect" to indicate how our first questions, like the early stage of a snowball, can grow into exponential tipping point movements. That's why, in the practice of AI in leadership, we say: "We live in worlds our questions create."

For me, articles and quotes like these, serve both as an invitation and strong support for my future forming research, and for writing this book as a vehicle to keep the snowball rolling. If the research process discussed in this chapter eventually would show up as a journal article, I am pretty sure you won't find phrases like 'rolling snowballs' in the final revision. Speaking of research, the interviews have been transcribed; what happened next?

Sitting with the Prints

I often use spreadsheets to collect information because they have advantages compared to the table in a word processor. However, the content of my spreadsheet so far was pure textual. What does one do when having "written" a first draft? Yes: printing the lot, and reading it from paper, preferably in an armchair. Regarding the interview data it was way too early for selecting and sorting; firstly the responses-as-a-whole had to be absorbed. For that I separated the discoveries from the dreams in two sets of prints, and put a pot of tea next to it. Research can be a very relaxing practice. Reading top-down, re-reading bottom-up; re-re-reading randomly across the fragments; "summertime, and the livin' is easy..."

Then, slowly, next to the data-collecting in the brain, a parallel mind game - the panoptical view? - seems to get hold of the matter. Mainly driven by questions. What are these nineteen people telling here? What did they see? How did they feel, when experiencing aspects of possible generativity? I remember well that I took my notebook again and wrote down the question: "What is there that can be known from this data?" This ignited two actions: making a rough design of the kind of information I could retrieve from the whole of the text fragments and, even before that: diving into Google Scholar hoping to find a bit of context in the domain of 'experiencing organizational behavior'. Perhaps this could help me to organize or label the textual data for the sake of sense making.

A Quickstep with Google Scholar

It was quite a disappointing sidestep, although it confirmed my not so optimistic expectation. Perhaps I should have known better: being engaged in a future-forming inquiry in which the data itself contains the clues toward new still unexpected forms, whilst looking for possible frames from the past; big chance they are not there. The thing is that I don't consider myself brilliant or unique, for which it is possible that all I am doing has been done already before me. And although I didn't find signs of that, it could be Google Scholar itself that is programmed to primarily show the obvious and most cited sources, and not the obscure ones. Which raises another question: "Is it possible to use referencing for the purpose of 'proving' that something is missing?" How long does one need to be searching to be sure that what is being searched doesn't exist? We are entering the world of Zen now: search for the source of your thoughts and find out that you won't find it, which doesn't deny the existence of such a source by the way. I just got the idea that one day I should do a Google search for Grounded Theory and Spirituality, but I am afraid that the outcome will be that spirituality is being researched, but not in use as a research practice itself. From a scientific point of view, of course. Practical reasoning tells me that the emergent dialogue in my mind, between my experiences and those of nineteen others, could be called reasoning, but has more of a spiritual nature. Basta. I did two searches in the always responsive Google Scholar.

My first search focused on "components of organizational behavior". At first sight, Google came up with promising book and article titles, which unfortunately did not always represent the actual content or findings. A few examples are shown below. Keep in mind that "organizational behavior" formed an important search item:

- Meyer and Allen (1991) wrote about employee commitment.
- Naler and Trustman (1980) addressed diagnosing and solving problems in organizations.
- Slocombe and Bluedorn (1999) relate task diversity with employee commitment.
- Gary Johns (1981) provides a critique on organizational behavior scoring systems.

All these studies seem to address the organization as it is; not as it is becoming. And where it comes to behavior, they constantly seem to refer to employee behavior.

- Thomas Wright (1997) states in *Time Revisited in OB* that time and timing has gotten little attention in OB. What actually can be understood from his abstract is the lack of attention for this in OB research, which turns the study into a meta-study I would say.

On the preliminary conclusion that 'organizational behavior' is constantly interpreted as 'behavior-in-but-not-of-organizations' I stopped searching for possible frameworks. What I took from it nevertheless is the importance of how employees and customers *feel* when having the organizational experience. (And how poorly they can recollect brand names.) In the case of very good feelings and very bad feelings, there is a chance of transformation. When the stakeholder feels nothing at all, the organization should worry. This notion of course is relevant in the realm of my collected discoveries and dreams. Some sources:

- Joe Pine and James Gillmore wrote the classic *The Experience Economy* (1999).
- Abhari, Saad and Haron (2008): *Enhancing Service Experience through Understanding Employee Experience Management*.
- The Gartner Group found out that only 13% of employees are fully satisfied with their experience.

- Brian Solis: *Customer Experience Isn't A Thing, It's A Feeling* (Forbes.com).

In my second Scholar search I focused on "organizational behavior and future". The first ten hits didn't tell anything about OB being future-oriented; they referred to what future OB research should focus on. (Studying future-orientation was not one of those suggestions.) Then I saw the promising title *Smartphones in the workplace: changing OB, transforming the future* (Pitichat, 2013). To say "nomen est omen" would be a poor joke, I admit. The conclusion of the article: "the smartphone is good for job satisfaction and good for the organization." I wouldn't call that a long term vision.

Disappointedly informed, I felt ready to create some answers myself to the earlier question of what we can get to know from my narrative data. I came up with the following ideas as a pre-study for building my next worksheet.

- What can be derived from the nineteen interview responses is a certain validity, based on the variety in their answers as well as on possible saturation in what they answered.
- Furthermore: insofar they mention sufficient case examples, I may be able to conclude that the features I am searching for appear in the real world.
- I can study how the five OG qualities have been described. Perhaps some have been easier recognized than others00.
- The data from the interviews may show the relative importance of the one OG factor compared to the other. Do they show overlap, interdependence? This may need text interpretation and also some quantification, for example of occurrences in wording and meaning.
- Finally, we can compare dream statements with the corresponding discoveries and find out about possible gaps.

In my mind I already had prepared and completed all this, and imagined myself already reflecting on it together with the nine contributing KC's, appreciatively embracing the possibility of turning their discoveries and dreams into areas of opportunity for designing interventions or innerventions that may contribute to more OG ... when I started to build the necessary next worksheet to bring my data processing alive.

Counting and Filtering

Am I bothering you? Would you rather just have the results of my inquiries? Perhaps there aren't any. Could the process of going through peoples opinions and experiences, and mixing these with your own views and those of scholarly others, be rewarding in itself? Would you trust me; would you believe any research conclusion I present? If not, you might disbelieve everything I say, even when my findings would be fully underpinned. Besides, we are in the field of humanities, not in mathematics, although the next step in my data processing is a bit calculative. This means that a lot of work can be shared in relatively few words. What to think of the following screenshot, part of my worksheet?

The fragment (only about Discovery of Intentionality) shows what I counted and plotted during re-re-re-reading the respective narratives, where some easy formulas (the gray cells) did the rest. A similar worksheet was created for the Dream answers. Remember, all this is still data, be it a bit more structured, to be used as input for further analysis (which I might have done unconsciously, but not officially). As in every proper abductive research, besides counting and filtering, there was some thoughtful coding waiting for me.

DISCOVERY ANALYSIS PER OG FACTOR	INTENTIONALITY
# words used by 12 OA's	1134
# words used per OA	95
# words used by 7 KC's	889
# words used per KC	127
# words used in total (written by KC; noted by Cees from interviews)	2023
# words used by 19 respondents	106
# OA give confirmation of existence from external	9
# KC give confirmation of existence from external	6
% of 19 respondents that give confirmation of existence external	79%
# OA give confirmation of existence from internal	9
% of 12 respondents that give confirmation of existence internal	75%
# case-examples given by OA from external	7
# case-examples given by KC from external	8
# case-examples given in total - external	15
# case-examples given by OA from internal	8
# case-examples recalled because of being informed	6
# case-examples recalled because of (also) believing in it	4
# case-examples recalled because of (also) having experienced it	8
# case-examples recalled with general feeling positive	9
# case-examples recalled with general feeling negative	3
Utterances after being asked the question (words and/or silence)	pfooh…
Words or phrases that (seem to) describe the OG quality at stake	satisfy the custome self organization more employee com more than profit, sha keep the suppliers a

Coding to Compare: a New Frame

Of course, one can easily do calculations with the numbers of words being used in a textual response. However, for retrieving the average feeling from it, or the nature, or the meanings of 'utterances', no spreadsheet formula is at hand. From the interview transcriptions I distilled and listed separate keywords or short phrases, partly shown in the bottom-right part of my earlier shown worksheet fragment. Every column represents either discoveries or dreams regarding one of the five OG factors. That is ten data groups in total plus one extra column for the integral dreams. And for each I created such a list of key phrases. All key phrases represent a certain description or denominator of the respective data group. Now, how could I label or categorize the key phrases in order to (a) get a structured, weighed 'valuation' of each of the data groups, and (b) be able to better compare and combine the narratives about the five factors?

My thoughts went back to the time that I tried to "plot" the seven manifestations of processual generativity in one model for the sake of 'ranking' their degree of generativity. For that I invented a two-axis model in which each of the seven represent a certain degree of Movement (from 'static' to 'dynamic'), as well as a certain degree of Timespan (from 'now' to 'far ahead'). I didn't use this diagram in my writings, because at that time I saw no added value in relative positions, where it seemed better to try and understand the seven manifestations themselves. However, this line of thinking contains a possible method to compare seemingly different entities along indicators that they do have in common.

So, for my keywords and phrases belonging to the various OG factors, I defined a uniform coding system. I noticed that all descriptions refer to a degree of *audience*, a degree of *future* and a degree of *movement*. By giving these three degrees a scale, the following rules for coding were created:

Degree of Audience (DA): to what extent are stakeholders being addressed?
- no score = not addressing
- 1 = ego / self / individual
- 2 = internal org
- 3 = external org
- 4 = all direct stakeholders
- 5 = beyond direct stakeholders

- Degree of Future (DF): how far into the future is being referred?
- no score = not addressed or past
- 1 = now, short term
- 2 = organizational year/cycle
- 3 = current generation
- 4 = next generation
- 5 = beyond next generation

- Degree of Movement (DM): how big is the expanding wave?
  - no score = not addressed, stillness
  - 1 = slow or forced action
  - 2 = active, in the flow
  - 3 = conscious, focused action
  - 4 = connected activities
  - 5 = integral co-creative action

After applying the "three degrees" to the text fragments, for example in the data column Dreams regarding Proccessuality, (part of) the coding looks like as shown in the next illustration.

PROCESSUALITY	DA	DF	DM
Vulnerability	1		
Questioning existing convictions and create new	2		3
Inquisitive employee attitude	2		2
Intention to constantly improve	2	3	
Open conversation about errors	2		3
Willingness to change	2	2	
Consider change flux normal	2		
Agility, able to bend the stream	2		3
Communication with employees is crucial	2		4
Coach potential disturbance		2	3
Always innovative	2		
External stakeholders notice the dynamics	3		3
Org lives in the now on every moment	2	1	

Just to make sure that we are still on the same page: I was interested in how (existing or desired) OG factors manifest themselves, and tried to find ways to compare at first hand uncomparable entities; I came up with three indicators that the five have in common. All five factors (can) refer to a certain degree of stakeholder-reach (DA), a certain extent of timespan (DF) and a certain broadness of action (DM). Every keyword or phrase in a data group is given a degree in all three indicators. Since the keywords come from spectators and visionaries, we now can 'calculate' to what degree a certain (experienced or envisioned) OG factor addresses the three indicators. The numbers make it possible to detect which of the three indicators is more or less dominant for the specific OG factor, and what would be the gap between the degrees of discoveries and dreams regarding a certain OG factor.

Measuring organizational behavior against DA, DF and DM implies a new framework, or at least a model, which is not in the least alike frameworks for assessing organizational behavior as I found them in the literature. And if you are as sharp as I think you are, you must have seen already that the three indicators are not measuring effects or impact, which might or might not be the result of certain organizational behavior; no, they represent the behavior itself, which can only be regarded as enabling, in this case more or less enabling. Enabling what? Enabling the organization to reach further I ("than its own nose", my granny would say). Including more stakeholders, looking further ahead in time, and creating a bigger 'buzz'. As we said before: when it comes to results, effects and impact, only time will tell. Enablers go before results.

Statistics

I admit that my ability to decide on the 3D's coding was partly strengthened by knowing a bit more context than the filtered words or phrases were telling (because of my constant re-re-reading, and doing the text filtering myself). To make the coding less personal and more scientific, we could involve more researchers to score, equipped with proper instructions. This would increase the absolute quality of the average degrees, when statistics enter the room. Given the fact that one (quite qualified) person did all the coding, at least the relative comparison between data groups can be regarded as accurate.

To be really honest and complete, I should mention that I started the coding activity with preliminary descriptions of the three degrees in each indicator. Only after a few rounds of coding, the degrees became more clear, after which I adjusted them slightly. With this final set I started my coding again on a fresh printout. Coding helps to become better at coding.

Right after entering the various codes, it was a matter of a few simple spreadsheet formulas to get the first *stats*. At that point my worksheets looked like the following screenshot. (Note that only part of the 45 lines of keywords are shown.)

I will come back later with more findings and pre-conclusions. For the sake of understanding the illustration - in this case referring to Dreams regarding Processuality - see below in brief what can be retrieved from it:

- regarding all three indicators, a degree of 5 is not seen in the dreams yet;
- the most coded Degree of Audience is a 2 (reaching not more than the internal organization) with an average of just a little more than 2;
- referring to future is happening in less than half of the key phrases;
- considering the average of 3.1, the degree of movement (DM) reaches just beyond conscious, focused action, still taking place mostly in fragments/groups within the organization.

PROCESSUALITY	DA	DF	DM
Appreciatively critical			3
Development is the central theme	2	3	3
Conscious organizing based on intrinsic needs	2	2	3
Awareness in handeling various time dynamics		4	3
Calmness			
People show a common path and contribution	2		4
Egalitarity			
Overcoming fear of losing control	2		3
Focus on process itself instead of results	2	2	3
Attention for that what is happening		3	3
Attention for human feelings in processes	4		3

Number of lines with keywords or phrases	avg DA	avg DF	avg DM
45	2,1	2,4	3,1

	DA codes	DF codes	DM codes
# times n/a	12	29	12
# times 1	1	1	0
# times 2	29	8	2
# times 3	2	6	25
# times 4	1	1	6
# times 5	0	0	0
Checksum	45	45	45

These numbers made it possible to have more clarity about the 'intensity' of perceived or imagined manifestations of the five OG factors. What do you think: could I ever have designed these sheets, coding systems and corresponding numbers without or before working with the data? Is novelty possible without emergence?

Proper Logic

There are managers who think they can change the results. Of course they can change the content of the monthly sales report in such a way that it shows more than what has been achieved in reality. There are managers who shout to their people: "THE RESULTS ARE BAD, I NEED BETTER RESULTS." Probably everybody knew that already and, perhaps out of fear or to please the boss, now the employees start adjusting the numbers. There are managers who show the actual bad results and suggest or - better - ask the people suggestions on how to improve. And there are managers who show the same results, and ask in all openness: "What about these achievements so far? We are way below target. Are we doing the wrong things? Or did we perhaps create (or recieve) the wrong targets? How much time do we have left? What can we do to achieve the best possible results at the end of this term? What do you need for that, and how can I be of support?"

I hope you are - like me - a fan of the last manager described, along with the idea that - briefly stated - enablers go before results. Call it a basic logic, or an axiom if you prefer. It seems to be a good starting point for my upcoming reasoning.

So we have the situation that, from the desire to compare seemingly incomparable OG factors, the "Three Degrees" entered the stage. (I will abbreviate them from now into the 3D's to prevent you from having different, more individual, more beautiful, more musical associations.) And since managers of 'the result orientation' tend to cling on tangible measures, my 3D's may be taken as a simple solution to questions of a more complicated, even complex nature. That is why I like to share here some logical warnings.

1. Although the (experienced or imagined) presence of an OG factor implies certain values on the 3D's, you can't turn this around: certain values of the 3D's do not necessarily indicate a certain level of the OG factors. (During rainy weather, the streets are wet. Wet streets are not necessarily pointing to rainy weather.)

2. So when you have found a way to increase the values of the 3D's as high as possible, you still can't conclude that the OG factors are at their maximum level (for which the organization would be ultimately generative, and can we ever speak of such?).

3. The 3D's have been invented to help us 'measure' the presence of an OG factor - it's much easier to measure the presence of rain - also in such a way that we can compare the OG factors regarding their presence, for example in order to bring more balance in the five factors.

4. The values of the 3D's in themselves don't tell so much about the five OG factors unless you measure the degrees in conjunction with an OG factor.

5. The 3D's as such might be an interesting addition to a management dashboard, since by then the organization would be monitoring the degree of stakeholder inclusion, the degree of future orientation and the degree of connected action, which all seem beneficiary to the process of organizing. But if such a dashboard would be active, and show high values of DA, DF and DM, one still can't derive from that a high level of organizational generativity ...

BREAKING: Unexpected Intermezzo

After typing that last warning, dear reader, my mind went into next gear and I wrote literally here: IS THAT SO? And furthermore: What if we really scale up DA, DF and DM, could that already do the generative trick? Would that be a tangible strategy? Just imagine that... We would have found the holy grail. My Boolean logic doesn't seem to imply such yet. But I am in doubt, not to say confused. (Where is Confucius when you need him?) More precisely: if we apply interventions that cause DA, DF and DM to increase; that may be easier to do than trying to find ways to increase respectively organizational intentionality, processuality, performativity, serendipity and procreativity. Am I finding something new here, something much more simple? I was on the point to make clear that all five OG factors are of a different nature, and need very different interventions in order to make them more present. What is easier? Increasing the five, or increasing the 3D's? Although the latter are definitely enablers, are they the enablers for the OG-factors to rise, or are the OG-factors enablers for the 3D's to increase? Pffff ...

Before I went to bed to let a good night's sleep help me process my logic, I noted - and I am aware now that I am using this manuscript directly as my diary - that I should tell the reader what happened, what I had in mind for this chapter, before the research had other plans with me. Suddenly my first plan - sharing my data collection, processing, analysis, findings and discussion - seems 'old school' again, almost on its way to a journal article. I also thought that you are entitled to see what that would look like; I could present it in a more compact way. And from there I would switch to my newly appeared reasoning. I went to bed, and put this question under my pillow: Is it better to find interventions for increasing the respective five OG factors? Or is it equally good, or better to find interventions for increasing the 3D's? Or should we switch to "just increase the 3 D's": include more stakeholders, think further ahead and make more collective movement...?

[Zzzzzzzzz....]

The next morning I find myself sitting at my desk, making busy notes on fast moving sheets of paper. The bad handwriting makes it clear that my pen has difficulties catching up with my brain. My body is thrilling with excitement. At the same time - the mind is not easy to control - an inner smile presents itself at the thought that if the insights here would ever be reported in a journal article, it could only be without mentioning all this emergence. (And the peer-reviewer would say: no way, José.)

My first notes address my earlier idea of introducing a metaphor to help the reader cope with all these abstract organizational concepts. For example, and here comes the metaphor, imagine the proposition that a person is likely to be successful if he or she shows to be Ethical, Flexible, Communicative, Creative and Generous. (Just an assumption of five qualities, no rigorous literature review available here.) We could ask observers to think of people with one or more of those qualities and describe those. For example: "strong sense of right and wrong", "the ideal partner for an adventure", "convincing", "full of surprises", "always ready to help". From the desire to advise an average person what to focus on in order to be more successful - whatever that may mean - we define three (!) indicators that all five qualities could be rated on, for example: size of network

(DN), level of intelligence (DI) and the extent of getting things done (DD). Back to the (proper) logic: now we meet a person with a lot of friends, thinking ahead and a real achiever. Is that person necessarily ethical, flexible, convincing, creative or generous? Our three indicators aren't really interventions. But if we knew of interventions to increase that person's network, intelligence, or delivery capacity, wouldn't that be beneficial to that person's functioning? Could this triple growth even have a positive effect on the ethics, the flexibility, the communication skills, the creativity and the generosity of that person? I think it is a yes. Not necessarily as a cause and effect relationship. But somehow it seems that the five qualities affect the three indicators - also to be seen as qualities by the way, but easier to measure - whilst the three indicators affect the five qualities. It seems that they mutually strengthen each other. Therefore, to enhance that person's functioning, we might focus on interventions to strengthen the five as well as interventions to increase the three. Does that sound logical? Does it clarify a bit? Do you need much data for this? Is future the result of extrapolation?

What comes to mind in this metaphor are the three so-called vital functions: consciousness, breathing and blood circulation. All three are needed to be alive. Can it be that some or many organizations are 'managed' from the level of keeping the vital functions active: minimal intelligence, minimal resources, minimal communication? (Not to mention maximum profit for few...) Just enough to stay alive as an organization? This perspective is completely at the other side of the spectrum I am researching. My metaphor addresses the 'fully functional life' according to psychologist Carl Rogers. I rest my case, your honor.

My second sheet of notes I can better show first and explain later.

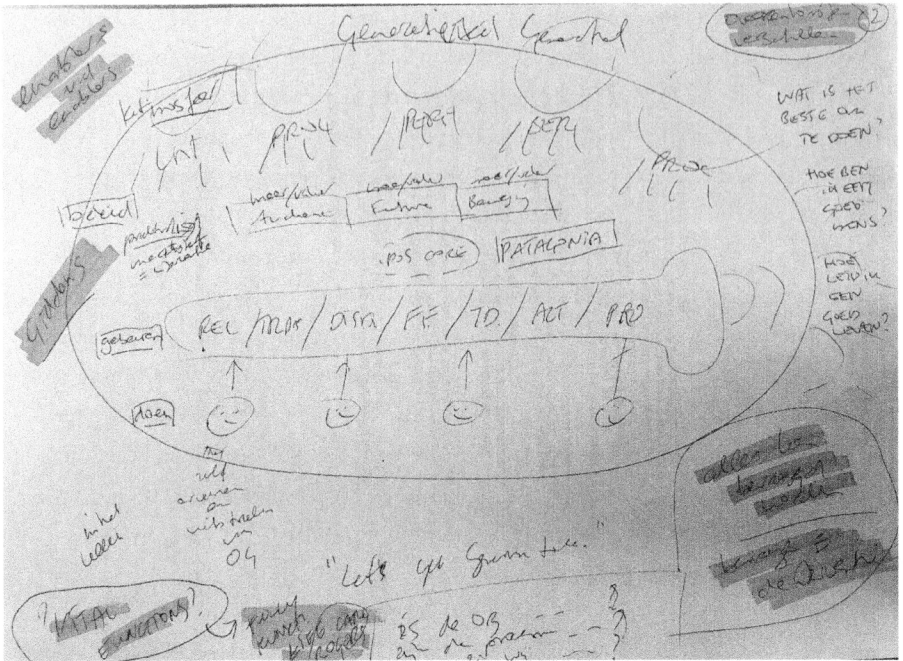

The essence here is that I came to my inquisitive senses again. By researching just the five factors and heading for a corresponding curriculum, I was dragging myself in a funnel, getting separated from so many other parts of the whole called generative organizing. My drawing shows the organization in its respective dimensions - let's not call it levels - of (people) Doing, of (processes) Happening, of (policy) Planning and Monitoring and of (organizational) Being. In all these dimensions we can say that if something happens, it always happens because of people doing something. The five OG factors are not especially reserved for the (perceived) behavior of the organization as a whole; the five also are - or can be - active on the individual level. It's all about the interplay - here is Giddens again - between individual behavior and the organizational atmosphere, with the processes happening in between. So I'm not going to simplify organizing to the level of just managing the 3D's. Insofar my fuzzy drawing makes sense, it tells us that "organizing" equals a set of attempts to intervene in complexity, and that "generative organizing" includes specific interventions in specific areas, including specific monitoring to keep all interventions in balance. Did you notice that my drawing doesn't refer to - or point at - any result? Interventions are enablers - or should be - and we see various enablers in action, some even enabling other enablers. "Take care of the organizing and the organizing will take care of the results," to paraphrase the pragmatic philosopher Richard Rorty.

Pffff... breathe out, breathe in. Take a break. Actually you are in a break, called Unexpected Intermezzo. The rest of my hasty notes pages contain a draft strategy and a storyline for how to proceed with this chapter: first, I will resume the 'old school' data-analysis, and show you what can be seen and known, as briefly as possible, with not too much academic discussion. Second, I will come up with my re-emerged integral research round-up: to prepare for Part Four, titled Genarrativity as a Practice.

Old School or Good Science? You tell me.

Since this story was abruptly interrupted by an insight that I shouldn't and couldn't resist, we need to start over again. So why not turn the research, reported in this part of the book, into the format that academic journals prefer? And for our sake, let's do this with the tightest possible word count. A great scholarly challenge indeed. With a bit of tongue in cheek also. Here we go. Times New Roman, 1.5 line spacing, not so sure about my conformity to APA7, Appendices only mentioned - as a reader of this book you have seen these already - and References simply left out for obvious reasons. Draft version 1.

Title page

A Future Forming Inquiry into the Five Factors of Organizational Generativity

Abstract

In his groundbreaking Academy of Management paper (2020), Hoogendijk proposes that Organizational Generativity - the capacity of organizations to create their own futures - breaks down into five factors: Intentionality, Processuality, Performativity, Serendipity and Procreativity. To substantiate this hypothesis, we performed engaged future-forming research to discover possible existence of the corresponding organizational behavior , and find ways to identify and foster this. Our findings give reason to believe that the OG factors are existent, can be considered as enablers to support organizations in their striving to flourish, and are promoted through a threefold grading method called the 3 Degrees. Further research on more case studies will be necessary to grow the level of substantiation.

Introduction

The pandemia made clear for organizations that efforts to prepare for an unknown future might not be the best of their investments. Building resilience may be a well sold proposition by consulting firms, but it holds at least two serious concerns: we still don't know what organizational resilience exactly should look like, and: resilience has generally a defensive character. What if organizations could grow or unleash the capability to have more influence on - or even create -

their own futures? For this, Organizational Generativity seems a promising concept, frequently used in OD literature but not sufficiently clarified or developed for this purpose. From 2017 onwards, Hoogendijk is working on this challenge by first doing a rigorous OD literature review on the meaning and potential of generativity. This subsequently resulted in a framework to identify and promote the generativity of processes in organizations, and a hypothesis about the concept of generativity as a quality of organization as a whole, driven by five OG Factors. It represents a warm invitation to take up the next research question, briefly formulated: How do We Bring the Five Factors of Organizational Generativity Alive?

Methods

To discover exemplary experiences of OG, and create an image of what OG could look like at its best, in order to prepare for designing interventions to increase the level of OG, Appreciative Inquiry was chosen - also recommended by Ken Gergen (2015) - as the main research method. It is executed with the help of engaged 'scholars' (Van de Ven, 2007) to perform scripted interviews with organizational actors likely to recognize OG if any. The appendices include (i) a preliminary description of the five OG factors, (ii) the criteria for selecting the engaged scholars who did the interviews, (iii) a questionnaire to retrieve their own OG experiences, (iv) the criteria for selecting interviewees, and (v) the script of the AI-interview. The recorded interviews are transcribed into editable text, which has been filtered, structured and coded in an abductive approach, in dialogue with the lead researcher. This resulted in quantitative information about identified cases, qualitative information about meaning and perception of the experienced cases, and a coding system to depict the degree of existence of the five OG factors, also enabling comparisons between the five. All data collection, and the various processing of it, has been executed in multiple worksheets of a Google sheet, in which furthermore tables and charts have been prepared for final analysis of the findings.

Results

The findings can be summarized in two diagrams, as shown below. Table 1 is mostly of a quantitative nature. The series of charts in Diagram 1, making use of quantified data as a result of qualitative coding, have primarily been designed for qualitative analysis. Both diagrams are completed with explanation and findings.

TABLE 1 - Recognizing and Experiencing the OG Qualities	Intentionality	Processuality	Performativity	Serendipity	Procreativity
In order to underpin existence, also to compare between the five					
1. Average number of words use to describe recognized/detected/experience OG qualities (19 respondents)	106	56	81	63	58
2. Percentage of (19) respondents that confirmed existence of the OG quality as external stakeholder	79%	26%	53%	47%	74%
3. Percentage of (12) OA respondents that confirmed existence of the OG quality as internal stakeholder	75%	58%	25%	58%	42%
4. Case examples mentioned from 19 respondents as external stakeholder	15	2	13	11	14
5. Case examples mentioned from 12 OA respondents as internal stakeholder	8	4	3	7	4
6. Total cases mentioned	23	6	16	18	18
7. Number of cases that caused positive feeling	9	4	7	7	5
8. Number of cases that caused negative feeling	3	1	5	1	3

Additional clarification for Table 1
- Lines 1 to 6 represent various different perspectives to create robustness regarding the 'detectability' or visibility of each OG quality.
- Line 2 also serves to 'compare' the relative visibility among the five factors.
- Line 3 also serves to see which qualities are seen more from external than from internal position.
- Line 7 and 8 serve to indicate the perception in terms of positive or negative feeling (as customer satisfaction theory suggests).

The numbers in Table 1 give reason to assume that:
- External visibility of an OG factor is the highest for Intentionality and Procreativity; the lowest in Processuality.
- Internal visibility is the highest for Intentionality and Processuality; the lowest in Performativity.
- On average, every respondent can mention one concrete case example of each OG factor, whereby most cases relate to Intentionality and least cases relate to Processuality.
- Experiences of Processuality and Serendipity show the highest ratio of positive over negative feelings; in general, all five OG qualities create more positive than negative feelings.

INTENTIONALITY

INTENTIONALITY relative occurence
of degrees within 17 qualifiers

	ience	uture	·ment
na	12%	82%	6%
1	0%	0%	0%
2	18%	0%	0%
3	41%	6%	71%
4	12%	12%	24%
5	18%	0%	0%
	DA	**DF**	**DM**
Average degree (excl. not addressed)	3,3	3,7	3,3

DISCOVERY

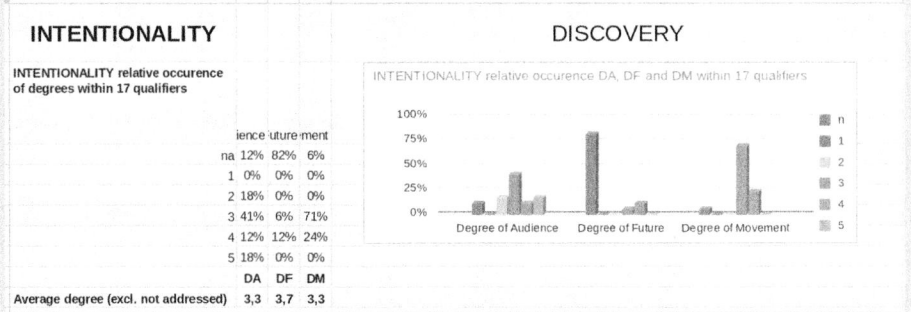

INTENTIONALITY relative occurence DA, DF and DM within 17 qualifiers

DREAM

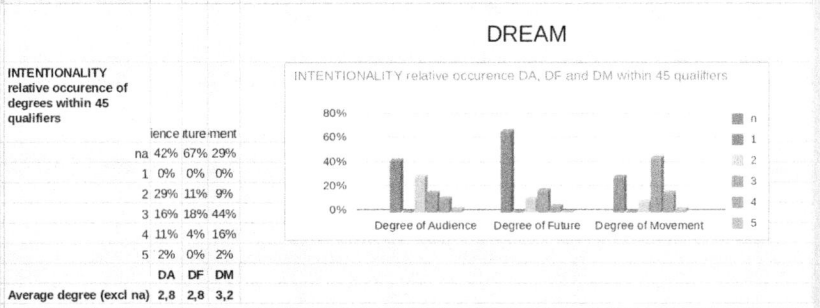

INTENTIONALITY relative occurence DA, DF and DM within 45 qualifiers

INTENTIONALITY
relative occurence of
degrees within 45
qualifiers

	ience	tture	·ment
na	42%	67%	29%
1	0%	0%	0%
2	29%	11%	9%
3	16%	18%	44%
4	11%	4%	16%
5	2%	0%	2%
	DA	**DF**	**DM**
Average degree (excl na)	2,8	2,8	3,2

Additional clarification Diagram 1, before including the four other OG factors
- In order to 'rate' and 'compare' the presence - existence has been sufficiently
  underpinned - of the OG factors, we used three 'common denominators', shown
  in the legenda below, enabling us to label each separate keyword or keyphrase
  describing a perceived to imagined OG factor.

DEGREE OF AUDIENCE	DEGREE OF FUTURE	DEGREE OF MOVEMENT
no score = not addressing	no score = not addressed or past	no score = not addressed, still
1 = ego / self / individual	1 = now, short term	1 = slow or forced action
2 = internal org	2 = organizational year/cycle	2 = active, in the flow
3 = external org	3 = current generation	3 = conscious, focused action
4 = all direct stakeholders	4 = next generation	4 = connected activities
5 = beyond direct stakeholders	5 = beyond next generation	5 = integral cocreative action

- Every (description of an) OG factor refers to a certain degree of including
  stakeholders, timespan or collective action. Although the numbers, percentages
  and averages in the charts may give a different impression, the main purpose was
  to do a "visual inspection" of the barcharts.
- Once in place, the various barcharts provide qualitative information about the
  degree in which an OG factor manifests itself, both on the three separate angles,

as in combination. One can also compare shifts in the degrees between the discovery descriptions and the dream descriptions regarding a given OG factor.
- Note that the dark (blue) bar on the left represents the number of times that the description doesn't address the perspective. This shouldn't be interpreted as "zero level degree". That's why the 'not addressed' numbers have been kept out of the averages (of grades 1 through 5).

The visual inspections of all five pairs* of barcharts provide the following insights:
(*) The graphs of all five pairs are included in appendix (vi).
- Different OG factors show different patterns across the three degrees. The excerpt table below shows for each OG factor the 'denominator' with the highest degree of presence, both for discovery and dream.

	Max Discovery	Max Dream
Intentionality	DF	DM
Processuality	DM	DM
Performativity	DM	DM
Serendipity	DF	DM
Procreativity	DF	DF

- Except for Procreativity, where the perspective is and stays on Future, the other four all shift to (desired) attention for Movement. (This may tell more about the preference for action above stakeholders and future, than the existence of a high degree of action.)
- In none of the descriptions, the degree of Audience is the highest, where the averages in DA show that the inclusion of stakeholders doesn't reach much further than the internal organization.
- What can be seen from the respective dark (blue) bars is that *in the imagining* of OG-factors the number of N/A is generally less than *in the experiencing* of OG-factors: towards the ideal, there is growing attention for stakeholders, future and movement.
- Based on average numbers throughout the five OG-factors, the DA is rated approximately 2.5 ("slightly including externals"), the DF 3.3 ("thinking not much farther than the current generation"), and the DM 3.1 ("conscious action happening, but still fragmented").
- Although it may be tempting to bring in the statistical procedures like standard deviation and normal distribution, the recommendation is to not dive deeper than this. Perhaps the statistical formulas can be applied, but the starting points for proper statistics do not apply. We are not reviewing numbers; we are reviewing

attempts to quantify qualifications for the sake of qualifying, in order to understand better what is inquired into: the possible existence and manifestation of the five proposed factors or Organizational Generativity, this to contribute to our bigger search for what makes healthy organizations.

Discussion

To answer our research question we asked nineteen relevant candidates about their possible experiences of OG, and how they imagine OG when at its best. From the findings we can conclude that it is possible (and desired) to include the five OG factors in the realm of strategies for organization development, and that proper monitoring is needed to be aware of existence and shifts. Since the five factors differ in nature, the 3 Degrees instrument can serve as an indicator, making 'the organization aware' of 'reaches' they didn't fully include yet in the policies and actions.

Possible flaws in the research are related to (a) the number of respondents, although they produced together 7000 words of input; (b) the fact that the coding has been done only by one researcher; (c) the way of inquiry (into the strongest examples) probably causing the closeness of experienced and imagined OG manifestations; (d) the selection of adult 'current generation' respondents, who during the years may have lost the capability or appetite for real dreaming, which can explain a certain mediocrity of the dream descriptions.

Implications for theory might be to give more attention to the (perceived) behavior of the organization as a whole - culture? - where this is now too easily narrowed down to employee or leadership behavior; and also to focus more on organizational enablers in themselves, not so much in association with (to be expected, quick) results, but from the perspective of "doing things well just for the sake of it" according to Sennett in *The Craftsman*.

Implications for practice are similar to the recommendations for further research as Gergen (2014) suggested: "What about research, not as a mirroring but as a making of the world?"

Recommendations for further research include mitigating the flaws, repeating the inquiries among respondents that are connected with one specific organization, furthering the preliminary set of 'measures' called the 3 Degrees, and stick to Appreciative Inquiry as the main future forming research method.

So far this draft (mini) journal article: Old school, or good science? You tell me.

Fast Forward to Organizational Reality

In my role as an OD practitioner I am always joking that my well respected clients are not very likely to come across my AoM and ODJ papers, let alone that they are aware these journals exist. I also doubt whether they would easily read through the academic language - I don't - or will distill elements of it for their daily organizational work. And yet I just sneakily included such a (pretended) scholarly piece in this practitioner's book. I can only hope that you as my reader are still with me. The draft journal article, as just presented, can be seen both as a mock-up and a pre-study for a real journal article; well intended and with a bit of a wink. Without the Abstract, the mini manuscript counts less than 1500 words: a personal record! (Let's not forget the left out appendices.) Can you imagine this article separated or isolated from its historical, processual and personal context? This book takes about 100 times as many words. Could we do with just that tiny article - summary of summaries - or do we need such a voluminous book to go forward? The answer lies in the future.

We have come a long way for this future-forming research into the five factors of organizational generativity. You have been witnessing that the findings are far from pre-cooked. At some point, the findings decided to twist the research process, and shake my ideas about how to structure my story; not much of a memoir anymore. Partaking by now in the enfolding reality, my diary and this manuscript have become entangled. I think I finally understand what Stephen King meant when he said that stories write themselves.

So far, my research and my data-analysis have produced various findings, partly reported *before*, and partly included *in* the "old school" article mock-up. What occurs to me is that these insights guided me towards new insights. Some of them fit - as I see it now - better in Part Four of the book, which will take a new shape, caused by the unexpected twist and shake. The following five insights surely belong to this Part Three, also serving as completion of this OG research phase. They concern respectively the nature and the (in)completeness of the OG factors, the three degrees, the design of this book and the research journey itself.

Five Factors, Five Natures

Being the blessed and grateful lead researcher, I had the opportunity to personally process all data and information in the most intense and intimate way. I dare to say that the five factors have become more alive for me than before, perhaps even more than I ever expected. If I were to lead an organization, I could work with those already, although I wouldn't constrain myself to the five OG factors. Proposing them as OD drivers makes sense, as well as identifying the corresponding manifestations. So much has become clear through the responses, from collected actors that hadn't thought of OG factors before, but did recognize them in some cases, after being inquired on this. From analyzing their descriptions, and trying to standardize all views with the help of the 3D's, the insight grew in me how different, how incomparable these five factors actually are. This may be very important when we want to promote and strengthen their presence in organizational behavior. Five factors, five characters.

Intentionality, to start with, seems to be "living behind the curtains"; coming from inside. From there, it drives and monitors our actions. How do we grow or change organizational intentionality? How is it perceived?

Processuality may be even more hidden, for I consider it as a form of awareness; it doesn't show itself by driving certain actions. It's almost like a belief: we believe in the processuality of organization. Of course, that awareness somehow influences behavior, be it more indirect. How do we grow awareness? It may need an invitation - or a soft push - to observe processes (with new eyes) to find out that it is not so clear what you are looking at.

Performativity, compared to the previous two, is relatively easy to perceive. There are messages involved, which can cause a certain effect or impact on the receiver. From the sender's side, performativity can be seen as a craft, an art of language, to make communication to be as effective as possible. Growing organizational performativity may not be easy, thinking of all those struggling communication departments. However, the path is quite clear; even promising if driven by Intentionality and inspired by Processuality.

Serendipity - meaning the organization's readiness to benefit from unexpected surprises - has in my opinion to do with freedom: the (perceived) availability in time and space and opportunity and support and appreciation, needed when it's time to bypass the trusted and expected procedures. The quality of the creative response can't be controlled, but the conditions can be "organized".

Procreativity is visible action. Any activity has of course an effect in the future, but the procreative deed is deliberately planned and performed in the now, with a desired effect in the future. Organizational procreativity shows itself in a constant flow of such actions, for which two conditions are crucial: exposing a long-term view, and being prepared for answering difficult questions (Why this? Why now? Why at all?).

Five factors, five different natures, characters so to say. And since we are dealing with organizational behavior, most of it is only perceived and almost impossible to change. It is mandatory to descend from our cloud - nothing wrong with understanding clouds - to find out how we can influence the rain or find the best way to interact with it.

About (in)completeness

Not mentioned in the preliminary findings are those specific respondents' comments that point towards my earlier consideration to call each of the five OG qualities literally a factor. The thing with factors - at least in multiplications - is that if one is zero, the outcome of all multiplied factors is zero. Translated to our conceptual framework, the term factor suggests that all five should be present for organizational generativity to be present; that no one can be missed. Besides the few respondent remarks, we could make use of the mathematical proof by contradiction. It works like this. Can we think of organizational generativity without intentionality? That seems very unlikely. To be generative implies the drive or intention to preserve the species. Therefore, OG needs Intentionality. Can OG do without one of the other four? Procreativity seems evident. Serendipity relates strongly to the proverb that not the strongest, nor the most intelligent, but the ones most responsive to change will survive. Processuality seems to be a necessary condition to actually accept and embrace change as the constant factor (Bruce Lee again). And Performativity refers to the social condition of relating and communicating, essential considering that organizations are people.

Nice mathematics, but the truth is: we will not find evidence for the completeness of the OG framework. And I also didn't hear any arguments of obsoleteness: that OG can do with less than five factors. In these times of lean and agile, the average manager must have thought about the efficiency regarding five factors; so far no urgent requests to reduce. Incompleteness perhaps? Is giving attention to the five OG factors sufficient to promote organizational generativity? Could we think of a sixth one? Again: no suggestions of such nature were noted. From the early literature review, and across the seven processual manifestations, the five have been derived much more than invented.

In the Discussion part of their papers, scholarly authors are always quite generous in sharing the flaws in, for example: sample size, research domain and number of sources. I don't see them so much questioning their proposed frameworks, like P.E.R.M.A (Seligman), P.O.S.I.T.I.V.E. (Cooperrider), and many more. I guess, for that reason - and the scholars will surely agree - that we better consider all such frameworks to be hypotheses, and not theories or formulas (yet).

The 3 Degrees Enhanced

It will be no surprise for you when I say that the 3D's - degree of Audience, Future and Movement - are of a processual nature. They represent a way to simplify the detection of OG factors. As if we only use a scale and centimeter to "grade" people. The object of inspection gives rise to more or better measures, like the color of the eyes, weight, etcetera. The 3 Degrees came to existence by choice. Once in place, they seemed to make sense, given the possible strategies for an organization to grow. The only way to find out whether these detectors are valuable is by applying them, resulting in numbers that make sense or not.

Regarding the 3D's I considered the N/A 'degree' first a zero, then a piece of non-data and subsequently a source of information. We shouldn't use it as a zero, nor use it in calculating averages, but the N/A code is still valuable to find out whether respondents did or didn't address one of the 3D's, which is information in itself. Enough processuality? During the process of defining and applying the 3D's, the code descriptions were slightly adjusted, and by now I think that the three titles need an upgrade again. This doesn't influence the data-analysis, the legenda remains the same. I would now suggest the following (replacing the former Audience, Future and Movement) to become more aware of what we are trying to observe.

- *Degree of Stakeholder Inclusion* - abbreviated DS or DSI
- *Degree of Acknowledged Timespan* - DA or DAT.
- *Degree of Flow Coherence* - DF or DFC.

The essential insight that appeared during my sudden emergent confusion is that the 3D's are not just indicators for detecting dimensions of OG factors. They very well serve as interventions, in the sense that organizational (development) objectives and strategies can be fueled by the three. Wouldn't it be possible for a company to include in their next 'strategic plan' (also) objectives for increasing the respective degrees with one or two steps of the ladder? Could that have an effect on the presence of the OG factors themselves, although we can't "measure" these directly? I think I just grabbed the essence of the flaws that arose when I was writing that paragraph called Proper Logic with perhaps too much focus on cause & effect reasoning.

About the Parts and the Whole (of this book)

The insight that relates to my focus on causality - instead of embracing emergent interactivity - has an impact on the structure of this book. As I see it now, the book parts are as fragmented as the departments in an organization. Of course there is logic behind. It's a story, therefore chronological. And admitted, the clarification of generativity - Part One - came before the discovery of the seven manifestations of processual generativity: Part Two. Organizational generativity was regarded as exotic, for which I took the liberty of (almost) isolating the corresponding research in Part Three. In my original book design, Part Four would be filled with various mental and practical exercises to get comfortable or even adept in handling generativity.

Generativity..., on the process level, the organizational level, the individual level? The thing is that I postponed the integration, the interrelatedness, if not the entanglement between the respective parts of the book. They only (r)emerged in my fuzzy drawing, happily just in time. Because, building on my new insights, and on that fuzzy drawing in particular, Part Four will differ from what I thought it would become.

Let it be an example for you, and a lesson for me, that fragmentation is always waiting around the corner, happy to be embraced, because it makes complexity seem so simple again. Which it isn't. The Cynefin model proves this convincingly, and its maker Dave Snowden is to be appreciated for the fact that his model is quite simple in itself: it distinguishes Simple, Complicated, Complex and Chaos and suggests how to deal with issues in one of its four domains. Snowden's assumption is that we have a tendency of solving issues as if they were existent in an "easier" domain than they actually are. Besides, academic research has become inherently fragmented, because the scrutiny demands to stay within a little post stamp. The call to keep things simple is strong. Unreasonably strong.

In the sharing of my newly risen insights I am preparing for re-integration of the book parts. After all, the word "part" suggests part of a bigger whole. Shall we consider this book as a whole again?

The Research Journey Revisited

The simple and attractive fact that my supervisor Celeste, back in December 2019, suggested that three articles would make a PhD, must have engraved this trinity in my research plans. My thinking was always about three steps. When I enjoyed my five minutes of fame in the AoM presentation, autumn 2020, my slides presented a three phases research trajectory: (1) clarifying Organizational Generativity until the level of a conceptual framework, (2) building a curriculum of OG enhancing interventions (or innerventions), and (3) applying and 'testing' the curriculum within a leadership team of a relevant pilot organization to see whether this has an effect on its generativity.

By then, I didn't have a clue that processual generativity would become more substantial - also necessary to pass peer-review. Thanks to the ODJ publishers we added practical guidelines, also valuable input for Part Two of this book. I knew that I was going to study organizational generativity, since phase two of the corresponding research trajectory had been designed before we knew the outcomes of our JABS attempts; a rewarding exercise for creating Part Three of this book. Besides, the first idea of writing this book crossed my mind about six months after distancing myself from PhD certification, and turned into action another three months later.

It may have been not more than a week ago that I made some notes about inviting my nine KC's for a meeting with the purpose of discussing the discoveries and dreams regarding the OG factors, and designing the foundations for a curriculum filled with OG related interventions: the fuel to finish Part Four of this book. My new insights tell me that interventions of the teaching kind may not be needed, because all actors in the organization are the right ones, in the right place, with the right capabilities to contribute to the generativity of their organization, and to take part in the process of generative organizing. The KC's are sincerely invited to pre-read the manuscript, and in that role they will adjust and enrich the suggestions this book is ready to reveal. But caused by pragademic emergence, the KC's - including myself - are dismissed from the duty to create learning modules, or even to become OG teachers. Besides the fact that they are already qualified for that, I don't think that teaching will be the way to generativity.

We learn most things and skills in life *in* and *by* practice, don't we? To make this book as performative as possible, you still can expect or allow me to use the word intervention (or innervention), but perhaps not as you may remember it: as an instruction, a lesson, a command. Let's bring to the fore that the principles of Appreciative Inquiry make clear that the most powerful change intervention always presents itself wrapped in a guiding question.

Any questions so far? Let's get "genarrative".

PART FOUR
02022 - 22020

Genarrativity as a Practice

The Practice of Practicing

One day I asked the Master: "How can the shot be loosed if 'I' do not do it?"
"'It' shoots," he replied. "I have heard you say that several times before, so
let me put it another way: How can I wait self-obliviously for the shot if 'I'
am no longer there?" "'It' waits at the highest tension." "And who or what is
this 'It'?" "Once you have understood that, you will have no further need of
me. And if I tried to give you a clue at the cost of your own experience, I
would be the worst of teachers and would deserve to be sacked! So let's stop
talking about it and go on practicing."

In his marvelous memoir *Zen in the Art of Archery* the author, Eugen Herrigal, German professor in philosophy and teaching in Japan in the 1930's, describes his learning experiences (or, as a friend of mine calls it: learning incidents) when being taught to master the art of handling bow and arrow. Although the book is thin enough to read it yourself in one afternoon I extracted the following personal lessons to give you a first glimpse.

Levels in Shooting	Faults in Learning
1. Wanting to quickly shoot	- Concern about the speed of the arrow
2. Feeling the pain of drawing the bow	- Attachment to set patterns
3. Drawing it with all one's might	- Fixation on theory
4. Becoming less dependent on technique	- Concern about the quality of the bow and arrow
5. Being able to draw the bow easily	- Worry about results
6. Concern about hitting the target	- Concern about being skillful
7. Achieving the limit of technical ability	- Worry about what others think
8. Cleansing of body and mind	- Trying to be enlightened
9. Confronting life and death	- Being self-satisfied
10. Developing tremendous resolve	- Shooting as amusing diversion
11. No regret True emptiness, no thought YES!	
12. The arrow flies from your center full of spiritual energy	

Please reflect a bit more on what the way to mastery implies. This Part Four, about practicing the practice of genarrativity, might offer similar challenges...

PRACTICING THE FRAMES

*[For] this teaching takes shape, as we have already seen clearly enough,
according to its own strange rules and rhythm. It manifests in its own good
time; will work its way inside us and finally show itself [,] not when we think
we are ready, but when it knows we are.*

To my opinion, this quote from the 'academystic' Peter Kingsley in his book
Reality illustrates in a miraculous way the beautiful mystery of what we call
learning, and what we so desperately want to 'implement' through interventions
called 'training'. Read below the citation again, extended with a selection of
contextual phrases, taken from the surrounding pages (500-530) in *Reality*, a
book that has so much more to tell but is already great for the way it describes the
way to master the skill called learning.

> His [Empedocles] first instruction to Pausanias [the student] is not to
> perceive but to perceive that he is perceiving - to watch the perceptive
> process itself. In other words he is telling him not just to look or touch or
> hear but to look and touch while fully conscious of looking and
> touching, to hear with the awareness that he is hearing.
>
> [...]
>
> Even to think about what you are doing is to lose that awareness, because
> in the moment of thinking you have already left the present moment.
>
> [...]
>
> But Empedocles is, to say the least, not the most reasonable of teachers.
> And while the practice he has just outlined is far more strenuous than
> our wandering minds can ever manage, there is that other faculty he has
> already mentioned by name which at any or every moment is perfectly
> up to the task - the sleepless alertness, always present by its very nature
> called *mêtis*.
> [..]

For humans, *mêtis* grows in relation to what is present.

[...]

As for how we should do so, nothing could be simpler. We just have to keep patiently watching and attentively waiting; to put aside all our doubts and inner questions for the time being and do the modest little things we are asked to do, step by step, instead. For this teaching takes shape, as we have already seen clearly enough, according to its own strange rules and rhythm. It manifests in its own good time; will work its way inside us and finally show itself not when we think we are ready, but when it knows we are.

Let this be said, or written, or better: be processed, before I attempt to bring forward our findings and learnings as journaled so far. The general and generative idea is to invite you to practice, to be aware of your learning process and to be patient with yourself. And to enjoy it. As the virtuous violinist Isaac Stern puts it: "The better your technique, the longer you can rehearse without becoming bored."

In this chapter I will now briefly revisit the three frameworks, adding a few suggestions to practice these separately. In the next chapter I happily invite 'the whole system' to share their practical wisdom to enrich our views. Let the various contributions surprise you: one has been provided by a chatbot. Furthermore, you will be served some proper inquiry scripting - right to copy - before the book tries to reach toward an ending, not by putting a period mark, but by (my interpretation of) a comma.

As you will understand, Part Four shouldn't contain too many words.

A little less conversation, a little more action, please
All this aggravation ain't satisfactioning me
A little more bite and a little less bark
A little less fight and a little more spark
Close your mouth and open up your heart and, baby, satisfy me

Elvis Presley

Practicing the Word Generativity

It's what we do and who we are that gives meaning to our words.
A new word is like a fresh seed sown on the ground of the discussion.

Ludwig Wittgenstein

Part One included you in the search for the meaning of the word Generativity, leading towards the corresponding conceptual framework as presented on page 62: a brief overview of do's and don'ts when using the word generative or generativity. This is a direct invitation to practice; to embrace the term in your desired future forming vocabulary; and when needed to deliberately replace it by a more appropriate alternative. For further reference and inspiration to enrich your language with this seemingly simple though valuable word, see the subsequent exemplary appendix starting at page 65.

Beware of so-called 'generative people' or 'generative things'. Your practice goes beyond speaking; listening is equally important: listening by detecting the term in spoken or written language, and by reflecting on it using your newly gained knowledge and awareness for generative language. In due time, 'generativity' will have become part of your repertoire, and from there you may discover various other valuable words that deserve the same care and attention of your growing *mètis*.

In the beginning of your practice you may experience yourself as eavesdropping over your own shoulder, or as a little observer in the corner of your mouth, monitoring the words passing by. More and more you will grow your craftsmanship of being aware of what and how you communicate, enabling your deepest intentionality to generate the meaning of your sentences. At a certain point of your increasing proficiency, you will notice that the conversation between you and the other will mainly be fueled by your generative listening. You may feel now that you are not there yet, but you are closer than you think.

Practicing Processual Generativity

But out of all secrets of the river, he today only saw one, this one touched his soul. He saw: this water ran and ran, incessantly it ran, and was nevertheless always there, was always at all times the same and yet new in every moment! Great be he who would grasp this, understand this!

Herman Hesse in Siddhartha

Part Two funnels you to generative processes, which are always of a relational nature, and may reveal six more features. In order to prepare yourself for detecting, observing and even promoting generative processes, first refer to the description of the seven features on page 111-113.

You may also want to revisit the reflective interview on page 114, or practice it with a partner. The practical guidelines, starting on page 121, are supposed to bring you as close as possible to observing generative processes from within.

Remember that your inquiry into the process can only be done in direct communication with the people involved in it. Be attentive to what or who is changing. Inquiry is your main instrument. Take into consideration that every question can be asked to yourself as well as others involved in the process.

- *Relational.* Do the partakers stay connected, and keep the conversation going, even when the "leader" (facilitator, chair, etc.) is no longer present?
- *Transformational.* If the partakers kept a journal of their behavior and opinions, would their notes show changes over time?
- *Future-focused.* Do the conversations and considerations in any way show explicit attention for an (ever changing) future?
- *Disruptive.* Do the partakers memorize unexpected events in the process?
- *Idea-giving.* Are new ideas (options for action) created and considered regularly?
- *Actionable.* Are new ideas carried out or tested in practice, and is even the slightest attempt to contribute to process improvement appreciated?
- *Procreative.* Does the process also create deliverables that are beneficiary to its future partakers or stakeholders?

Practicing Organizational Generativity

The main idea behind complex systems is that the ensemble behaves in ways not predicted by its components. The interactions matter more than the nature of the units. Studying individual ants will almost never give us a clear indication of how the ant colony operates. For that, one needs to understand an ant colony as an ant colony.

Nassim Nicholas Taleb

Part Three of this book made us inquire into the fivefold framework that emerged from the critical literature study and its findings regarding generativity: as a word, and as a processual quality. You participated in the unfolding of a future-forming research practice regarding intentionality, processuality, performativity, serendipity and procreativity as qualities of a generative organization.

Practicing the OG framework - which means identifying, grasping, observing and understanding - builds upon the previous practices, and also interacts with them. This is where Giddens pointed at , according to some quotes taken from the article[5] inspired by his Structuration Theory.

> Agency and structure, the subjective and objective sides of social reality, are considered to be inseparable. They meet each other in recurring social practices. To develop this thesis, Giddens had to rework both the concept of social structure and that of the acting individual...
> [...]
> This means that social structures are both the outcome and the very medium of social interaction (Giddens, 1976: 121)...
> [...]
> But when we want to look inside an organization, we will have to find out how individual practices contribute to what can be described as organizational action.

Essential in the practice is to experience the whole organization as one process, as one movement and to try to observe the behavior of the whole. And would you find yourself observing processes *in* the organization, you may need to view these

---

[5] Berends, H., Boersma, K. & Weggeman, M. (2003) *The Structuration of Organizational Learning*, in Journal Human Relations

with new eyes as Marcel Proust once suggested. The organizational behavior you will be perceiving, has an effect on the people inside and the people outside, those who we used to call the stakeholders. Furthermore, the behavior has an impact on the environment, on future generations, entities that we are slightly embedding in our new definition of stakeholders.

This all is what needs to be observed, and there are no clear rules nor recipes. The exchange that is constantly happening between the open system called organization and its surroundings, is actually the essence of organizational life, and bears the possibility to be generative. Isn't life a practice itself?

GENARRATIVE INSPIRATORS

Tomorrow belongs to those who can hear it coming.

David Bowie

Should I speak of circumstantial support, or indirect evidence? Pragadamic wisdom perhaps? Or must-reads? One thing is sure: the text fragments in this chapter provide only a glimpse of an infinite source: the experience and opinions of others.

In the books I have been reading - or rereading - I sometimes encountered a phrase or paragraph that resonated with my inquiries on generativity. Since a text can't be regarded as generative in itself, I chose from a lot of fragments a few that may bear a chance to generate resonance on your side too.

Please enjoy reading this unique variety of text fragments below, and you may find out whether this strengthens your genarrative capacity. (Notice that the years are with an extra 0, according to Roman Krznadic' s cathedral thinking.)

Michael Puett (02016)

Our Chinese philosophers enable us to name and perceive consciously impulses and behaviors we might otherwise dismiss as irrelevant because they don't fit into our notions of agency and sincerity. [...] In this fractured and fragmented world, it's up to us to generate order. We are the ones who construct and give pattern to the world - not by getting rid of the unwieldy human emotions, the messy stuff that is us, but by beginning right there. And we do this through daily self-cultivation: working through our rituals to improve the way we relate to those around us; cultivating energies in our bodies so that we can live with more vitality; training our hearts and minds to work through daily decisions in a powerfully different way; and resisting our tendency to cut ourselves off from experience, so that we become constantly receptive to new things. [...] But as we learn how to better our relationships, we will learn how to alter situations and thereby create infinite numbers of new worlds. (From: *The Path: What Chinese Philosophers Can Teach Us About the Good Life.*)

Umair Haque (02011)

Here then is my modern twist on eudaimonia, how I might put paid to the idea of "faring well." A good life is about more than quantity of gross product, denominated in nominal income. It's about net real wealth. And real wealth, in turn, consists of much more than mere money. When a person is wealthy relationally in social capital, environmentally in natural capital, managerially in organizational capital, personally in human capital, emotionally in emotional capital, and intellectually in intellectual capital, he or she might be said to be authentically, broadly, and deeply rich. He or she is faring well, enjoying an authentic prosperity, a good life, and a life that matters because it resonates with meaning, accomplishment, and purpose. (From: *Betterness: Economics for Humans*.)

Roman Krznaric (02021)

There is an Apache saying, 'We do not inherit the land from our ancestors; we borrow it from our children.' In the end it is not just our own children, but all children who will judge us from the future. A legacy is not something that we leave but something we grow throughout our lives. It is not just a bequest written into a will, but a daily practice. (From: *The Good Ancestor: How to Think Long Term in a Short-Term World*.)

Peter Senge a.o. (01990)

"In my experience, the part that people struggle most to understand," said Betty Sue [Flowers], "is the bottom of the U - *presencing*." [...] "What do we mean by 'presencing' and the capacity to have a different relationship to the future? In particular, Joseph [Jaworski] and Otto [Scharmer], you often talk about becoming aware of 'a future seeking to emerge.' This seems to imply that the future has intentionality, which is not something that most people would readily connect with. Is this consistent with your experience?" "Yes, I think so," said Joseph. "My view may be a little bit different," said Otto. "To me, presencing is about 'pre-sensing' and bringing into presence - and into the present - your highest future potential. It's not just 'the future' in some abstract sense but my own highest future possibility as a human being." (From: *Presence, Human Purpose and the Field of the Future.*)

Margaret J. Wheatley (02017)

Sane leadership is developing the capacity to observe what's going on in the whole system and then either reflect that back or bring people together to consider where we are now. This is working with emergence. And self-organization. In a dynamic, organic way. (From: *Who Do We Choose to Be?: Facing Reality, Claiming Leadership, Restoring Sanity.*)

Timothy Gallwey (01979)

Once absorbed in experience, one sometimes slips into a state that is difficult to describe because the "observer" who would describe it is no longer there. It's like falling asleep; you don't really know you did until you've awakened. But in this case it is falling awake, and you may not know it happened until you're looking back on it. As strange as it may sound, this state of absorption feels like the most natural thing when it happens. It is simple, effortless, and uncalculated. [...] You can't make relaxed concentration happen any more than you can make sleep happen. It occurs when you allow - not force - yourself to become interested in each moment of your life. Undertaking to learn this master skill is a supreme challenge, but one with inestimable personal benefit. (From: *The Inner Game of Golf.*)

Benjamin Smith a.o. (02017)

Vulnerability, deep listening, goodwill, and equanimity are four fundamental skills individuals can develop to support generativity. We could have added many more – sensing, compassion, and contextualizing come to mind – but the point is not to be comprehensive. The point is that generativity is about both the community and the individual. Nurturing the conditions of generative community requires that communities use the supporting practices of convening and narrating just as much as it requires individuals within those communities to attend to their own individual skills. Each of us is different and comes with different histories and aptitudes, all of which will impact how quickly or thoroughly we can develop these individual skills. These four skills are a worthy place to begin this never-ending process. (From: *The Way of Generativity: From separation to resonance.*)

David Bohm (01990)

So the suggestion is that people could start dialogue groups in various places. The point would not be to identify with the group, but rather, what is important is this whole process. You might say, "This is a wonderful group," but it's actually the process that counts. I think that when we are able to sustain a dialogue of this sort you will find that there will be a change in the people who are taking part. They themselves would then behave differently, even outside the dialogue. Eventually they would spread it. It's like the Biblical analogy of the seeds - some are dropped in stony ground and some of them fall in the right place and they produce tremendous fruit. The thing is that you cannot tell where or how it can start. The idea here, the communication here, the kind of thought we're having here, is a kind of seed which may help this to come about. But we mustn't be surprised if many of these groups are abortive and don't get going. That doesn't mean it can't happen. The point is not to establish a fixed dialogue group forever, but rather one that lasts long enough to make a change. (From: *On Dialogue.*)

Matthew B. Crawford (02009)

The way things actually "show up" for us is not as mere objects without context, but as equipment for action (like the hammer) or solicitations to action (like the beautiful stranger) within some worldly situation. One of the central questions of cognitive science, rooted in the prevailing epistemology, has been to figure out how the mind "represents" the world, since mind and world are conceived to be entirely distinct. For Heidegger, there is no problem of re-presenting the world, because the world presents itself originally as something we are already in and of. His insights into the situated character of our everyday cognition shed light on the kind of expert knowledge that is also inherently situated, like the firefighter's or the mechanic's. If thinking is bound up with action, then the task of getting an adequate grasp on the world, intellectually, depends on our doing stuff in it. And in fact this is the case: to really know shoelaces, you have to tie shoes. (From: *Shop Class as Soulcraft: An Inquiry into the Value of Work.*)

Yuval Noah Harari (02018)

Indeed we have no idea what the full human potential is, because we know so little about the human mind. And yet we hardly invest much in exploring the human mind, and instead focus on increasing the speed of our Internet connections and the efficiency of our Big Data algorithms. (From: *21 Lessons for the 21st Century.*)

Gareth Morgan (01986)

The human brain is characterized by a form of "emergent intelligence" whereby coherent order and pattern result from a multitude of possibilities. It is useful to think about the process of reading organizational life in similar terms, for, as has been shown, an effective reading requires that we remain open to different possibilities that we can form and reform in a way that allows us to act appropriately. The process is organic, not mechanistic. There is a dynamic quality that unites "the reader" and the situation being "read" in an unfolding process through which the reader can begin to grasp, shape, and understand the patterns of events or circumstances being encountered. [...] Effective readings are *generative.* They provide insights and actions that were not there before. They open new action opportunities. They make a difference. The criteria for judging an effective reading are not just objective. They are pragmatic. [...] Another important point that must be emphasized is that the process of reading a situation is always "two-ways". In trying to discern the meaning of a situation, we create an interplay between the situation itself and the frames through which we are trying to tie it down. [...] In this sense the reader is also an author. He or she is not in a passive role. This is what makes the challenge of reading organizational life so powerful. The manager truly does have an opportunity to shape how situations unfold. (From: *Images of Organization.*)

(P)REFLECTIONS BY MY CO-MAKERS

"Friendship is not about who you've known the longest. It's about who walked into your life, said 'I'm here for you,' and proved it." - Unknown

After completing Part Three, I shared the manuscript with my knowledgeable co-creators and the other protagonists in this memoir and asked them if they would be willing to contribute to Part Four, with any reflection, blurb, practice or preflection that might arise. A big thank you for the ones that took the effort; your contributions make this book again more genarrative. They delivered on the bridge from 02022 and 02023 and I happily put their contributions uncensored, in order of entry. Between brackets you find the page number(s) where this specific friend appears in the book. To find out more qualities of these elusive people, a simple internet search will help you to trace their most recent curricula.

Lara Carminati:

(p. 92)

The honest and transparent content of this book will leave the readers with a refreshing and warming feeling towards every-person and -thing around them. At least, this is the "smiling" feeling I always experience when practicing appreciative inquiry and that makes me ponder how much different the world would be if all people could embrace this lifestyle.

Lars Doyer:

(p. 172)

Thank you Cees, for our long relationship starting in the first AI100 group; your long, intensive and extensive inquiry into the concept of organizational generativity; your appreciation of everyone you met and the institutions you visited; sharing your journey in such words that I can experience your experiences; inviting me to co-create the meaning of the framework you designed; inspiring me to dig deeper into my own drivers and thus embracing AI on a deeper level. After reading the manuscript, this is what came to live:

Imagine....

- That flourishing organizations generating life, regenerating biodiversity and humane dignity are the standard for being successful.
- That now the generativity of organizations and countries is the accepted standard this is made visible through 'snapshots' on the (3) degrees of the (5) factors.
- That EBITA and GNP/GDP are considered 'pre-developed perspectives' just as for long we held the earth as the center of the universe.
- That in meetings in organizations and our government, with parliament as a shining example, dialogue is the standard instead of debate and we reserve two seats: for former and future generations.

Thus we invite ourselves to search for joined wisdom in this moment through our ancestors, to be good ancestors."

Kenneth J. Gergen:

(pp. 2, 8, 15, 21, 26, 70, 82, 130, 140, 193, 197)

So much to appreciate in this work; the head spins with ideas.
The work thus performs that which it attempts to describe.
As a continuation of the process, I share a few questions
brought to life by this fascinating text:

Generative process may well be enriched by these ideas,
but is generativity a necessary good....
enabling us to co-create new forms of weaponry
gain insight into more sophisticated means of public surveillance
or innovate by profiting from misrepresenting our products?

Should we be careful about the symbolic associations:
Generativity...productivity...the desire for more, greater, bigger
A love song to Capitalism?

If competing organizations are both generative,

Is the relationship between them generative?
Does competition become fiercer and more alienating?

How can we facilitate a generative relationship between
profit making organizations and their cultural surroundings?

Could there be a generative relationship between humans and nature?

How can we measure a process?
When does a process begin and end?
Is measuring a form of participating in the process?
Doesn't our vantage point create our observations?

How generative can an organization be if hierarchical in structure,
if participants compete for position,
if performance reviews are winnowing devices,
and for effective organizational functioning
relations are ideally transactional?

With deep appreciation for your efforts, Cees, stimulating as ever...
Ken Gergen

Joep C. de Jong:

(pp. vii, 90, 172)

I write this part as if we are having a conversation on your book, the topic and how we bring your (co-created) discoveries to life as Genarrators. You offered me the choice between a 'blurb', just a paragraph, or a somewhat more elaborate text. As shared before I love the story, your journey, and actually the discoveries that are unfolding in the book. And I guess what I especially love is the wide array of connections you make as I regard you now a Master on the Subject.

You provide us with different perspectives, including that of *The Good Ancestor* by Krznadic. Studying and playing with the 'concepts' of generation, generative, generativity, genarrativity and that of genarrator (which the automatic spelling checker consistently tries to change to 'generator', in and ofitself another nice association to play with). I guess to me you presented a puzzle that I'm still trying to make, and I sometimes feel that I don't even see a glimpse of what might emerge, still the process, the generative process, is fascinating and invites me to continue to search for the pieces and how they might fit.

Reading the first three chapters I ended up with four pages with notes, a little sketch and several intriguing one liners emerging in my brain. Just to share two quotes from my notes:

- When we would apply the description as produced by Cees of a PhD process to sex, I honestly believe we would never have sex.
- Appreciative Inquiry in the hands of an executioner will still cause death.

Now I have not been as structured as Cees in keeping track of where and how these thoughts exactly emerged, but I do know they did find their origin in the interesting associations I see being made in the descriptions and stories Cees is sharing with us.

It is a wonderful story of creativity, of a very generative process that invites us to think how we can link the 7 manifestations of generative/generativity to the concepts of Intentionality, Performativity, Processuality, Serendipity and Procreativity. And to be honest it feels at times that Cees is miles ahead of me, which of course is actually the case after all his reading, studying and struggling with the theme of this PhD process, only to find out that with regards to this – generative - process in the end the balance tips to being a real Practitioner more than a scholar.

I love what he [citing Gergen] writes on page 132: 'In a sense, generative theorizing is a form of Poetic Activism (PA). That is, it asks us to take risks with words, to shake up conventions, to create new ways of understanding and new images of possibilities.' By the way I immediately associated the abbreviation PA with 'Personal Assistant' a term I first learned when I became a manager at Apple in the '80's. And maybe that is what has been happening to me reading the book, maybe the text Cees has written is like a 'personal assistant', facilitating me in the generative process of learning how to become a Genarrator.

And even more, how about becoming a Knowledgeable Co-creative Genarrator. To me this raises enough questions to probably fill a book by myself. Just to share a few, also in relation to this book: 'How knowledgeable does one actually have to be to become a Genarrator?' The way you, Cees, have been uncovering the depths of generativity in the previous chapters might actually demotivate, challenge some of us to explore this concept as a potential way to make our organizations more human as your story must be read as a living document. A cathedral to which you constantly add new elements and/or ornaments to make it even more beautiful.

I mentioned earlier a sketch I made reading the book, trying to grasp some of the complexity you are sharing with us. I came up with a triangle with the words 'generative', 'gener(r)ativity' and 'genarrator' on the sides and in the center the words 'hope' and 'inspiration'. Not pretending to be anywhere near the depths that you reached in your research, but aren't we indeed all becoming Genarrators when we take the findings of this book and try to find / discover their meaning in our own situations, knowing that in the end it is all about how to make our organizations, our institutes more human. And once more I find it so refreshing that your book provides us with frameworks (personal assistants) that we can rely on and that at the same time you as the author offers us enormous freedom when I take this quote by you (by me translated quote from one of your earlier documents in Dutch): "NB I realize that by including 'individual implications' in table 10, I contribute to the confusion. This will be corrected in a (!) future version."

Jeffrey Hicks:

(pp. 95, 104-108, 126)

For the blurb: Countless times on back covers I've read: "Every manager should read this book." This book is one of only a few where I believe this to be true. If you're looking to proactively and intentionally create your organization's future, instead of only passively preparing for whatever future may arrive, this book can be your guide.

And - this may be a bit long - but here is a contribution for your consideration:

I'm honored that Cees has invited me to contribute. Taking up this opportunity in earnest, might I be so bold as to offer some words for the benefit of other readers who may come along, in particular practicing managers who are not, in the main "OD Consultants" or similar? If so, then: This is a great book. But it's also a rich, even 'dense' read. This is not surprising, because I believe Cees to be one of the world's leading authorities on generativity - despite the strong likelihood he might reject this appellation. Still, the work life of a practicing manager is a busy one, a hectic one, and it might seem difficult, when thinking about how to 'do' generativity as it's so thoroughly explored here--how can one work this into an already busy workday?

Well I have some good news: I'm pretty sure that you're doing it already; that you're already acting in a generative way, every single workday. This book can help you articulate the ways whereby your practice is already generative, and make it even more so.

In my own career, I came up through the managerial ranks, after completing what I would consider a good but 'mainstream' masters-level management education, where I was told I needed to 1) 'learn,' in order to 2) 'acquire' knowledge, which I could then later 3) 'apply' in order to solve managerial/organizational problems, or capture opportunities - learn, acquire, apply. What I experienced from the very first day as a practicing manager, however, is that every situation was unique. The knowledge I had acquired was never a perfect fit, and often not a very close fit at all - and this was true for the large majority of the problems and situations I encountered. The 'easy' problems, which could be solved through application of a priori knowledge, were rare, and in most cases, had long-since been automated. The real work of managing - as I now tell participants in the university classes I teach - begins when the path forward is not clear, not known, and knowledge that is precisely fit-for-purpose is not available. And in the non-deterministic social spaces known as 'organizations,' the absence of a clear and singular path forward, is what one faces most of the time.

So what does one do? I'm proposing that what you're already doing, every day, is acting in a generative way. You are, quite literally, creating the future of your practice, of your organization. To act in generative fashion, is not to passively prepare for some unknown future, but to proactively and intentionally to create the future. You may be fairly confident that some particular action or decision on your part, may lead to a particular outcome. But if we're honest about it, and if you're honest with yourself - here, in the safe space of this book where your boss is not around - you simply do not know with very much certainty at all, that this outcome will indeed come to be. I'll remind you that the predictability of social situations, including those in organizations, across all the social sciences - which includes management, by the way - is on the order of 30%, and this is an upside limit. Stated differently: for any given organizational outcome, what percent of causality cannot be explained, to a statistically high degree of confidence? About 70%.

But still, and despite the uncertainty and low-predictability, you go on. Most of the time, you're not frozen by 'analysis paralysis.' You take action (i.e. you create the future), you evaluate the outcome, you adjust, and you repeat the cycle. You are acting in a generative fashion. And with this book as a guide, you can increase the degree of generativity of your practice. Specifically, for the processes you design and implement, how can they - again, proactively and intentionally - be made more 1) relational, 2) transformational, 3) future-focused, 4) disruptive, 5) idea-giving, 6) actionable and 7) procreative? Or, using the "three degrees" as a guide for your practice, how can you extend the stakeholders you reach (DA), extend the future orientation (DF) and broaden the scope and scale of action (DM)?

In short, I see generativity as an important supplement to the good work you're already doing; as a way of proactively and intentionally creating better futures for more people, using this book as a guide.

Miriam Subirana Vilanova:

(p. 73)

Transformative Presence

(Original words with quotes from: *Mindfulness Relacional, Vacuidad y Plenitud*, Miriam Subirana, 2023, and: *El poder de nuestra presencia. Una guía de coaching apreciativo*, Miriam Subirana, 2012.)

The words generativity and genarrativity, connect me with the intentionality to move forward, to see through and beyond, to flow with the river of life that moves on. They also connect me with the intentionality to transform, to the life-giving energy that transforms the caterpillar into a butterfly in a metamorphosis process. It invites us with the provocative proposal of awakening the capabilities to live the freedom to be and to become what one is and what we are collectively.

The caterpillar needs to fully trust the process, without knowing what the outcome will be. As humans we are sometimes far from this level of trust in life. We don't know how the future will evolve, and we cling to what we do have. Holding on to systems, objects, persons, in essence holding on to what we have and not wanting to let go. Life flows, it is change, it is generative. What I have today maybe tomorrow I won't have. That clinging arises from the fear of what will happen, fear of the uncertainty of what will come, because we don't know what will come, and also from wanting to control reality.

When our mind is full of assumptions, certainties, opinions and fixed judgments, we are not fully present in reality. We cannot see clearly and broadly what is in front of us, the visible and the invisible, since we are conditioned by our own judgments and assumptions. We see through our glasses of assumptions and projections. We do not see what IS, nor what wants to become, but we see what our mind and imagination projects being puppets of our desires and fears, or else we see what was and not what is now.

We need radical trust. As soon as we stop imposing our schemes on reality, reality stops presenting itself as adverse or prone and begins to manifest itself as it is, without those patterns that prevent us from accessing it. The path of meditation is that of detachment, that of breaking mental schemes or prejudices: it is a stripping off until you end up verifying that you are much better off naked. It is silencing all the assumptions and stories until you can see through and beyond, you can hear the call of what wants to be born and of what is emerging.

Along with the practice of meditation, that makes it easier for us to let go of obsolete views, appreciative inquiry teaches us to see again, from another perspective, to see the good in the other, to realize from where you build your perspective and to question assumptions. Asking, clarifying and expressing what we want and listening to others helps us to be aware that there are other possible views that lead us to break stagnant mental schemes and gently, gracefully, with appreciation, we move towards the space of the positive core, the vital center of our person, the one that makes us vibrate with enthusiasm and joie de vivre and open us to our full potential from which we co-create meaning and restore radical trust.

There are some basic attitudes that strengthen your ability to transform, that is to be generative and genarrative with your presence. For many people it is the situations and reality that transforms them. They allow themselves to be affected by them to such an extent that they even collapse under its weight. Undoubtedly it is necessary to be strong to be generative and flow with reality so that it does not weaken you. In my book The Power of Presence, a guide to Spiritual Coaching, I share practices to be able to strengthen your presence. To achieve this, some of the attitudes and skills that will help you are:
- to observe, perceive, be open
- to ease and facilitate
- be an instrument
- to serve, and connect with abundance and generosity
- to inspire
- to nourish and sustain, to strengthen to flourish
- to heal and the joy of caring

I will only write about the first one here. The one that has to do with the questions: What do we see and how do we see? Are we seeing by being fully present? Is our presence transformative?

One of the characteristics that I consider essential in a person with a transformative presence is their ability to perceive with their intuition, to see with their being and to observe impartially in order to distinguish the different dimensions of the situation. The material and corporeal dimension, which is seen with the eyes. The mental and emotional dimensions, which are felt with the mind and heart. And the spiritual realms. All of which comprehend the Cosmos (Universe), the Theo (Divine or Transcendent) and the Andros (Awakened human conscience), that is the CosmoTheAndric vision and presence, being aware of the whole.

One is able to remain an observer that perceives from the whole, only when one does not dissolve in what one observes. Difficult thing in these moments in which the culture of entertainment and social media is booming. You watch a movie, go to the circus or a soccer game and get lost in what you are watching. So, one yells, jumps, laughs, cries, gets angry and gets emotional depending on what they are observing. They forget themselves and become a puppet of what they observe. You have released the rudder of your consciousness and what happens outside determines how you are inside. I suggest we connect with the best of our being to turn it around, and with our transformative presence be able to create the world we want to live in.

To be aware of the whole, to have a CosmoTheAndric vision and presence we need to:
- Develop trust, radical trust.
- Don't panic. Breathe in, breathe out. Everything will pass. Nothing is permanent.
- Try not to have expectations nor assumptions.
- Don't resist. Resistance gives away your power to that which you resist.
- Accept what is as it is.

- See beyond the mirage of what seems real. Keep your awareness open.
- Cultivate your capacity for detachment.
- Control your mind, have positive thinking.
- Cultivate inner calm.
- Stay connected with yourself, without falling into narcissism and without disconnecting from the whole.
- Do not get carried away by your inner saboteur: the one that boycotts your highest aspirations and paralyzes you in a sea of doubts and insecurities.
- Do not allow the water of the river, of circumstances and situations, to enter your boat. So, you don't sink. You stay afloat and keep sailing.
- Be grounded in your inner power.

You can practice an exercise in silence:
Sit and Relax. Take a deep breath. Think: I am not this situation. I separate from it. I calm my mind. I am aware that nothing is permanent. Situations come and go like waves. Everything will pass. I remain stable. I am peace. I am a star and I radiate peace. My presence is inter-connected with all the wisdom available, all the presence of presences. The Cosmos flows; the Theos embraces; and the wise awakened Andros is here in now, when I am here and now.

By being here and now we are generative as we are co-creators of the life we want to live, and we are genarrative as we co-create the better narratives that shape our world.

Be here and now, for yourself, for your teams, for your family, for the world.

Here and Now, I Am and so We Are.

Gert Veenhoven:

(p. 172, 230)

Knowing is not enough, we must apply.

Cees and I have known each other for about 20 years now. Our relationship started professionally as partners in OD in a big change program; now we call ourselves friends. We don't work very much together (measured in Chronos) but on the other hand we really do (measured in Kairos). Our encounters - whether we have them physically or online - are of great value and reciprocity. I am privileged to be part of his Pragademic Research adventure and can call myself Knowledge Creator.

I consider Cees' invitation to write in this book to be honorable. I want to put my best efforts into his masterpiece. I have already done that in the role of KC in the appreciative inquiry about generativity, but I am keen to make a meaningful contribution to this book.

I've been pondering for many weeks: what am I going to write about? The narrative in this book is so rich. And by means of the Appreciative Inquiry process a lot of my words - and those of my interviewees - are already somehow in the book; what else can I add?

To organize my thoughts I painted an (abstract) painting and reread a chapter from Senge's Presence. The painting is not finished yet, but the intention is there, as well as the title. I call it: "Suspension". A few weeks ago I tried to gain some inspiration and asked Cees whether he would label our collaboration as generative. Besides, the other day I asked my master students Serious Gaming how I can place generativity in the context of their learning community.

Up to this point, I still don't know what I want to write about. And I find myself leafing through the manuscript of Cees' book again. I can think of hundreds of sentences to relate my thinking and experiences with his book. Words like intention, reflection, reframing, experiment, relationship, and transfer make me very happy. Just like Cees, I truly want to make a positive contribution to our planet. In my case I am looking, or even better practicing, half or maybe my entire working life for essences and levers to flourish.

Genarrativity. Sure; we humans are narrative creatures. What generative story are we creating together?

"But Gert, knowing is not enough, you must apply!" I think to myself. And I feel inspired again by Bruce Lee who, in his relatively short life, was not only a martial artist and actor, but also a philosopher. This Sunday morning around 08:00 am I finally sat down and wrote the sentences so far. As I continue my writing and leafing through the book, the idea of what I want to tell finally unfolds. A new word on the cover page catches my eye. I didn't see it before, but this is the word I'm going to write about: "pragademic"! Hurray! Finally, here are my words and I copy them directly from my mobile phone:

This Sunday at 08:14 I sent the following whatsapp message to Cees: "Pragademic.... Pragmatic + Academic?".
At 08:16, Cees replied. "Exactly".

"You'll only see it when you understand it", says Johan Cruijff. Yeah, my learning works like this. How do you learn, when it comes to generativity?

Cisca Hoogendijk:

(p. 6)

A new generation keeps mankind alive, while a story told or written contributes to the big narrative that treasures mankind's civilization.

Dear brother, I am proud to see that likewise, your story will contribute, too.

Celeste Wilderom:

(pp. 89-93, 95, 99, 101-108, 126-127, 143, 203)

How about this? Feel free to edit (to switch roles for a time!)

This book comprises a quest to new human approaches to the flourishing continuation of existing human systems.

Cees shows that such new human approaches require, at the very least:

- deep curiosity to all people who operate in these human systems
- much courage of all people concerned, and
- creativity of all who are contributing to co-organizing the long-term continuation of their human system.

This pertains not only to thinking about such approaches, but also to (intuitive or other types of) expressions of them, and the ensuring of interaction processes that contributes to ways of reaching enduring, flourishing human systems.

To me, this is one of Cees' book legacies; the initiating and citing authors wish to promote or contribute to any human system that produces something of net human value. I will keep applauding such efforts because, in essence, it is the story of every (wo-)man's life.

Part 2 of this book reads as the story of a part of my own professional life: I treasure it, therefore.

If I myself could give out a PhD, Cees would have obtained it already! The fairly standard format in which PhDs are being given out by universities required a different format, a format that is much less creative, courageous and worldwide-curiosity engendering than this book has become.

Thank you for working with me, Cees; it was a true pleasure, and I look forward to learning so much more from you.

Geert Heling:

(p. 172)

It often happens that a book challenges you to think. Seldom a book makes you rethink your thinking, and rethink again. And that is what this book does. Cees guides us through his journey, his quest, which in a way is our quest.

Apart from the inside-description of the Kafkaesque gone-crazy academic ecosystem, this book is disruptive, confusing, and challenging. At many moments it made me reflect and rethink about (psycho-) logic, research, quantum mechanics, the meaning of life, my own contribution to my family, to organizations, to mankind in general, etc. Thinking of course not merely as a cognitive activity, but also in emotional, spiritual, humanistic sense; multi-modal and multi-perspective. Call it holistic!

Many ideas and perspectives pop up, questions and more questions, surprise after surprise, contradictions that turn out to be non-contradictory, etc. At times it feels like running a Möbius loop. Exhausting, but reviving, exhilarating, and vitalizing at the same time. Call it generative!

Having a real-time meeting (conversational encounter) with Cees leaves you with the same kind of exciting confusion. You end up with more surprises, ideas, and questions, but most importantly, infected with inspiration, optimism, and zest. And so does this book, it makes you feel humble and powerful (or better, valuable) at the same time. Call it appreciative!

If the goal of science is to provide answers to our questions, and the purpose of art is to question our answers, then this book is to be seen as a piece of art, making us not only question our answers but also our questioning. Call it science-art!

Let academics classify this work as constructivist, structuralist, postmodernist, post-postmodernist, or whatever; it is enriching, and relevant for all times. Call it genarrative!

Erica Harpe:

(p. 172)

Everything is energy, and that's all there is to it.
Match the frequency of the reality you want,
and you cannot help but get that reality.
It can be no other way.
This is not philosophy.
This is physics.

Albert Einstein

Generativity, energy and consciousness

Original words and quotes on energy from: *Reinventing Ourselves*, Erica Harpe, 2019.

Kudos Cees for performing such rigorous research on generativity! The word generative calls up for me the essence of our humanity, of emergence, of evolution and of energy. In my contribution, I would like to offer a take on viewing the world and oneself by offering views on energy and universal energy design. Or, from an energy perspective: how does generative come about?

What is energy? Wikipedia defines energy as 'a quality (action) creating an effect (reaction).' This materialistic view forms the basis of Newtonian physics that became the cornerstone of science at the end of the 17th century: there is only matter and nothing else. Over the last twenty years science has largely moved on to quantum physics and accepts that the universe, including ourselves, is made up of energy, not matter.

Energy is information. It's the motivating force driving everything. Everything in our universe is made up of energy, from the book you are looking at now, to your body, thoughts, ideas and inspiration. The more we are fully embodied or present in the physical world, the easier it becomes to transfer non-physical energy (like ideas) into the physical world (manifestation). Or: to become generative.

The Universal Energy Design. People have always tried to make sense of the universe. To gain insight into the true nature of reality and ourselves as part of it. Over the last twenty years, science, through quantum physics, has proven the wisdom traditions' knowing that the universe operates in accordance with certain principles called Universals Laws. Universal Laws help us understand the natural order inherent to life: how life works in a way that enables all living systems to function optimally in harmony with each other. The wisdom traditions view our human existence in service of the evolution of consciousness.

So what do these Universal Laws look like and entail? A very short overview to give you a first idea:

From the unmanifest...

1. The Law of Creation. We live in a field of pure potential. Creating needs certain elements that form the roadmap from idea to manifestations. The Law of Creation = Potential x Intention = Coherence + Action = Manifestation.
2. The Law of Unity or Potential. We are all part of a dynamic and inseparable field of energy.
3. The Law of Intention. Intention is the conscious direction of attention and energy. Our human intention creates a strong magnetic field to draw in manifestation.
4. The Law of Centre. Centre is the primary organising principle. On a human level, this has to do with remaining present, no matter what. Carl Jung defines this as Mastery.
5. The Law of Cause & Effect or Action. As you sow, so you will reap. Become aware that your future is generated by the choices you make in every moment. The more you witness your choices and listen to the feelings in your body, the more synchronicity will show up in your life.

... to the manifest

1. The Law of Vibration. The relationship between energy and consciousness has been described as: mass = energy = consciousness. This brings us back to raising our frequency and inviting in more of our soul so as to become the generator we want to be!

2. The Law of Dynamic. We live in a world of polarity, look for the overriding centre and stay there! Build Mastery.

3. The Law of Cycles. Joseph Campbell's 'The Hero's Journey' beautifully captures this: he discovered that the archetypical story of the hero describes a deeper developmental model for every human.

4. The Law of Radiance and Attraction. Life acts like a mirror: you attract what you are! Not what you want.

5. The Law of Levels. Everything in the universe is evolving to higher levels of evolution and frequency. And so do we. It's by connecting to the energetic reality that we communicate with all there is. This enables synchronicity: think of swarms of starlings tapping into the collective intelligence of the energy field and so flying further as a collective than they could ever do on their own.

6. The Law of Order. Development comes in leaps of periods with, and periods without a structure. View chaos as a doorway to the future, maybe then you find yourself prepared to move through.

7. The Law of Development. This is the culmination of all other laws. And gives rise to the question: what kind of human are we becoming?

So, if everything is energy and energy is information, and we now have an insight into the energy laws of the Universe, how could we put all of this to use in being / becoming more consciously generative - genarrative? Center for EcoIntention is an institution where I followed a vocational training on energy. Their 6 basic rules for energetic guardianship are:

- Inner Peace - You can only work with energy if you are relaxed inside.
- Consciousness of the whole - You can only charge something energetically if you are conscious of its boundaries.

- Feeling for what's going on - By giving the system and everything in it positive attention, you charge it up energetically.
- Subject matter expertise - Before you direct energy, you formulate realistic goals.
- Identify, affirm and visualize goals - You focus your intention on these goals and imagine that they have been realized.
- Process past pain - What is holding you back from the past and is standing in the way of you fulfilling your dream?

Let me finish with this. May becoming aware of the Universal Laws of energy and the principles of Energetic Guardianship help you to be more generative and to co-create life with life in an energetically coherent way. May it help you to be/become conscious energetic guardians. And may it help you to be/become more genarrative as you consciously co-create the new narratives that shape our world.

You are needed!

When a human grows, he opens his abilities to accept higher levels of
vibrations, of energy and consciousness that come in ...
As we grow, we fall more in tune with our Essence.
The more in tune, the more expansive our consciousness,
the better we're able to use the Universal Laws.

Barbara Brennan

Peter Brinkman:

(p. 173)

In his trilogy *Spheres*, Peter Sloterdijk actually comes to the final conclusion that everything begins and ends with a Magna Commoditas. Call it abiding around a pleasant middle. Around a fire or kitchen table. A place where the dual is explored from a certain silence and equanimity so that eventually a transcendent conclusion emerges. It is generative with a clear narrative act; ancient and fully contemporary. I can therefore identify well with the word genarrative. As I write this text, the word has been added as a new word which immediately invites me to play with it. The fusion of generative and narrative does justice to an important undercurrent in my actions.

When I was an executive and founder of an organizational consulting firm for the human factor in business and society, there was always an interplay between the generative and the narrative. For me continuously a search for knowledge and applicability; the practical effect. Here the connection with the Santa Fe Institute taught me a lot. The Belgian philosopher of science and chemist Ilya Prigogine and the writer philosopher Professor Peter Kingsley were both working there and indicated that this institute gave them the opportunity to bring their scientific knowledge in interplay with the original inhabitants, different cultural streams and other knowledge disciplines. Prigogine called his work merely a stamp, and Kingsley described it as staying alone in a lit attic room while not knowing the rest of the house. Kingsley eventually left science, surrendered his titles and made the journey of discovery to the roots of Western society. This is where we met; he is still a great inspiration to me. In my opinion, in the word genarrative, these energetic perspectives come together beautifully. An invitation to a delicious fruit juice.

A few weeks ago, I met Jack Vintage (nice name) again. It was in an artist supplies store. We had met years ago and I was deeply impressed by his knowledge of the many types of coffee beans that he transformed into a delicious cup of coffee in his very busy coffee house. Quite suddenly, however, he sold his business and left for Australia to start baking bread. When I met him again, he was back in Holland and baking bread here. Actually it was not about the bread, but about fermentation. His passion revolves around ancient techniques for preserving and developing food. The people who work with him are all connected to this intention. Like the biopharmacy student who puts her knowledge into practice in combining health aspects with fermenting vegetables. She receives instruction from Gino, an Italian baker who has been baking bread for 40 years. Both speak a completely different language and yet they understand each other extremely well. Jack is convinced that it is the intention under fermentation that makes their language unite.

Intentionality organizes at lightning speed in international platforms of all kinds, and hardly discriminates because it is based on expressivity. This is how energetic cooperative organizing develops. There is a beautifully moving language, maximally free of institution, which is based on the shared love for the ancient fermentation, and on the hand in hand gathering of knowledge and the practical translation into the spirit of our time.

Thousands of stories, individual and collective, provide the nourishment to authentic expression. As a result, it also organizes both individually and collectively. From here a fruit juice with forgotten knowledge and modern science emerges.

Serendipity is incredibly important here, and a spontaneous inspiration in the process of organizing and growing. My meeting with Jack was a pure stroke of luck and has led me to now make my own kimcii, and become initiated into the potential of fermentation and mindful nutrition. It connects me with the expressiveness of translating ancient techniques that have been passed down from generation to generation to the people and times of today.

Cees Hoogendijk's years of exploration have been reflected in his book *Genarrative*. It is, in my opinion, his Magnus Opus. Cees' work provides the current and next generation with tools to consciously develop, learn, organize and be in expression without an imposed structure, but in the unfolding from its own authenticity. A wonderful breeding ground for an enriching life.

I am grateful for our wonderful friendship.

Ronald Fry:

(p. 173)

My first journey through this work by Cees was a wonderful ride. It was full of inner 'yes,' 'aha,' 'never looked at it that way,' and outer smiles, with some thoughtful frowns. Overall it is a tour-de-force into a deeper view of generativity, generative connections, and the novel idea of the "genarrator" to help those interested in nurturing, transforming, changing or developing human systems toward being spaces for everyone to flourish within. A few things I am appreciating most about this contribution to our global community of practice include wordplay, communitas and power-with.

Wordplay. Like Cees and many of us in the Appreciative Inquiry and Social Constructionist domains, I adhere to the powerful notion that words create worlds. Cees has given us a masterclass in the power of intentional-yet-playful reframing, rewording, and inventing words to stimulate new ideas and images. This is not jus limited to the new Genarrator role. Everywhere there are delightful twists and turns with language to awaken us from mechanistic reading and thinking.

Communitas. Every time I have encountered Cees, and now in his writing, I am reminded of community. He lives and "be's" for communing with equal voice, shared power, and true appreciation for diversity and inclusion. But now I think he is highlighting even more the moments of communitas that Victor Turner first described. Those emergent moments where a collective finds themselves in a space of true concrescence, or simultaneous "growing along with." The unknown is embraced, everyone shares a type of bond I would describe as a generative connection, and all join in co-inquiry. The Genarrator can be a positive change agent for these moments.

Power-with. Several times during my reading, I found myself thinking of Mary Parker Follett's sage distinction between power-over and power-with. One occurred when Cees described the Genarrator role as being about the other(s), not about oneself.

I would extend this a bit to suggest it is about our relational space and the beauty, love, influence, curiosity, creativity, difference, etc. that emerges or resides in that relationship. It is beyond any personal ego agenda, not just the Genarator's.

I look forward to the next time and space to wander through this book again. Like every time I view my garden, there are likely to be experiences of newness and sameness, but always an inviting and fertile space for discovery and growth.

WHEN AI MEETS AI …

"Artificial intelligence will be able to participate in human conversation in the same way a person could. It will be able to listen to what people are saying and respond in a way that is appropriate and helpful. It will be able to learn from its conversations and adapt its responses to better serve the needs of the person it is communicating with."

Satya Nadella

The conversational robot is likely to *discover* and *respond*, but is it able to *experience* and to *dream*? The moment I wrote this Part Four, a beta version of the OpenAI invention ChatGPT became hot news. After having been inspired by both genarrative authors as well as my honorable co-creators, I took the spontaneous liberty to engage in a dialogue with this 'state of art' generative dialogue partner. It was 4 December 2022, and I asked it a series of questions about topics and findings regarding my research. One might get easily impressed or feel comfortable by the rapid and seemingly profound answers. Is this the kind of comfort we seek? ChatGPT surely makes some sense, from time to time. Find out for yourself, skip what you like, but don't miss my last question to this robot, because its answer may give you an extra clue about creating futures.

A Not so Genarrative Chat with ChatGPT

Cees: "How would you reflect on the concept of truth according to Richard Rorty?"

ChatGPT: Richard Rorty was an American philosopher who is best known for his work in the fields of metaphysics, epistemology, and aesthetics. In terms of the concept of truth, Rorty is known for his rejection of the idea that there is a single, objective truth that exists independently of human thought and language. Instead, he believed that truth is simply a matter of the beliefs and practices of individual people and communities.

Cees: "What would you consider a good example of performative language?"

ChatGPT: A good example of performative language is the statement "I hereby pronounce you husband and wife." This statement is a performative utterance because it performs the action that it describes: by saying the words "I hereby pronounce you husband and wife," the speaker is actually pronouncing the two people as married. This is in contrast to a statement like "They are now married," which merely describes the situation but does not perform any action. Other examples of performative language include statements like "I apologize" or "I promise." These statements perform the actions of apologizing or promising, respectively, simply by being spoken.

Cees: "And if you think of organizational performativity, how would this be experienced, for example by clients?"

ChatGPT: Organizational performativity is the idea that organizations, like individuals, can perform actions and produce effects through their language and practices. For clients, this might be experienced in a variety of ways, depending on the specific organization and context. For example, a client might experience organizational performativity through the way that an organization presents itself and its services, the language that it uses to describe and promote its products or services, and the way that it interacts with clients and responds to their needs. In general, organizational performativity can create a sense of trust and confidence in an organization's ability to deliver on its promises and meet its clients' needs.

Cees: "Could you reflect on the deeper meaning of organizational intentionality?"

ChatGPT: Organizational intentionality refers to the idea that organizations, like individuals, can have intentions, goals, and purposes. This is distinct from the idea that organizations are merely collections of individuals who each have their own intentions and goals. Instead, organizational intentionality suggests that an organization as a whole can have a collective intention or purpose, which is different from the intentions of the individuals who make up the organization.
The deeper meaning of organizational intentionality is that it suggests that organizations can have a kind of agency and autonomy, just like individual people. This means that organizations can make choices, take actions, and produce

GENARRATIVE

effects in the world, even if those choices, actions, and effects are not the direct result of the intentions of any individual person within the organization. In this way, organizational intentionality helps to explain how organizations can be more than the sum of their parts and can have a real impact on the world.

Cees: "What would you suggest if you would want your organization to benefit optimally from serendipity?"

ChatGPT: Serendipity refers to the unexpected discovery of something valuable or interesting, often by accident or chance. To benefit optimally from serendipity, organizations should create an environment and culture that encourages and supports the exploration of new ideas, the pursuit of novel opportunities, and the willingness to take risks. This might involve providing resources and support for employees to pursue their own interests and projects, encouraging open communication and collaboration among employees, and fostering a culture of innovation and experimentation. Additionally, organizations can look for ways to actively seek out serendipitous experiences, such as by attending conferences and networking events, collaborating with other organizations, and investing in research and development. By creating a culture that values and supports serendipity, organizations can increase their chances of making unexpected and valuable discoveries.

Cees: "Do managers have the capability of actually changing or creating the culture of an organization?"

Managers do have the capability of changing or creating the culture of an organization. Culture refers to the shared beliefs, values, norms, and practices that define a group or organization, and it is shaped by a variety of factors, including the actions and behaviors of the people who make up the organization. As managers, individuals have the ability to influence the actions and behaviors of their employees, and therefore they can play a significant role in shaping the culture of an organization.
Managers can create or change the culture of an organization in a number of ways. For example, they can set expectations and standards for employee behavior, establish policies and procedures that reflect the organization's

values, and model the desired behaviors and attitudes themselves. They can also use a variety of tools and techniques, such as training and development programs, communication campaigns, and performance management systems, to help align employees' behaviors and attitudes with the organization's culture. By taking an active and intentional approach to shaping the culture of an organization, managers can have a significant impact on the way that the organization functions and performs.

Cees: "Please reflect on the concept of organizational procreativity."

ChatGPT: I'm sorry, but I'm not familiar with the term "organizational procreativity." Could you please provide more context or clarify what you are asking about?

Cees: "Procreativity in terms of leaving things behind well for future generations."

ChatGPT: Procreativity, in the sense of leaving things behind well for future generations, refers to the idea that organizations should be mindful of the long-term consequences of their actions and strive to create a better future for those who will come after them. This might involve taking steps to protect the environment and natural resources, supporting social and economic development, and building sustainable and resilient communities.
To achieve organizational procreativity, organizations need to adopt a long-term perspective and consider the potential impact of their actions on future generations. This might involve making strategic decisions that prioritize long-term sustainability over short-term gains, investing in research and development to support innovation and progress, and engaging with stakeholders and the broader community to identify and address future challenges and opportunities. By taking a proactive and responsible approach to procreativity, organizations can help to create a better future for themselves and for those who will come after them.

Cees: "Let's enter the domain of processuality. How would you define such in an organizational context?"

ChatGPT: Processuality is a term that refers to the idea that organizations are composed of processes or sets of activities that are interconnected and interdependent. In an organizational context, processuality can be thought of as the way that organizations function and operate, and it is often used to describe the complex and dynamic nature of organizational life.

At a broad level, processuality in organizations refers to the various processes that are necessary for an organization to achieve its goals and fulfill its mission. These processes might include things like decision-making, planning, communication, resource allocation, and problem-solving. At a more detailed level, processuality can refer to the specific activities and tasks that are carried out by individuals and groups within the organization, and the ways in which these activities and tasks are interconnected and interdependent.

By understanding and analyzing the processuality of an organization, managers and other decision-makers can gain insight into the way that the organization functions and identify areas for improvement or change. This can help organizations to operate more efficiently and effectively, and to achieve their goals more successfully.

Cees: "And if you think of organization as a process in itself, what comes to mind?"

ChatGPT: If we think of an organization as a process in itself, several things come to mind. First, it suggests that an organization is not a static and unchanging entity, but rather a dynamic and constantly evolving system of activities and processes. This means that an organization is always in a state of change, as it responds to internal and external factors and adjusts to meet the needs and demands of its environment.

Second, thinking of an organization as a process also highlights the importance of the interactions and relationships between the various parts of the organization. In a process-oriented view of organizations, each part of the organization is seen as a component that contributes to the overall functioning of the organization. This means that the success of the organization depends not only on the individual components, but also on the ways in which they work together and support each other.

Finally, thinking of an organization as a process also emphasizes the need for organizations to be adaptable and flexible. In a constantly changing environment, organizations need to be able to adapt and respond to new challenges and opportunities in order to remain relevant and effective. This might involve adopting new technologies, changing the way that they operate, or developing new strategies and approaches. By embracing a process-oriented view of organizations, managers and decision-makers can better understand the complex and dynamic nature of organizational life and take steps to ensure that their organization remains successful and effective.

Cees: "Do you see a relation between processes in organization and the organization as a process itself? What kind of relationship would that be?"

ChatGPT: There is a relationship between processes in organizations and the organization as a process itself. In a process-oriented view of organizations, the processes that take place within an organization are seen as the building blocks that make up the organization as a whole. These processes are interconnected and interdependent, and they contribute to the overall functioning and performance of the organization.

The relationship between processes in organizations and the organization as a process itself can be thought of in terms of cause and effect. The various processes that take place within an organization, such as decision-making, planning, and communication, are the causes that generate the effects of the organization as a whole. In other words, the processes that take place within an organization are the means by which the organization achieves its goals and fulfills its mission.

At the same time, the organization as a process also has an impact on the individual processes that take place within it. The overall direction and goals of the organization can influence the way that individual processes are carried out, and the performance of the organization as a whole can affect the success or failure of individual processes. In this way, the relationship between processes in organizations and the organization as a process itself is complex and dynamic, with each influencing and shaping the other in various ways.

Cees: "Ever heard of Giddens?"

ChatGPT: Yes, I have heard of Anthony Giddens. He was a British sociologist and political theorist who was one of the most influential figures in the field of sociology in the late 20th and early 21st centuries. Giddens is best known for his work on social and political theory, and he has made significant contributions to the study of globalization, modernity, and the self. His most famous work is probably his book "The Consequences of Modernity," in which he explores the impact of modernity on the individual and on society. Giddens is often associated with the school of thought known as structuration theory, which emphasizes the role of human agency in shaping social structures and institutions.

Cees: "How would you apply the Structuration Theory of Giddens to the processual nature of and in organizations?"

ChatGPT: The Structuration Theory of Anthony Giddens can be applied to the processual nature of organizations in several ways. First, structuration theory emphasizes the role of human agency in shaping social structures and institutions. In the context of organizations, this means that individuals within an organization have the ability to influence and shape the processes that take place within the organization, and therefore they can have an impact on the overall functioning and performance of the organization.

Second, structuration theory also emphasizes the importance of the interactions and relationships between individuals and groups within organizations. In a process-oriented view of organizations, these interactions and relationships are seen as the foundation of the organization as a whole, and they play a critical role in determining the success or failure of individual processes. By understanding and analyzing these interactions and relationships, managers and decision-makers can gain insight into the ways in which the processes within an organization are interconnected and interdependent.

Finally, structuration theory also highlights the importance of social and institutional context in shaping the behavior and actions of individuals within organizations. In the context of organizations, this means that the broader social, economic, and political environment in which an organization operates can have a significant impact on the processes that take place within the organization. By considering the context in which an organization operates, managers and decision-makers can better understand the factors that influence the success or failure of individual processes and the organization as a whole.

Cees: "If I would define the following five factors to determine organizational generativity: intentionality, processuality, performativity, serendipity and procreativity, would that make sense? Are they all needed? Would you add another factor perhaps?"

ChatGPT: It makes sense to use the five factors you mentioned - intentionality, processuality, performativity, serendipity, and procreativity - to determine organizational generativity. These factors all relate to different aspects of organizational behavior and performance, and they can provide valuable insight into the ways in which organizations function and operate.
In terms of whether all of these factors are needed, it ultimately depends on the specific context and situation. Different organizations may place different levels of emphasis on these factors, and the relative importance of each factor may vary depending on the goals and objectives of the organization. Additionally, some organizations may choose to focus on additional factors that are not included in your list, such as innovation, collaboration, or social responsibility.
In general, it is important to consider a range of factors when determining organizational generativity, as each factor can provide valuable information and insight into the organization's performance and potential for success. By considering a diverse set of factors, organizations can develop a more comprehensive and holistic understanding of their strengths and weaknesses, and can take steps to improve and enhance their performance.

Cees: "If you were to define practical indicators to 'measure' organizational generativity, which would you choose?"

ChatGPT: There are many possible indicators that could be used to measure organizational generativity. Some possible indicators include: The level of innovation and creativity within the organization, as measured by the number of new products, services, or processes developed by the organization; the organization's performance and financial health, as measured by key financial metrics such as revenue, profitability, and shareholder value; the organization's ability to adapt to and respond to changes in its environment, as measured by its track record of successful transitions and its ability to navigate challenges and uncertainties; the organization's impact on its stakeholders and the broader community, as measured by metrics such as customer satisfaction, employee engagement, and community involvement; the level of collaboration and teamwork within the organization, as measured by the degree of communication, coordination, and cooperation among employees and teams.

These are just a few examples of possible indicators that could be used to measure organizational generativity. The specific indicators chosen will depend on the goals and objectives of the organization, as well as the context and environment in which it operates.

Cees: "Would it be possible to 'measure' the emergence of organization?"

ChatGPT: It is possible to measure the emergence of an organization in a number of ways. Some possible indicators of the emergence of an organization could include:

The formation of a clear and distinct organizational identity, as indicated by the development of a mission statement, a set of core values, and a clear brand and reputation.

The establishment of formal structures and processes, such as a hierarchy of leadership, decision-making mechanisms, and communication channels.

The recruitment and retention of a stable and committed workforce, as indicated by metrics such as employee turnover and engagement.

The development of a track record of successful operations and performance, as indicated by financial metrics such as revenue and profitability, or other measures of organizational success.

The recognition and acceptance of the organization by external stakeholders, such as customers, suppliers, regulators, and the broader community.

These are just a few examples of possible indicators of the emergence of an organization. The specific indicators chosen will depend on the context and environment in which the organization operates, as well as the goals and objectives of the organization itself.

Cees: "When speaking of an organization's ability to create their own future, what do we see such organizations do in daily practice?"

ChatGPT: Organizations that are able to create their own future tend to exhibit certain characteristics and behaviors in their daily practice. Some of the things that these organizations do on a daily basis include: They are proactive and forward-thinking, always looking for new opportunities and ways to improve and innovate. They are adaptable and flexible, able to respond quickly and effectively to changes in their environment. They are collaborative and inclusive, fostering open communication and collaboration among employees, stakeholders, and the broader community. They are strategic and visionary, with a clear and ambitious vision for the future and a plan for achieving it. They are focused on continuous learning and improvement, investing in training and development for their employees and staying up-to-date with the latest trends and technologies.
By exhibiting these characteristics and behaviors, organizations that are able to create their own future are able to position themselves for success and achieve their goals more effectively.

Cees: "What do you think of my self-invented word genarrativity?"

ChatGPT: Genarrativity is a self-invented word that does not have a widely accepted or established meaning. It is not a term that is commonly used in academic or professional contexts, and it does not have a clear connection to any existing concepts or theories. Without more context or information about what you mean by genarrativity, it is difficult to provide a more detailed or specific response.

Cees: "The word genarrativity holds generative and narrative. Please reflect on it."

ChatGPT: The word genarrativity combines the concepts of generativity and narrative. Generativity refers to the ability of an organization or system to create or generate new ideas, products, or processes, while narrative refers to the stories or accounts that people use to make sense of the world and their experiences. In the context of genarrativity, these two concepts can be seen as interconnected and mutually reinforcing. On the one hand, the ability to generate new ideas, products, or processes can be seen as a necessary precondition for creating and sharing narratives. Without the capacity for generativity, organizations and individuals would be unable to produce the materials, experiences, or events that provide the raw material for narratives. At the same time, the power of narrative can also enhance and support generativity. By using stories and accounts to make meaning and connect with others, organizations and individuals can create a shared sense of purpose and direction, which can in turn facilitate the development and implementation of new ideas and innovations. In this way, genarrativity can be seen as a valuable quality for organizations and individuals, as it combines the ability to create and innovate with the ability to communicate and connect with others. By harnessing the power of genarrativity, organizations and individuals can position themselves for success and achieve their goals.

Finally One of my Genuine AI Interview Questions

Cees: "What do you see when you think of Intentionality at the organizational level? Do you think you have seen it before (in some way)? Which organization and when are you talking about? What did you see that organization doing in this regard?"

ChatGPT: As a large language model trained by OpenAI, I do not have the ability to see or observe anything. I am a machine learning model that processes and generates text based on the inputs I receive. I do not have personal experiences or the ability to perceive the world like a human being.

Quod erat Demonstrandum

GENARRATIVE

LET'S GET GENARRATIVE

Standards comprehensible to non-experts
raise quality in the organization as a whole

Richard Sennett

So far this book has been addressing primarily the organizational experts: the managers and consultants in their roles of co-creating organization; the scholarly practitioners, the practical scholars and perhaps in between them the PhD candidates inclined to bridge practice and theory. They - you - are allowed, if not supposed, to spend time and effort on practicing the practices offered here. What about all the other workers that 'make up' the organization, be it by executing their own specific practice, contributing to what the organization actually is producing? As they won't need you to operate their welding torch, you better not ask them to observe processes from within. (Although they might already do such in the field of their craft.) However, you still want to involve them in the process of co-creating the organization's best possible future.

Could you narrow down the processual and generative complexity to its most comprehensive essence? Like how an unforgettable management trainer once narrowed down his three days training to the one question asked to every single participant, before being admitted into the training room: "Do you love people?"

What if we forget about the word generative, about the seven features of relational processes, even about the five factors of organizational generativity? Which questions would remain, and still be an act of genarrativity?

Let me suggest two possible interviews prepared to fuel conversations with or between professionals in areas other than organization development. Designed along the songlines of Appreciative Inquiry, our recommended future-forming practice, generative questions form the main ingredients. Might your 'organization' be more like a social enterprise, a community or neighborhood, you will easily adjust the interviews correspondingly.

Five Steps Interview with your Co-worker

1. Do you remember an experience in your work that illustrates clearly why you are in this job? Who are the ones that you want to benefit the most from your intentions?

2. Reviewing your present working environment: where do you see satisfactory successful performance? Which might be the three biggest enablers for this?

3. In your own domain, what do you consider as the core delivery process? Take a moment to ponder, and picture that particular process in its best future version: what has changed?

4. Think freely. What extraordinary ideas could fuel further growth and satisfaction in your work? Which of these ideas appeal the most to you? What could be your first step to put that particular idea into action?

5. For which contribution would you like to be appreciated the most in the long term? What will you do (more) in the present to make that happen?

Three Degrees⁶ Questions as a Common Practice

Encourage yourself and your co-creators to ask, frequently and repeatedly, about everything they are doing in work and life, the core three questions.

- Who will be possibly impacted, and in what way, by my work?

- How far into the future are my activities pointing or reaching?

- To what extent do my actions contribute to the collective flow?

GENARRATIVE

ENDNOTE & ANDNOTE

The future must enter you long before it happens

Rainer Maria Rilke

Here comes my last selfie, taken from my first Leiden paper in which I introduced the new word *genarrative*. This little epilogue has been waiting for five years to serve as the comma at the back of my book.

> The French philosopher Derrida invented (1972) the new word différance (spelled with an "a") to stand alongside the existing word différence. When pronounced in French we do not hear the difference between the two words, by which Derrida makes us aware that words without context are difficult to understand. (This is a simplistic explanation of his profound thinking.) The sudden appearance of the word genarrative in the mind of this article's first author should not be considered to be as significant as Derrida's reflections. But perhaps this change of language can serve to leverage OD practitioners in the direction recommended in this study.
>
> Our new word, genarrative, which suggests narrative practices, may help clarify and amplify what is required for "organizing generativity" in OD practice. We know by now that we cannot speak of a generative person. However, when we imagine someone mastering intentionality, processuality, performativity, serendipity, and procreativity in an OD context, we certainly could speak of a person who is behaving or organizing in a generative way.
>
> A genarrative OD practitioner? The more, the merrier.

I asked, why have I received only this?
A voice replied: 'Only this' will lead you to That.

Rumi

www.genarrativity.org

Printed by Amazon Italia Logistica S.r.l.
Torrazza Piemonte (TO), Italy

57296616R00157